D0146495

Globalgothic

Manchester University Press

INTERNATIONAL GOTHIC

Each volume in this series contains new essays on the many forms assumed by – as well as the most important themes and topics in – the ever-expanding range of international 'Gothic' fictions from the eighteenth to the twenty-first century. Launched by leading members of the International Gothic Association (IGA) and some editors and advisory board members of its journal, *Gothic Studies,* this Series thus offers cutting-edge analyses of the great many variations in the Gothic mode over time and all over the world, whether these have occurred in literature, film, theatre, art, several forms of cybernetic media, or other manifestations ranging from 'Goth' group identities to *avant garde* displays of aesthetic and even political critique.

The 'Gothic Story' began in earnest in 1760s England, both in fiction and drama, with Horace Walpole's efforts to combine the 'ancient' or supernatural and the 'modern' or realistic romance. This blend of anomalous tendencies has proved itself remarkably flexible in playing out the cultural conflicts of the late Enlightenment and of more recent periods. Antiquated settings with haunting ghosts or monsters and deep, dark secrets that are the mysteries behind them, albeit in many different incarnations, continue to intimate what audiences most fear in both the personal subconscious and the most pervasive tensions underlying Western culture. But this always unsettling interplay of conflicting tendencies has expanded out of its original potentials as well, especially in the hands of its greatest innovators, to appear in an astounding variety of expressive, aesthetic, and public manifestations over time. The results have transported this inherently boundary-breaking mode across geographical and cultural borders into 'Gothics' that now appear throughout the world: in the settler communities of Canada, New Zealand, and Australia; in such post-colonial areas as India and Africa; in the Americas and the Caribbean; and in East Asia and several of the islands within the entire Pacific Rim.

These volumes consequently reveal and explain the 'globalization' of the Gothic as it has proliferated across two-and-a-half centuries. The General Editors of this series and the editors of every volume, of course, bring special expertise to this expanding development, as well as the underlying dynamics, of the Gothic. Each resulting collection, plus the occasional monograph, therefore draws together important new studies about particular examples of the international Gothic – past, present, or emerging – and these contributions can come from both established scholars in the field and the newest 'rising stars' of Gothic studies. These scholars, moreover, are and must be just as international in their locations and orientations as this Series is. Interested experts from throughout the globe, in fact, are invited to propose collections and topics for this series to Manchester University Press. These will be evaluated, as appropriate, by the General Editors, members of the Editorial Advisory Board, and/or other scholars with the requisite expertise so that every published volume is professionally put together and properly refereed within the highest academic standards. Only in this way can the International Gothic series be what its creators intend: a premiere world-wide venue for examining and understanding the shape-shifting 'strangeness' of a Gothic mode that is now as multi-cultural and multi-faceted as it has ever been in its long, continuing and profoundly haunted history.

Globalgothic

Edited by Glennis Byron

Manchester University Press
Manchester and New York

distributed in the United States exclusively
by Palgrave Macmillan

Published by Manchester University Press
Oxford Road, Manchester M13 9NR, UK
and Room 400, 175 Fifth Avenue, New York, NY 10010, USA
www.manchesteruniversitypress.co.uk

Distributed in the United States exclusively by
Palgrave Macmillan, 175 Fifth Avenue, New York,
NY 10010, USA

Distributed in Canada exclusively by
UBC Press, University of British Columbia, 2029 West Mall,
Vancouver, BC, Canada V6T 1Z2

British Library Cataloguing-in-Publication Data
A catalogue record for this book is available from the British Library

Library of Congress Cataloging-in-Publication Data applied for

ISBN 978 07190 8795 0 hardback

First published 2013

Typeset in Arno Pro by Servis Filmsetting Ltd, Stockport, Cheshire
Printed in Great Britain by TJ International Ltd, Padstow

Contents

List of contributors

Katarzyna Ancuta is a lecturer at the Graduate School of English at Assumption University in Bangkok, Thailand. She has published on the interdisciplinary contexts of contemporary gothic and horror, (South)-East Asian (particularly Thai) cinema and supernatural anthropology. She is currently working on a book on (South)-East Asian horror film and a multimedia project on Bangkok gothic. She is also involved in a number of film-related projects in South-East Asia, co-ordinating Asian Cultural Studies Association based in Bangkok and editing *Asian Journal of Literature, Culture and Society*, published by Assumption University Press.

Colette Balmain is a film critic, lecturer and writer specialising in East Asian cinemas and cultures. In particular, she is interested in gender theory and whiteness studies in relation to non-Western cultures. She is the author of *Introduction to Japanese Horror Film* (2008), the editor of *Directory of World Cinema: South Korea* (2012), finishing a book on South Korean horror cinema (2012) and in the preparatory stages of a project on East Asian gothic.

Fred Botting is Professor of Literature and Theory in the School of Humanities and Executive member of the London Graduate School, Kingston University. He is currently writing on horror and zombies and has published extensively on gothic fiction and literary theory, including *Gothic Romanced* (2008) and *Limits of Horror* (2008).

Steven Bruhm is Robert and Ruth Lumsden Professor of English at the University of Western Ontario, where he teaches courses in nineteenth-century literature and culture, queer studies, and the gothic. He is the author of *Gothic Bodies: The Politics of Pain in Romantic Fiction* (1994) and *Reflecting Narcissus: A Queer Aesthetic* (2001), as well as co-editor of *Curiouser: On the Queerness of Children* (2004). He is currently at work on a book exploring the queer temporalities of gothic dance, of which the work on Japanese butoh is a part.

Glennis Byron is Professor of English Studies at the University of Stirling. She is the author of *Gothic* (with David Punter, 2004) and the editor of *Dracula: New Casebook* (1999), *Spectral Readings: Towards a Gothic Geography* (with David Punter, 1999). Recent publications include essays on various contemporary gothic texts, including Malaysian horror fiction, Zafón's *La sombra del viento*, Ishiguro's *Never Let Me Go*, Cronin's *The Passage* and Meyer's *Twilight*. She was the principal investigator for the AHRC-funded Global Gothic network.

James Campbell is a PhD candidate at the University of Stirling. His research concerns the American gothic and globalisation, and includes such topics as the phantasmagoria, the global village in the Pacific North-West and the trope of the dark carnival. An article on the Southern gothic novelist formerly known as Poppy Z. Brite is forthcoming.

Ian Conrich is a Fellow in the Department of Literature, Film, and Theatre, at the University of Essex; previously he was the founding Director of the Centre for New Zealand Studies, Birkbeck, University of London. He is the author of several books, including *Easter Island, Myths, and Popular Culture* (2011), and *New Zealand Cinema* (2012); co-author of *Culture and Customs of New Zealand* (2012) and *Gothic Dissections: The Body in Parts in Film and Literature* (2013); and editor or co-editor of a further eleven books. He has contributed to more than fifty books and journals, and his work has been translated into French, German, Norwegian, Danish, Polish, Hungarian and Hebrew.

Justin D. Edwards is Professor and Director of Research in the School of English and Languages, University of Surrey. He is the author of several books, including *Gothic Passages: Racial Ambiguity and the American Gothic* (2003), *Gothic Canada: Reading the Spectre of a National Literature* (2005) and most recently *Postcolonial Literature*

(2008). He is also the co-editor of *Pop Goth: Gothic in Contemporary Literature and Popular Culture* (2012).

Avril Horner is Emeritus Professor of English at Kingston University, London. She is co-author, with Sue Zlosnik, of *Daphne du Maurier: Writing, Identity and the Gothic Imagination* (1998) and *Gothic and the Comic Turn* (2005); and, with Janet Beer, of *Edith Wharton: Sex, Satire and the Older Woman* (2011). She is editor of *European Gothic: A Spirited Exchange, 1760–1960* (2002) and co-editor of *Le Gothic: Influences and Appropriations in Europe and America* (2008). She was co-president of the International Gothic Association between 2005 and 2009.

Barry Murnane has been Assistant Professor in German Studies at the MLU Halle-Wittenberg since 2007. He has published on German literature and culture and Anglo-German cultural transfer. He has published widely on the gothic, including a monograph on Franz Kafka (2008), and two edited volumes on German Gothic, *Populäre Erscheinungen* (2011) and *Popular Revenants* (in English, 2012).

Charles Shirō Inouye is Professor of Japanese Literature at Tufts University. He is the translator of Izumi Kyōka's novels and stories. His most recent publications include *Evanescence and Form, an Introduction to Japanese Culture* (2008), 'Promoting Virtue and Punishing Vice: Tarantino's *Kill Bill* and the Return of Bakumatsu Aesthetics' in *Postscript* (2009) and 'Japanese Gothic' in David Punter's *New Companion to the Gothic* (2012).

Aspasia Stephanou obtained her PhD in English Studies, entitled *Our Blood, Ourselves: The Symbolics of Blood in Vampire Texts and Vampire Communities*, at the University of Stirling. She has published on issues pertaining to race and the vampire in Justin Cronin's *The Passage* (with Glennis Byron), on the use of blood in Ron Athey and Hermann Nitsch's artistic performances, and on Black Metal Theory. She is co-editor of a collection of essays on *Transgression and Its Limits* (forthcoming 2012).

Isabella van Elferen is assistant professor of Music and Media at Utrecht University. Isabella has published widely on baroque sacred music, film and TV music, videogame music, and gothic theory and sub-cultures. She is the author of *Gothic Music: The Sounds of the Uncanny* (2012), *Mystical Love in the German Baroque: Theology – Poetry – Music*

(2009) and the editor of *Nostalgia or Perversion? Gothic Rewriting from the Eighteenth Century until the Present Day* (2007).

Sue Zlosnik is Professor of Gothic Literature at the Manchester Metropolitan University. With Avril Horner, her publications include *Daphne du Maurier: Writing, Identity and the Gothic Imagination* (1998), *Gothic and the Comic Turn* (2005), the edited collection *Le Gothic: Influences and Appropriations in Europe and America* (2008) and an edition of Eaton Stannard Barrett's *The Heroine* (2011). Alone, she has published essays on Meredith, Stevenson, Tolkien and Palahniuk. Her most recent book is *Patrick McGrath* (2011).

Acknowledgements

This book emerged from the work of the AHRC Global Gothic Network (2008) and I would like to acknowledge the generous support of the AHRC in facilitating the meetings and discussions of the Network members. I would also like to thank the members of the Network for all the work that they put into this project; there may have been a few fraught moments, but it was certainly one of the best experiences of my academic life. In addition to those represented in this collection of essays, there were many other scholars who, at one stage or another, were part of the network activities and whom I would like to thank for their contributions: Elizabeth Andrews, Francesca Billiani, Betsy Fuller, Ken Gelder, Giulio Giusti, Terry Hale, Andrew Hock Soon Ng, Marilyn Michaud, Amy Palko, David Punter, Brian Rock and Dale Townshend. Particular thanks to Abigail Lee Six, who was always an invaluable and most agreeable member of the network, and whose translation skills were greatly appreciated by all.

Thanks also to Tony Wakeford of Sol Invictus and Tursa Records for permission to quote from 'English Garden'; John Bundrick of Creation Books and Meital Hershkovitz for permission to reproduce *Outcast Samurai Dancer*.

Glennis Byron

Introduction

The dead travel fast and, in our contemporary globalised world, so too does the gothic. Since the 1990s critics around the world have increasingly begun to locate their own traditions of the strange and the supernatural, sometimes, but by no means always, traditions emerging out of earlier Anglo-European forms. But although the late twentieth century saw a growing number of articles and books appearing on new national and regional gothics, from Kiwi gothic to Florida gothic, Barcelona gothic to Japanese gothic, the wider context for this had not really been addressed. What were the conditions that had produced such a proliferation of gothics and what were the general implications of this proliferation for what the West had previously understood as 'Gothic'? There was also increasing evidence of the emergence of cross-cultural and transnational gothics that called out for attention and which suggested that, despite the emergence of so many national and regional forms, in the late twentieth and early twenty-first centuries gothic was actually progressing far beyond being fixed in terms of any one geographically circumscribed mode. Most importantly, perhaps, it was clear that these developments in the increasingly diverse and problematic genre labelled gothic were intricately connected to historically specific conditions, to the development of an increasingly integrated global economy.[1]

The Global Gothic network, founded in 2008 and funded by the AHRC (Arts and Humanities Research Council, UK) was formed in order to consider the issues and questions arising from these developments. Between January 2008 and September 2009, the network hosted three major international symposiums, a postgraduate conference and an International Horror film weekend in collaboration with the Macrobert Theatre in Stirling to celebrate Halloween and the Day of the Dead in late October, early November of 2008. The first symposium saw the gathering of over thirty of the top gothic scholars from around the world at the University of Stirling to initiate discussions, and, while funding restrictions made it impossible to maintain such an impressive international mix throughout, the network benefited immensely from the discussions initiated here.

In addition to contributing, in the broadest of terms, to a greater understanding of the effects of globalisation upon cultural products, the network initially had four primary objectives. Firstly, to consider the extent to which these new forms of gothic were the product of a neo-imperialist movement, with the homogenising of culture and the rewriting of local tradition as commodity. Secondly, to consider if, alternately, there was a more dynamic process of transnational exchange with new forms being produced or old forms revitalised. Thirdly, to examine specifically the role technology played in producing these new gothic forms. And, finally, to consider not only how the processes of globalisation were facilitating the cultural exchanges that were producing new forms of gothic but also whether globalisation itself was being represented in gothic terms, with traditional gothic tropes being reformulated to engage with the anxieties produced by the breakdown of national and cultural boundaries. The chapters in this book suggest some of the conclusions we reached – and, inevitably, we did not always completely agree – and some of the new directions in which our debates took us. As discussions progressed, our growing emphasis on the contemporary processes of globalisation meant that some of the work of the network members, valuable as it was, could not ultimately be included here, but, as the publication of such works as Abigail Lee Six's *Gothic Terrors in Spanish Narrative* (2010) suggests, these network members are nevertheless continuing to impact upon gothic studies today in many other ways.

While gothic is obviously not unique in registering the effects of globalisation, it does appear to have a particularly intimate relationship with its processes, offering a ready-made language to describe whatever anxieties might arise in an increasingly globalised world. From Appadurai's cannibal culture to Beck's zombie concepts to Hardt and Negri's golems and vampires, the discourses of globalisation repeatedly turn to gothic tropes in articulating the social, cultural and economic impacts of a new world order. This is a point more fully developed in the first chapter of this book, 'Theorising globalgothic', in which Fred Botting and Justin D. Edwards situate what we are calling the globalgothic within some of the existing theoretical paradigms of globalisation.

While globalisation discourse may call upon familiar gothic tropes, globalisation is nevertheless transforming and defamiliarising these tropes as the increased mobility and fluidity of culture leads to the emergence of new gothic forms. As many of the chapters in this book show, gothic has energetically participated in the cultural flows and deterritorialisations that characterise globalisation. It is no doubt significant that the majority of the chapters focus upon gothic representations produced within the first decade of the twenty-first century. Globalisation literature of the period from around 1980 until as late as 2000 often focused upon critiques of neo-liberalism, American hegemony and fears of cultural homogenisation. A greater number of essays looking at works of earlier periods may have led to a similar emphasis in this collection and offered more in the way of dystopian visions of a Mcglobal-Mcgothic monoculture. To the extent that such issues as neo-liberalism and American hegemony remain questions of concern, they no longer assume a dominant role. It is not impositions, however, whether American, European or otherwise, that are the central concern of these chapters, but flows. In the new phase of globalisation the narrative that once conflated globalisation with Americanisation or Westernisation has been replaced by a new emphasis on multidirectional exchanges. Demonstrating a greater focus upon and acceptance of such flows, we have moved from 'the West and the rest' to what a *Washington Post* reporter dubbed the 'Trend to Blend' (Weeks).

Not only has Western gothic travelled but one of the effects of the increasing mobility and fluidity of people and products in the globalised world has been a growing awareness that the tropes and strategies Western critics have associated with the gothic, such as the ghost, the vampire and the zombie, have their counterparts in other cultures, however differently these may be inflected by specific histories and belief systems. Consequently, the flows have by no means been one-directional. This is part of our reason for coining the term *globalgothic*. Binding the words together is a way of attempting to signal a disconnection between the contemporary global manifestations we are examining and the 'Gothic' in its traditional Western sense as the shadow side of Enlightenment modernity. These forms are gothic in that we recognise their use of specific tropes and conventions. Nevertheless, they are produced and read in new temporal, geographical and political contexts. By using globalgothic as opposed to Global Gothic or Global-Gothic or any other possible permutation we hope to decentre notions of 'Gothic', tacitly placing the term under erasure and marking the confluence, in globalised space, between divergent cultural traditions. At the very least we want to register a sense of a gothic inextricable from the broader global context in which it circulates rather than a gothic tied to past notions of Enlightenment modernity.

One other point may suggest a need to decentre the West when considering globalgothic. I noted above that in the majority of chapters here the examples of globalgothic offered are twenty-first-century forms. The exceptions to this rule may be of even more significance than the general rule itself: interestingly, the globalgothic manifestations discussed from earlier periods are primarily Japanese. This may well have something to do with the profound growth in Japan's postwar economy and Japan's early participation in developing contemporary globalisation and advanced technologies. In terms of the emergence of what we are calling globalgothic, Japan, it might well be argued on a number of levels, led the way.

It is also significant that there is a predominance of chapters considering film and other visual cultural products. These are necessarily best suited for thinking about the globalgothic because they – obviously – move more easily than literary texts beyond linguistic boundaries and lend themselves to the marketing of a popular culture that can be easily commoditised, sold and consumed. The more visual forms of cultural production have therefore inevitably become more multidirectional than others.

One of the most striking features of Western gothic has always been its propensity to prey upon itself, to delight in consuming and recycling certain persistent motifs: those ubiquitous vampires, for example, or the continual returns to the monstrous potential of science or technology. This would also seem to be true of many other traditions of the strange and the supernatural throughout the world. One might think, for example, of the constant recycling and development of the pontianak in Malaysia, of Nang Nak in Thailand, and the *onryō* in Japan. The transnational flows that characterise globalisation have functioned both to reinvigorate and to intensify this tendency by opening up multiple new fields of play, and gothic has taken up what has been dubbed the 'Trend to Blend' with notable enthusiasm.

At the same time as it takes full advantage of the transnational flows, however, globalgothic frequently exploits the flows precisely in order to give form to anxieties attendant upon the processes of globalisation: anxieties about such issues as the stability of local or national identities and cultures, about the impact of transnational capitalism or the workings of technology. And so, as many of these chapters demonstrate, while the *products* made available through globalisation are eagerly appropriated, they are frequently exploited in order to articulate the *processes* of globalisation as monstrous, spectral, cannibalistic: as objects of anxiety and suspicion. Globalisation itself, then, becomes a gothic manifestation, a material and psychic invasion, a force of contamination and dominance. It is, above all, the combination of these two responses to globalisation – the exploitation of what globalisation enables and produces combined with the frequent demonisation of its processes – that characterises what we are here calling globalgothic. The conjunction of the two terms, then, enacts a kind of reversal and transvaluation in which, as Botting and Edwards point out, gothic is globalised – reproduced, consumed, recycled – and globalisation is gothicked – made monstrous, spectral, vampiric.

The chapters that follow Botting and Edward's 'Theorising globalgothic' are test cases that we hope will open up the field for further debate. We begin with three chapters considering manifestations of transnational and/or cross-cultural gothic. Steven Bruhm's 'Butoh: The dance of global darkness' offers one of the earliest examples of globalgothic with an analysis of a global dance practice, 'Ankoku butoh' ('dance of utter darkness'), first performed in Japan by Tatsumi Hijikata in 1959, on the eve of Japan's signing of the US–Japan Mutual Defense Treaty. Butoh, Bruhm points out, is a dance devised in such a way that it is not delimited by a particular nationality or subjectivity while using its globalism to resist the mechanics of globalisation. Using a familiar gothic semiotics of dying, haunting and suffering, butoh can, for Bruhm, nevertheless function as globalgothic only if we move from considerations of the politico-geographical to the politico-corporeal, to the universal and gothicised butoh body: a body in crisis, one that both suffers and causes suffering (31).

In the next chapter, 'Maori tales of the unexpected: The New Zealand television series *Mataku* as an Indigenous gothic form', Ian Conrich reflects upon *Mataku* as an active engagement between non-Western and Western cultural practices. Beginning with a survey of the ways in which Indigenous cultures have been appropriated for gothic screen fictions, Conrich then turns to forms of Indigenous gothic. As Conrich points out, it would be inappropriate to label Maori beliefs, superstitions and legends as gothic. 'They are distinctly removed from the emergence of the gothic in the West', and 'Maori culture in this context is not manufactured or the result of a commercial enterprise; instead its values are ingrained within the relationship this Indigenous culture has to *whenua* (the land) and the surrounding natural environment' (41). For Conrich it is when Maori values, beliefs and mythologies are combined with Western narratives of horror fiction that there is the production of an Indigenous gothic that can be considered a manifestation of globalgothic.

As national and regional myths and folklore are increasingly appropriated, recycled and commodified for a global audience, there a growing need to reassess the relationship of these forms with the gothic in today's globalised world. The question of how traditional folklore and myths are transformed in globalgothic narratives is also considered in the next chapter, '"She saw a soucouyant": Locating the globalgothic', in which Justin D. Edwards discusses a Canadian-Caribbean narrative, David Chariandy's *Soucouyant* (2007). Noting how *Soucouyant* draws upon and yet differs from Caribbean works that represent spectrality and possession 'without invoking the language of monstrosity or terror' (51), Edwards examines the ways in which the soucouyant is reframed in order to articulate a sense of fractured identity. Edwards considers globalgothic in terms of the migrations or displacements that engender social dislocations and cultural changes, and *Soucouyant,* he demonstrates, exemplifies the ways in which gothic tropes and narratives travel with the movements of people and the flows of cultural production, becoming dislocated from specific regions or places and yet at the same time connecting with new narratives, forming new transregional or transnational alliances.

Representations of mobility in contemporary globalgothic texts are linked to the fluidity of a space-time continuum whereby vast spaces are not always separated by distance or dislocation. Drawing on a history of gothic depictions of the Arctic (Shelley, Coleridge, Poe), Sue Zlosnik's reading of Michel Faber's 'Fahrenheit Twins' examines a text that is set, quite literally, on top of the globe. Here the uncanny cartography of the now charted Arctic terrain is simultaneously familiarised and defamiliarised through the conflations of time and space: the categories of habitable and uninhabitable, here and there, north and south are ruptured in the wake of rapid global movements and the new technologies of travel. The unlocated 'vagabonds' of Faber's text, Zlosnik suggests, are not only doubles (twins) of a gothic trajectory; they are also globalgothic figures of environmental change, hyper-modernity and what it means to be unhomed in the multivalent contexts of globalisation.

Rapid flows in the globalised world mean that globalgothic is as likely to focus upon such figures as soucouyants, La Llorona, pontianaks and *onryō* as upon the ghosts, doubles and so on familiar to readers of Western gothic, but the vampire nevertheless continues to hold its own and to demonstrate what might appear to be an unnerving global reach. In the next chapter Aspasia Stephanou approaches the question of cultural exchanges with specific reference to virtual networks and online vampire communities. More particularly, in 'Online vampire communities: Towards a globalised notion of vampire identity' Stephanou considers the degree to which these vampire communities reveal cultural homogenisation and the imposition of Western forms and the degree to which there is hybridisation and a productive melange of cultures. While demonstrating that there are indeed multidirectional flows, as she shows most notably with respect to Eastern spiritualities, ultimately Stephanou remains unconvinced that these produce a global community. The experience of blending, she suggests, is both superficial and fleeting, following the dictates of a Western consumerist logic; vampirism remains a predominantly Western phenomenon, whether in cyberspace or offline, and limited to a global mobile elite.

Isabella van Elferen's 'Globalgoth? Unlocatedness in the musical home', also interrogates questions of communities and location. Like Stephanou on vampire groups, van Elferen acknowledges that Goth is a predominantly Western affair, and the internet frequently not as global as it would seem, often functioning primarily to strengthen location-based communities. At the same time, however, van Elferen suggests that Goth nevertheless 'negates the possibility of geographical location: it is *unlocated*'. The 'gothic glance is a nostalgic one', (94) with Goth residing 'there' and 'then', never 'here' and 'now', and van Elferen shows how this not belonging, this nostalgia and evasive subjectivity which characterise the subculture, are expressed in the music of Sol Invictus and Sopor Æternus, with musical inversion turning globalised media into sites of gothic unlocation.

Barry Murnane next looks at Michael Haneke's *Funny Games* (1997) and his remake *Funny Games U.S.* (2008), to ask where the uncanny may be located today. In the first film the space of the home/the local, the Alpine setting, is overwritten with foreign cultural signification:

the signifiers of Hollywood slashers. Global culture, as Murnane puts it, 'has created a signature phantasmagoric spatial experience which is uncanny' (114). The remake, as he shows, then goes on to reproduce this process on the material level of production, distribution and reception.

Questions of the global and the local are central to the following three chapters, all of which identify the instability of these concepts in the contemporary world. Colette Balmain focuses upon the Japanese *Kwaidan* and the South Korean *A Tale of Two Sisters* (2003) to consider the merging of the global with the local in the construction of 'Pan-Asian gothic'. Myth and folklore again become a key issue, with the return to premodern and oral traditions showing a resistance to the global at the level of the local. Looking specifically at the self-Orientalism of the two films, 'the holding up of visuality both as resistance to the logic of domination and an acquiescence to its "to-be-looked-at-ness"', Balmain argues, necessitates a new way of thinking about the gothic on a global scale.

In 'Cannibal culture', I turn to Fruit Chan's *Dumplings*, to cannibalism and to those rather odd bedfellows, China and Hong Kong. Beginning with a reading of the ways in which difference has been exploited to demonise the supposedly 'primitive' local associated with China and to celebrate a progressive global city with Hong Kong, I offer a close reading of the relationship between Mrs Li and Aunt Mei to show how distinctions between the local and the global collapse with a merging of two worlds, equally driven by consumption, the prevailing imperative of the global economy.

In 'Ghost skins: Globalising the supernatural in contemporary Thai horror film', Katarzyna Ancuta argues that the increasing globalisation of the Thai economy has had a strong impact upon Thai horror films, affecting not only their production and distribution but also their themes, tropes and narrative structures. As she demonstrates with specific reference to the *phi tai hong*, the spirit of the violently dead, and Sophon Sukdapisit's 2008 debut feature *Coming Soon*, this does not reveal a process of Western imperialism but rather a conscious negotiation of values. The figure of horror produced is neither local nor global but simultaneously both. Nevertheless, for Ancuta, it is localities that 'have the last word, shaping and transforming foreign influences to fit their specific contexts' (154).

Next are two chapters that, in quite different ways, engage with globalgothic and the question of the nation with particular reference to the United States. Looking at two canonical antebellum texts and one contemporary, James Campbell traces the development, rise and decline of American gothic and the transition to a globalgothic in which America is just a part, concluding with *Silent Hill*, exemplifying a globalgothic America made in Japan that has nothing to do with what is generally considered 'American gothic'. Each of the texts Campbell considers shows the American nation state to be built upon unstable foundations, leading effectively into Avril Horner's chapter on *The Dark Knight*. For Horner what this film most chillingly illustrates are the threats and uncertainties that result from what Zygmunt Bauman has termed 'liquid modernity'. In particular *The Dark Knight* engages with anxiety over a sense of growing impotence, a concern with America's changing status after the attack on the World Trade Center and the so-called 'War on Terror', with 'American economic, scientific and political power' seen to be 'rendered ineffectual through global movements and phenomena' (184).

Fred Botting then turns to what has been one of the central gothic figures of the twenty-first century: the zombie. In 'Globalzombie', Botting traces changes in this figure from *White Zombie* onwards. In particular he considers Max Brooks's *World War Z* with its depiction of the emergence and defeat of global swarms of living dead, swarms which are both reactionary images of Western fears of immigrants and manifestations of the excessive and destructive effects of global capital. Myths and their transformations have provided an underlying connection for many – indeed in one sense or another for perhaps all – of these chapters, and Botting's conclusion takes us to what may be the greatest myth of all. By returning to 'human values and community, recentring the human figure in a global world that thought it had passed beyond humanity', *World War Z* ultimately returns, Botting suggests, to 'a basic humanist fantasy': 'that there is an idea of person that transcends myth, culture, ideology' (200).

In the final chapter Charles Inouye begins by directing our attention to Japan, a dominant source, as he points out, of globalised popular culture. His main concern, however, is to offer some account of why we have been seeing a proliferation of gothic, and the emergence of a globalgothic. Considering the global reach of J-Horror and the relentless monstrosity of anime, manga and video games, Inouye suggests that the postwar period has seen the movement away from a rationalism associated with modernity, and a resurgence and proliferation of monster-friendly expression, a resurgence of 'animism', the reanimation of the world through a globally shared, highly visual semiotic field. For Inouye, therefore, what we are calling the globalgothic is a contemporary revival of non-realistic expression, something 'sustained by high figurality and nourished by numerous cross-cultural flows' (212).

Note

1 In the mid-1990s David Punter and I met with much bemusement from publishers when we proposed a series on the topic of the Global Gothic. Such a series was simply not considered feasible in financial terms. It is a sign of how much interest has grown, therefore, that Manchester University Press is now launching a series on the International Gothic.

Reference

Linton Weeks, 'Frappe society: the trend to blend'. *The Washington Post*, 31 January 2002. C1–C2.

1

Fred Botting and Justin D. Edwards

Theorising globalgothic

'Die, die you witch. We can't get work because of you': in September 1998 a crowd returning from a march in Pretoria throw three migrant workers to their deaths (Comaroff, 2002: 788). Jean and John Comaroff cite this example as one in many of the recent reports that document a rise in cases connecting witches and zombies to class, inter-ethnic and economic tensions in southern Africa. Contemporary figures of dread are, they suggest, conjured out of the economic upheavals and shifts in immigration motivated by new labour practices. Witchcraft and zombification, then, are linked to African 'immigrants from elsewhere on the continent, whose demonization is an equally prominent feature of the postcolonial scene. Together these proletarian pariahs make visible a phantom history, a local chapter in a global story of changing relations of labor to capital, of production and consumption' (Comaroff, 2002: 783). Indeed, like so many postcolonies, post-apartheid South Africa has been dramatically changed by the social, cultural and economic impacts of globalisation. The rush of new commodities, consumption, products and money is tied to an increasingly illusive economic system that has been, at times, aligned with the sorcery of witches, zombies and disembodied, dispirited phantasms. Hence seemingly archaic figures for postmodern times – witches, zombies, monsters, ghosts and vampires – spring up in numerous and diverse locations, crossing geographic, cultural and medial divides. But these figures also adopt various guises: they are markers of otherness, articulations of the threatening changes of economic and imperial power, signifiers of techno-scientific innovations, as well as representations of personal and communal losses and traumas. By enunciating these changes through creatures of collective dread, this fixation with the living dead signals more than a figurative or symbolic response to the impacts of globalisation. It constitutes a tangible reaction to the distress and anxiety of a globalised system that erupts within or from public cultures across the world. Globalisation, then, has led to a new way of thinking about gothic production: globalgothic.

But what is globalgothic? And how might it be theorised? One starting point for addressing these questions is to acknowledge that, despite huge variations in cultural-historical factors, spatial and temporal modes and the significances tied to locality and specificity, there are certain continuities and commonalities between imaginary supernatural, spectral and monstrous forms in fiction, film, fashion, media, music and culture. But even this recognition raises further queries. What do these forms represent, if they represent anything? What do they do? What are their effects? And what might they have in common? These are tricky questions, particularly when we consider that figures from the gothic genre are imaginary and metaphorical, revenants, often vague in form, shifting of shape, and have for centuries screened and screened out otherness and fear. Yet a shared sense, itself dark, uncertain, of the world can be located through the diverse uses of gothic tropes disseminated widely in media networks: in print, on screens, online, over airwaves and satellite systems. Exported Western images move across the world, manifesting a global market in which cultures produce, consume, appropriate, and transform stories, images and characters. Dance forms in Japan mesh local customs and concerns regarding death with traditional and imported aesthetic and cultural theories, hybrid challenges to form and sense that raise political anxieties about imperialism; mergings of myth and media in New Zealand acknowledge the permeability of borders while the interfections of media forms embody the clashing and inmixing of social realities and cultural crossings. Global events, the collapse of blocs and borders, the emergence of transnational and economic unions, spectres of superstates, transform the West from within, such events, moreover, having large-scale political effects as well as small-scale subcultural ramifications. The traffic in images and tropes is not unidirectional given the scale and audiences for media and cinematic production across the world. The varieties of Asian cinema offer abundant examples of different forms and figures of haunting and spectrality, different axes of media, tradition, embodiment and anxiety that are exported, appropriated, remade.

The multidirectional traffic exposes the limitation to ideas of Western cultural hegemony in the face of competing and globally dispersed patterns of consumption. Here, always mobile, travelling with migrations and through the flows of global media, boundaries between life and death, real and unreal, self and other, normality and deviance become defamiliarised as they are shifted across geographical, virtual and cultural planes, global and local at the same time.

The global market of signs, images and commodities energises globalgothic interactions. As a result globalgothic operates as a locus, frequently an obscure locus, of world exchanges, and also points to the context in which messages, meanings, responses and reactions take shape. For the rapidly changing and highly mobile network called globalisation presses upon the security and stability of all cultural, political, national systems and structures. This new market is, in our thinking, a new world order that can no longer be simply aligned with the consumerist and homogenising pressures of modern – Western or US – capitalism. Transnational capitalism, for so long associated with Western or US imperialism, respects no national border in its pursuit of profits and markets. Changing patterns of ownership, investment and corporate structure over the last forty years – and now the growth of new economic superpowers and new global financial crises – situate the nation in a subordinate, even subaltern, position, at the mercy, rather than at the centre, of fluctuations of capital. As a decentred and deterritorialising apparatus of governance, capitalism progressively transforms, reshapes and incorporates the entire global realm within its open, expanding frontiers (Hardt and Negri, 2001: xii). Such decentring turns modern ways of thinking, believing, being, and narrating inside-out and upside-down, generating a new sense of anxiety about borders, identities and futures. This anxiety is, perhaps, one of the bases for the reappearance of gothic and supernatural motifs and tropes. But it is an anxiety that selects its metaphors, reading figures of disturbance, haunting and liminality, ephemeral figures of strangeness, as well as violence and death, in a range of cultural productions, from contemporary Japanese dance to American zombie narratives, music and online bloodsucking. Global manifestations of the gothic, we suggest, touch on the sense of the unnerving, unpredictable and uncontrollable scale of world changes that impinge diversely and relentlessly on different locales and peoples. The darkness of real and imagined ecological disasters, overproduction, pollution, climate change, is rendered both sublimely unthinkable and culturally and emotionally specific in its devastations. In attempting to broach the scale of change, the globalgothic mode registers an ill-formed grasp of the consequences attendant on the dissolution of old securities, clear-cut jurisdictions, stable structures and comforting boundaries, be they national, social, cultural, scientific or subjective.

The rise of recent reports of zombies and witchcraft in southern Africa is connected to the 'implosion of neoliberal capitalism' and a 'global crisis' that engenders anxieties about immigration and unemployment (Comaroff, 2002: 779). Violence between citizens of neighbouring postcolonial nations, then, is not merely the byproduct of local tension. It also stems from the 'structural adjustments' that have imposed global market forces on developing nations and enforced a dependency on economic fluctuations (prices, investments) and the resulting shifts in employment and migration. Following the Comaroffs, Michael Hardt and Antonio Negri cite a growing number of reports of ritual murder, occult practices, witchcraft, monsters and zombies from Africa to Indonesia, Russia to South America. From a European perspective these events may be dismissed as a resurgence of primitive premodern practices. Hardt and Negri, however, caution against such a response, arguing that these reports are manifestations of contemporary forces and effects, postmodern more than premodern or primitive. They seem to share a common element: supernatural sightings often appear when 'new dreams of wealth in the global capitalist economy have for the first time been plunged into the icy realities of imperial hierarchies' (Hardt and Negri, 2001: 126). Such reports offer, for Hardt and Negri, a way of understanding how 'each of these contexts' shares a 'contradictory social situation': singularity at a local level finds 'global commonality' in the fluxes and flows of a new Empire (126). Pushing at the constraints of a residually Enlightenment ontology that reproduces a master logic and places Europe at the centre of thought, history and being, Hardt and Negri importantly try to articulate the effects of what they call the new world order at economic, political and cultural levels. They identify a changing global habitus, a transnational digitally enhanced network which transforms spaces, times and, significantly, ways of thinking, demanding a greater and more effective understanding of globalisation's complex and fluid relationships. Articulating these phenomena with numerous reiterations of gothic figures, they observe the interpenetration of the local and global, self and other, while avoiding the static models of binary opposition and hierarchical difference that have been challenged so effectively in postcolonial reversals of Western subalternisation. It is here, among and across the liminal spaces of a new world order, that gothic figures are articulated as immaterial presences with physical effects and the globalgothic grasps and connects antitheses by engaging with doubles, ambivalences and multiplicities.

In *Specters of Marx* Jacques Derrida envisions this new economic order as monstrous, techno-scientific, quasi-messianic: it is seen to be introducing a 'new disturbance' and an 'unprecedented form of hegemony' to which older modern categories no longer apply except in spectral misrecognitions (1994: 50). Fredric Jameson's more measured – economically speaking – Marxist account plots a similar trajectory towards something systemically inhuman. For him finance capitalism's general and cannibalistic tendency to exploit crises enables it to move from failing economic practices (such as industrial production) to absorb 'ever greater zones of social life (including individual subjectivity)' (Jameson, 2000: 264). Abandoning the national industrial competition of an imperial stage, capital discovers profit beyond material goods in financial transactions alone to become 'free-floating', separated 'from the concrete context of its productive geography' (259). Its dematerialisation parallels the operations of virtuality, informatics and posthumanism and transforms the globe in the light of its digital abstractions. Objects and things are rendered secondary to flows of information, signs and services. Here globalisation is envisaged as 'a kind of cyberspace in which money capital has reached its ultimate dematerialization, as messages that pass instantaneously from one nodal point to another across the former globe, the former material world' (268). The other side of such abstracted yet immanent connectedness is perhaps a very different sense of hauntedness. New ghosts, separated from material contexts and monetary realities, appear to redefine financial exchanges. Speculation becomes a spectral force: 'specters of value' vie 'against each other in a vast, world-wide, disembodied phantasmagoria'. A different, dark and dominating shape orchestrates the flows and movements of global capital: 'a play of monetary entities', abstracted, immaterial, that 'can live on their own internal metabolism and accrete without any reference to an older type of content' (273). In its ghostly form, capital moves outside of what we once might have considered a real world. Its disembodied and spectral presence now signals something other than an invisible hand conferring or withholding wealth. The new monster operates autonomously, in an inhuman way, disconnected from any relation that might once have benefited humanity.

Fredric Jameson's description of an indomitable capitalist monster machine revives the Marxist nightmare of a vampiric capitalism feeding off the living labour of the world's workers. Jameson's capitalist monster is, like the vampire-capital of Hardt and Negri's Empire, less reliant on the material life and vital bodies of Marx's metanarrative. Still, Jameson's writing is haunted by the revenant of modern oppositions – particularly class conflict – and thus romanticises resistance in terms of heroic collectives, indigenous cultures or individuals struggling against a callous and dominating system. But this assumes that modernity is stable and successful in always maintaining its divisions and hierarchies. Such a vision fails to acknowledge that modernity's enlightened, progressive, rational, scientific and productive forces were always double and haunted by the past, strangeness and otherness. For modernity has always been dependent on the antitheses it invoked and suppressed, on the subjects it constructed and excluded through the demonisations of class, gender and racial difference.

Modernity's formation works on the basis of doublets: empirical and transcendental, liberty and discipline, spirit and spectre, self and other, norm and monster, consciousness and unconscious, progress and regression, mind and body, light and dark, surface and depth, sameness and difference. It was, as such, formed on the basis of an originary division-elision, a hybrid-uncanny structuring, which Homi Bhabha relates to the hegemonies of European imperialisms. For Bhabha it is the very ambivalence and undecidability within modernity that reveals its plurality, its interstitial, transnational and translational shiftings, its doubleness and strangeness. A 'contentious internal liminality', he writes, can be located in the 'antagonistic and ambivalent moments within the "rationalizations" of modernity' (1994: 171). Thus, if modern culture is *heimlich* in its disciplinary generalisations, its mimetic narratives, its homologous empty time, its seriality, its progress, its customs and its apparent coherence, then it is also *unheimlich* in its encounters with heterogeneities, otherness, discontinuities and differences that are, for all its occlusions, its own. For in order for modernity to distinguish itself and to signify, it must be translated, disseminated, differentiatiated, and hence it must become 'interdisciplinary, intertextual, international, inter-racial' (136). By extension 'cultural globality is', for Bhabha, 'figured in the *in-between* spaces of double-frames: its historical originality marked by a cognitive obscurity; its "decentred subject" signified in the nervous temporality of the transitional, or the emergent provisionality of the "present"' (216). Gone are the fixed meanings of binary structures, clear borders, cultural coherence or causes and effects. In their place we find flows and disjunctions in the 'stubborn chunks' of cultural identification, as well as a reiteration of migrations, displacements, translations, deterritorialisations and reterritorialisations. Unsurprisingly, it is in modernity that gothic is invented, signs of Western culture's 'internal liminality' and its increasingly futile attempts at holding otherness at a distance.

In recognition of modernity's failed suppressions, haunting has been used throughout postcolonial theory to bring an awareness of colonial history to the present while also revising the conceptions of contemporary regional, national and cultural relations. Spectral coloniality often figures the relation of otherness, of occlusions, of limitations, and of desires to acknowledge, see and hear others, the marginalised, the silenced. Indeed haunting is persistent within the postcolonial consciousness precisely because of its affective feature, a feature that conjures a sense of looming importance that is both present and unsettling. And a spectre is also conjured in the imagined origins of a 'pure' tradition killed off in the incursion of colonial forces. Though haunting can signal the return in spectral forms of cultures and pasts that have been pushed aside, those revenant pasts return often as sites of loss, nostalgia, guilt or betrayal. More importantly, postcolonial hauntings reveal powerlessness when faced with the possibility of resistance. Memories are not always mobilised and insurgencies are often written over by an ever increasing transnational condition that denies or obfuscates situated or positioned resistance. And this is where globalgothic is significant. For the use of haunting in postcolonial theory also signals a placeless yet always present mode of resistance that betrays an underlying fear about how disputes and encounters are diffused within the often elusive character of new transnational realities and postcolonial forms of oppression. Seen from a globalgothic perspective, then, the use of haunting in postcolonial theory reflects a suspended condition, in-between because it is indicative of an era hovering between the traces of a defeated colonial history and vague transnational structures of hierarchy and subjugation. With the rise of new forms of empire and transnational capital, the active imperialisms witnessed in tangible and positioned structures of conflict related to nation states have declined, and it is not always easy to locate tangible forms of empire, particularly given their transnational nature.

In *Spectral Nationality*, for instance, Pheng Cheah explores postcolonial anxieties about the possibility of mapping or situating resistance under conditions of transnational empire and globalised incarnations of imperialism. Drawing on Derridean hauntology and Benedict Anderson's work on imagined communities, Cheah examines how contemporary theories of freedom, including postcolonial nationalisms, are underwritten by a metaphor of the organic body. While this metaphor is essential to modern theories of freedom, it is also inherently unstable and prone to perform its own unravelling. The actualisation of freedom, a concept that is politically and philosophically anchored in modernity, is always incomplete, and the nation signified within this 'organismatic metaphor' figures a pledge of freedom that remains spectral, neither simply living nor simply dead (Cheah, 2003: 19). Put simply, nationalism is part of a body politic that cannot simply be killed off by a new globalism or a utopian cosmopolitanism. It is too deeply embedded in modern thought. Rather, the nation state becomes involved in a series of hauntings: 'the state is an uncontrollable specter that the national organism must welcome within itself, and direct, at once for itself and against itself', and the nation, too, 'must be seen as a specter', haunted by and haunting the state (390, 395). In this the only nation that can be conjured is spectral: assertions of nationalism have failed to reappropriate the body of the neocolonial state from the grasp of contemporary forms of empire, confirming that 'the metaphor that has replaced the living organism as the most appropriate organism for freedom today is that of the ghost' (383).

Globalgothic, however, registers something different, something that is harder to define and yet to be formed. It reflects the dark and shadowy contours of a new world order that is mediated, networked, militarised and corporatised but offers no clear-cut image of itself, flickering between a series of dissolutions and displacements. The speeds of cultural change, new technologies, media exchanges and financial fluidity augment liminal and uncanny zones, making ephemeral spaces pervasive and generalised. The in-between moves outside. Hence the structures that once held modernity's doublets in place are dissolved. Fixed boundaries become fluid as unstable networks, mobile assemblages, complex clusters and nodal singularities engender rapid movements across a viral and transversal diffusion of borders and fields. Globalgothic registers the effects after the interpenetration of global and local has rendered the separation of both poles redundant, thus exploding the myth of a pure globality and shredding the nostalgic fantasy of a return to an untainted local culture. An early example of this arises in reports of Malay *hantu* possessing the bodies of women workers in the established free-trade zones of Malaysia. Here haunting and possession insist on the power to 'attack the real', exploding the polarities of local and global, as the shop floor is reterritorialised by the threatening spirits of traditional, regional narratives. 'In the 1970s', writes Mary Keller,

> hundreds of incidents were recorded in the free-trade zones of Malaysia in which women who worked in the technically sophisticated manufacturing plants were possessed by *hantu*, spirits, often harmful to human beings, associated with a place, animal, or deceased person. Fifteen women, possessed by *datuk*, an ancestral male spirit associated with a sacred place, closed down an American-owned microelectronics factory . . . The possessed women were so volatile that the male supervisors could not control one woman. (2002: 1)

In this context, where the spirits of a folkloric tradition take possession of the factory, an altered reality arises out of heterogeneous experiences and the means of production becomes, if only momentarily, unmanageable. By taking possession of the workplace, these women transform the physical and temporal dimensions within a sphere of activity that has been established through Kuala Lumpur's investment in global capitalism.

Of all the forces evident in the transformation of the world, consumerism (or 'Western consumerism') is perhaps most vividly identifiable as having powerfully imposed economic and cultural practices as a global norm and dominant expectation or aspiration. To consume is to be able to play one's part in the contemporary world. It is also most obviously – and most often condemned – as part of the homogenising imperative of new imperial, corporate culture, a 'McDonaldisation' of cultural differences. At the same time, cultural differences are repeatedly consumed and transformed, to be sold at the delicatessen counter, in 'World Music' or 'World Cinema' racks or in tourist brochures. Consumerism, coming to the fore in the West in the twentieth century, overturns practices and morality in which work and prudence are privileged over luxury and indulgence. It transforms Western cultures as well as those of the developing world. A marker of what is called a shift to 'post-industrial' practices, it is a move away from an emphasis on production and towards economies based on the circulation of goods and services. In many ways, and in its function as the double of bourgeois modernity, consumption has been figured in gothic terms, its darker and more destructive features visible in the contagious bite of the vampire. For Marx capitalism itself was voraciously undead, feeding 'vampire-like' on living labour (1976: 342). Anne Rice's vampire, Lestat, notes how the pattern changes as the twentieth century draws to a close. Awakening near the end of that century after going into hibernation at the end of the nineteenth, when consumption was linked to sexuality and decadence (see Dijkstra, 1986), Rice's eponymous hero praises the way US consumer culture exudes an 'Oriental loveliness' and manifests a society in which all people have a 'right to luxury' (Rice, 1995: 14). These rights of consumption, though registered in residually nineteenth-century terms, are very much part of a new world order in which consuming imperatives have become the norm (Goux, 1990). No longer is the fat cigar-smoking capitalist the one who stands behind vampire capitalism, with its repulsive aspect in respect of the living, human workers of the world. Enjoying the freedoms of consumerism, every member of Western culture is enjoined to feed on the rest of the world, expropriating the resources and labour of other countries, presiding, unaware perhaps, over those stripping forests or slaving all day in sweatshops to deliver the outsourced objects of consumer desire. In Western youth culture, moreover, the vampire signals these new and seductive norms of economic individualism and consumption; all assume the shape of 'consuming mall-rats' (Latham, 1997: 131). As with the figure of Lestat, however, the enjoyment of this new world of consumer plenitude comes at a price: not only others' slavery to global forces of production and unequal distribution but also a subjection and transvaluation of the idea of humanity. In consumer culture all life gives itself and its dignities up, willing or not, to vampiric corporate powers for whom humans are victims of exploitation comparable to the very burgers they consume (Zanger, 1997).

The effects of modernity's movement beyond itself are not just virtual. For the acceleration of economics, science and technology have *real* consequences for *real* bodies, cities, nations, cultures, spaces and histories. 'In the context of the flexibility demanded by contemporary capitalism', writes Arjun Appadurai, 'there has been a great compression of time and space, and the body comes to be seen as a chaotic, hyperflexible site, ridden with contradictions and warfare' (1996: 44). Hypermodernity, then, cannot simply be conflated with the homogenising processes that transform specific economic, martial or technological elements and effects. Rather, it is better understood as a radical destabilisation and unanchoring of interrelationships as part of fluid and shifting networks of powers (Harvey, 1996). Thus 'national security' shifts fluidly into 'global security' as the call for a universal peace is calibrated against a 'global civil war' and local resistance is redefined as international terrorism. Furthermore the same modalities and technologies that produce economic forms of globalisation also support global terrorism, not just in the fluid transfer of funds for acts of resistance but also in the communication technologies that enable networks to develop across distance, time and space.

Globalgothic asks vital questions about the decentring of power. For while it can be packaged, marketed and sold, globalgothic can also reveal the terrors of global terrorism or how oppositional movements might challenge the powerful hegemonic discourses of free market, neo-liberal ideologies. Gothic conventions situate terror as happening 'out there'; its position is elsewhere, outside the self, something that takes place away from the security of the homely. But the proximity of terror does not always remain at a distance, for terror refuses to be contained within the borders of a particular jurisdiction. Indeed, in a globalised world, the terror of terrorism brings the reminder that borders are permeable, exploding binary models of terror and proximity. 'If the displaced become instruments of terror', writes Tabish Khair, 'it is as much because we, who have decided to stay home or who have the privileged option of making the entire globe our home, have for too long averted our eyes from those who are "elsewhere" or who come from "elsewhere"' (2009: 109). Put simply, terrorism forces us to recognise that 'elsewhere' is 'here', not only because the formulation of the distinction was always located in the privileged site of power but also because we can no longer refuse to see the shadows we have cast. Bombs on the London Underground, exploding trains in Madrid, the crash of the World Trade Center – all of these acts spawn terror in developed nations, prompting a reallocation of resources in the name of security.

Chasing ghosts is, for Paul Virilio, a by-product of transpolitical militarisation that moves beyond nation states. In this new world order 'peace' and 'security' are privileged over 'defence' and, as a result, the 'enemy' disappears, 'making way for the indeterminacy of constantly redefined threats' to life and ways of life. 'The enemy of the constitution is', he continues, 'thenceforth less an "internal enemy" of the national state than a "threat" to the civil peace, a danger to the *constitution of internal pacification*' (2005: 160–1). Hence the enemy is no longer a specific nation or threat, but 'banalized (reduced to an object of continued police repression) and absolutized (as the Enemy, an absolute threat to the ethical order)' (Hardt and Negri, 2001: 13).

Globalisation has produced major social divisions through the 'overvalorization of corporate capital and devalorization of disadvantaged workers' (Sassen, 1999: 88). Class distinctions, though, are not ahistorical, and the asymmetrical relations in globalisation involve 'new movements and new instabilities, from "transmigration" of capital and people to new contexts that are "fragile" in being centred on an economy of high productivity, advanced technologies and intensified exchanges' (Sassen, 1999: 102). From this perspective globalisation is 'multiscalar': it occupies places and non-places and denationalises state institutions. Here a global proletariat exists, but in 'dispersed' and 'mobile forms' (Harvey, 1996: 423). As frontiers and borders shift to form internal boundaries and virtual non-spaces, the distinctions between global and local interpenetrate and transform each other in a fluid and dynamic relation. As global forces and media – capital, advertising, commodification – are absorbed into the local, a new interior is hollowed out (Appadurai, 1996: 42). For US geopolitical strategy identifies globality with the 'interior' of a finite world, while local issues are exteriorised, pushed to the periphery. This process signifies 'a great globalitarian transformation which extraverts localness – all localness' and deports 'living spaces' and spaces of economic subsistence. It also engenders 'a global de-localisation, which affects the very nature not merely of "natural", but of "social" identity, throwing into question not so much the nation-state, but the city, the geopolitics of nature' (Virilio, 2000: 10).

Globalisation is, as Appadurai notes, a cannibalising force: sameness and difference, East and West, begin to consume each other in a 'cultural flux' which destabilises identities, disturbing migrant communities from within (1996: 43–4). In turn, transnational settings challenge traditional expectations and identifications. This can, in some cases, generate a sense of 'rage' and 'betrayal' in translocal ethnic contexts due to misunderstandings about the relationship between appearance and reality, particularly when it is revealed that one's neighbours are not necessarily identified with the same communal, ethnic or political values. 'This sense of betrayal is', Appadurai writes,

> about mistaken identity in a world where the stakes associated with these identities have become enormously high. The rage such betrayal seems to inspire can of course be extended to masses of persons who may not have been intimates . . . [but] it remains animated by a perceived violation of the sense of knowing who the Other was and of rage about who they really turn out to be. This sense of treachery, of betrayal, and thus of violated trust, rage, and hatred has everything to do with a world in which large-scale identities forcibly enter the local imagination and become dominant voice-over in the traffic of ordinary life. (1996: 154)

identity and otherness between members of what appeared to be the same community not only blurs but also motivates rage and violence. This is an effect of (mis)perception and unreal expectations, but also an effect of translocation in which traditional values are pressed by the tensions and desires of a different culture. David Harvey explains this as part of 'the new imperialism' in which cohesive components of the body politic are left to die in the name of profit. 'Communities', he argues,

> built to service now defunct manufacturing industries have been left high and dry, wracked with long-term structural unemployment. Disenchantment, dropping out, and quasi-legal means to make ends meet follows. Those in power rush to blame the victims . . . If those marginalized happen to be an ethnic or racially marked minority, as is all-too often the case, then the stigmatization amounts to barely concealed racial bigotry. (1996: 404)

Responses include urban violence, rage, frustration, depression and disillusion. But as geophysical boundaries dissolve, as historical structures are torn down or realigned, and as the cultural contours of modernity collapse, the proximity of otherness gets closer and closer. Economically rich and poor regions of the world were never very far apart. But in globalisation the insecurities between self and other are heightened as once stable spaces undergo radical shifts and reversals. The assumptions propping up the notion of separate regional and economic spheres have been jettisoned by the migrations, unemployment and homelessness arising out of contemporary transformations of financial markets. Our post-industrial regions, then, mirror the old colonial world (Virilio, 2000: 55) and the 'Third World does not really disappear in the process of unification of the World market but enters into the First, establishes itself at the heart as ghetto, shantytown, favela, always again produced and reproduced. In turn, the First World is transformed into the Third in times of stock exchanges and banks, transnational corporations and icy skyscrapers of money and command' (Hardt and Negri, 2001: 253–4).

If, as we suggest, globalisation engenders a context of unbelonging through the rupture of communities, then what function does globalgothic perform? The answer is twofold and enfolded: first, it registers the anxieties that arise from national, social and subjective dissolution, including an endless media-critical interrogation of identities, genders, races and classes; second, it constructs an otherness that screens out the excesses of anxiety while turning the mirror back on itself . . . globally, darkly, monstrously.

References

Appadurai, Arjun. 1996. *Modernity at Large: Cultural Dimensions of Globalization*. Minneapolis: University of Minnesota Press.

Bhabha, Homi. 1994. *The Location of Culture*. New York: Routledge.

Cheah, Pheng. 2003. *Spectral Nationality: Passages of Freedom from Kant to Postcolonial Literatures of Liberation*. New York: Columbia University Press.

Comaroff, Jean, and John Comaroff. 2002. 'Alien-nation: zombies, immigrants, and millennial capitalism'. *South Atlantic Quarterly*, 101.4: 779–805.

Derrida, Jacques. 1994. *Specters of Marx*, trans. Peggy Kamuf. New York: Routledge.

Dijkstra, Bram. 1986. *Idols of Perversity: Fantasies of Feminine Evil in Fin-de-Siècle Culture*. Oxford: Oxford University Press.

Goux, Jean-Joseph. 1990. 'General economics and postmodern capitalism'. *Yale French Studies*, 78: 206–24.

Hardt, Michael, and Antonio Negri. 2001. *Empire*. Cambridge, MA: Harvard University Press.

Harvey, David. 1996. *Justice, Nature and the Geography of Difference*. Oxford: Blackwell.

Jameson, Fredric. 2000 (1997). 'Culture and finance capital'. In *The Jameson Reader*, eds Michael Hardt and Kathi Weeks. Oxford: Blackwell, 255–74.

Jameson, Fredric, and Masao Miyoshi. 1998. *The Cultures of Globalization*. Durham, NC: Duke University Press.

Keller, Mary. 2002. *The Hammer and the Flute: Women, Power, and Spirit Possession*. Baltimore: Johns Hopkins University Press.

Khair, Tabish. 2009. *The Gothic, Postcolonialism and Otherness: Ghosts from Elsewhere*. Basingstoke: Palgrave.

Latham, Rob. 1997. 'Consuming youth: the lost boys cruise mallworld'. In *Blood Read: The Vampire as Metaphor in Contemporary Culture*, eds Jan Gordon and Veronica Hollinger. Philadelphia: University of Pennsylvania Press, 129–47.

Marx, Karl. 1976 (1867). *Capital*, Vol. I, trans. Ben Fowkes. Harmondsworth: Penguin.

Rice, Anne. 1995. *The Vampire Lestat*, New York: Warner Books.

Sassen, Saskia. 1999. 'Globalization and the formation of claims'. In *Giving Ground*, eds Joan Copjec and Michael Sorkin. London: Verso, 96–105.

Virilio, Paul. 2000. *The Information Bomb*, trans Chris Turnes. London: Verso.

Virilio, Paul. 2005. *Negative Horizon: An Essay on Dromoscopy*. London: Continuum.

Zanger, Jules. 1997. 'Metaphor into metonymy: the vampire next door'. In *Blood Read: The Vampire as Metaphor in Contemporary Culture*, eds Jan Gordon and Veronica Hollinger. Philadelphia: University of Pennsylvania Press, 17–26.

2

Steven Bruhm

Butoh: The dance of global darkness

> Whether it's a squash blossom fading or a horse getting thin in the face, it all comes down to a tale of the body.
>
> Tatsumi Hijikata, 'Wind Daruma'

Imagine bodies hairless and pure white, except for black, deeply set eyes. Emaciated and weightless, they glide across a dark space as if on no legs. They join other such bodies, whose faces register the contact through hideously distorted grins or silent shrieks. All these bodies proceed to some stylised, repetitive movements, here frenetic, there glacial. They claw and scratch, they fall and writhe, they twist and maim their postures, at once the victims of torture and its perpetrators.

Ankoku butoh, literally the 'dance of utter darkness', was first performed in Japan by Tatsumi Hijikata and then developed by Hijikata and Kazuo Ohno (among others) into a global dance practice. Featuring dancers whose bodies appear as if they were cadavers refusing to die, butoh was born of death, or of many deaths: the death of a Japanese culture that was, in 1959, entering into a commercial and military treaty with the very country that had dropped two atomic bombs on it fourteen years earlier; the death, at the personal level, of female family members whose ghosts would haunt and inspire Hijikata and Ohno throughout their careers; and death at the ontological level of all coherent reference of subjectivity, of a self or an ego that might dance identity or emotion the way it does in modernist dance practice. For Hijikata the body is something of an active sepulchre: 'I would like to make the dead gestures inside my body die one more time and make the dead themselves dead again. I would like to have a person who has already died die over and over inside my body. I may not know death, but it knows me' (Hijikata, 2000a: 77). Butoh for him is an artistic practice that, like the gothic, turns the body 'into a material object, an object that is like a corpse' (Nanako, 2000: 17). Through this object certain personal and social disequilibria can find expression. And, since its invention in the mid-twentieth century, butoh has spread across the globe. With avatars in such popular videos as Marilyn Manson's 'Tourniquet' or Tool's 'Schism', butoh, in the words of dancer-artist Sandra Fraleigh, 'is fast becoming a borderless art for a borderless century' (2010: 1).

This chapter seeks to unpack a number of suggestions and assumptions that I have woven into my above description of butoh as a recognisably gothic aesthetic. By juxtaposing the living dead of an 'Eastern' dance practice with the animated corpse of the 'Western' gothic, I want to join two critical traditions that, to my knowledge, have not yet been considered together.[1] I take as a working premise that at least some aspects of the contemporary gothic aesthetic owe as much to butoh as butoh owes to an earlier Western dance practice, which itself owes much to the gothic tradition in literature, music and visual art. In so juxtaposing these expressive worlds, I want to use butoh to raise some questions about the notion of a 'globalgothic', where the signifier 'global' may too quickly or cleanly invoke the worrisome spectre of cultural imperialism and corruption, and of the hegemony of Western (usually US) ideological powers. Reading butoh as globalgothic must do justice to the different traditions that produced these cultural practices – critics such as Fraleigh, Juliette T. Crump and Michael Sakamoto see a salubrious Zen Buddhist healing practice in butoh that may be less evident to the West's audience for gothic[2] but it is precisely the 'nature' of the butoh, I shall contend, that makes it impossible and undesirable to be hived off from Western gothic. My project, then, has three straightforward questions. What sense might it make to read Japanese butoh within a tradition of Western gothic? What might we learn about the gothic by reading it within the practice of butoh? And, how might these two things come together to limn a phenomenon we want to call 'globalgothic'?

Butoh, Japan and the global

Any consideration of butoh as an art form – either geographically borderless or spiritually healing – must first locate it in Japan's archive of images of violence, protest and the riven body. If Fraleigh is right to contend that 'butoh retrieves something essentially Japanese' (2010: 3), that is because it found its birth in the body of a Japanese performer, Tatsumi Hijikata, who had built a dance upon a Japanese novel, Yukio Mishima's scandalously homoerotic *Kinjiki* (*Forbidden Colours*, 1953), a dance that was performed in Tokyo on the eve of Japan's signing of the US–Japan Mutual Defense Treaty (Klein, 1988:1). Hijikata's outrage at American commercialism and military arrogance was foremost an outrage at his country's capitulation to American influence under the guise of economic prosperity and military security. As Clark Lunberry puts it,

> During the transitional period of Japanese post-war history, from the late 1950s and on into the 1960s, it seemed that much of the nation was wholeheartedly embracing the speedy social, cultural, and economic transformations, and in particular the 'Americanizations' that were sweeping this recently defeated and newly compliant nation. However, already by the early 1960s there developed a specific cultural and aesthetic reaction against these widespread transformations, evinced in the heated and often violent confrontations regarding the 1960 military treaty with the U.S. (2006: 83)

The implications for 'Japaneseness' of this 'cultural and aesthetic reaction' are manifold. First, it was directed against a soulless and bloodless Japanese bourgeoisie that, in Hijikata's words, were 'inhabitants of the transparent, mechanical "world," without any ties to bleeding nature and even without smell. I could not help seeing them as corpses' (2000b: 43). And if this sort of spiritual zombification were not gothic enough, Hijikata casts himself in the role of zombie killer, a role that is, paradoxically, as tyrannically violent as it is socially healing. 'Isn't there some work that strews absolute putrefaction and graphic terror throughout the world?' he wonders. 'I have always thought I would like to put my hands to the axle of anger that sustains that kind of work' (2000b: 43). Playing Ben Huss to Tokyo's Living Dead, Hijikata sets himself the gothic task of ridding his country of foreign pollution.

But the 'axle of anger that sustains that kind of work' was not readily to be found in Japanese artistic tradition. If the butoh of the 1960s was busily rejecting the ideological infiltrations of the West, it was also rejecting the ossified stage practices of bourgeois Japanese theatre, such as kabuki and noh. Themselves arising from a tradition of imperial dynasties and performed in a sanitised urban theatre only for patrons toney enough to afford tickets, traditional Japanese drama styles were as much the culprits in the corpsification of Japan as any seductive

Western influence might be. For these reasons, then, Hijikata rejected Tradition (capital 'T' intended) by building on his body a series of gestures or choreographic poses that would signal an *other* Japan, a Japan not corrupted into rotting urban flesh and bloated decadence but rather corrupted by poverty and the ravages of nature and of radiation. The 'butoh body' was to be found in Hijikata's frigid northern birthplace, Tohoku, from which Hijikata took what is now the most legible stance of the butoh dancer (the *ganimata*): a semi-crouch, knees bowed and feet supinated, with torso leaning forward and shoulders slumped low, hands extended horizontally but limply. This pose condenses in the dancer a number of ravaged bodies: the rice picker in the paddy, the survivor of an atomic blast, the malnourished and maimed. What is 'essentially Japanese' about butoh, then, is what is 'essentially French' about *Notre Dame de Paris,* or essentially English about the Jacobin gothic: the poor, criminal and outcast made to display their suffering to a potentially sympathetic audience to advertise the crimes of the *ancien régime.*

Or so it would be if butoh were a nationally insular and centripetal force of aesthetic creativity. It is not. What is remarkable and richly paradoxical about butoh is the degree to which its tenets belie any desire to make it a local, essentially Japanese expressive practice. Hijikata's inaugural butoh performance may have been based on his countryman Mishima's novel *Kinjiki,* and it may use as its 'first position' the radiated rice picker of northern Japan, but Hijikata himself was relentlessly macaronic in his sources of inspiration. The German Expressionist Dance (*Neue Tanz*) style of Mary Wigman and Kurt Jooss reflects itself in his choreography as consistently as Jean Genet, Jean-Paul Sartre, Antonin Artaud, Friedrich Nietzsche and the Marquis de Sade permeate his writings. See, for example, the way Hijikata seamlessly stitches together a moment of butoh inspiration with a Sartrean existential crisis:

> A criminal on death row made to walk to the guillotine is already a dead person even as he clings, to the very end, to life. The fierce antagonism between life and death is pushed to the extreme and cohesively expressed in this lone miserable being who, in the name of the law, is forced into an unjust condition. A person not walking but made to walk; a person not living but made to live; a person not dead but made to be dead must, in spite of such total passivity, paradoxically expose the radical vitality of human nature. Sartre wrote: 'A criminal with bound hands now standing at the scaffold is not yet dead. One moment is lacking for death, that moment of life which intensely desires death.' This very condition is the original form of dance and it is my task to create just such a condition on the stage. (2000b: 46)

I will return momentarily to this strange ontology, but for now it is enough to say that, for Hijikata, such European inspiration is not accidental; it is part of a larger programme to devise a dance that would not be delimited by a particular nationality or subjectivity. As Lunberry argues of new Japanese dance, this 'movement presented a curious merger of internationalism and the newly formed "nativism" . . . this desired reemergence freely borrowed from the Western avant-garde in order to frame its own investigations and creations, and to articulate its own complex and often conflicting image of itself' (2006: 83). In what Lunberry calls 'a knot of enabling complications' (85) and a 'reverse migration' of influences from East to West to East (80), Hijikata's butoh freely allowed Japanese culture to penetrate and to be penetrated by global influences, and not simply to have those global influences be rejected in favour of local purity. 'For Butoh had in large part been formed as a hybrid mix of dance and theater that emerged in the ruinous aftermath of the Second World War', Lunberry notes, 'but a mix that was intricately composed of overlapping, intercultural strands of influence and tradition, individual resistance and cultural revolt' (77–8).

Butoh's relentless invocation of death, its wallowing in decay, dirt, criminality – all those gothic underworlds that the genealogy of civilised morals would have us deny – points to its own project of post-humanity and post-identity. As Sondra Fraleigh observes, butoh dancers 'consciously morph: from culture to culture and from birth to old age – transfiguring from male to female, from human to plant life, disappearing into ash, animals, bugs, and gods. Surprisingly, they transform without closure' (2010: 45). This lack of closure, for Fraleigh, is among other things a lack of political and national boundary, a borderlessness that the discourse of globalism tirelessly decries. Yet for her, as for me, butoh uses its globalism to *resist*, rather than *to fall prey to* the mechanics of globalisation. 'Concerning global scattering', she writes, 'pure identities are difficult to find in butoh. Hardly utopian, the muddy, ashen bodies of butoh disclose a shadow side of the global economy and negative consequences of technology turned toward material accumulation, thus ensuring that as an East–West synthesis it can never be recuperated in the interests of political globalization' (17). In butoh there can be no Japanese subject because there can be no subject at all. Hijikata's investment in darkness, Fraleigh claims,

> is his way of rejecting the forces of modernity, especially the secular idea of progress he saw sweeping from America into Japan after World War II. Hijikata's bodily transformations presented the amorphous materiality of the body, and his

> call for the end of genres set the stage for permeable boundaries in the international absorption of butoh methods. From the beginning, butoh artists produced postmodern amalgamations of East and West, moving their art beyond ethnic boundaries toward international participation. (45)

And such post-identity at the inter/national level is accomplished in butoh only through that recognisably gothic semiotics of dying, haunting, suffering, tearing, of vulnerable bodies framed against environmental mayhem. Hijikata's deconstruction of Japaneseness is based upon a deconstruction of humanness, where the butoh dancer is charged with the task of becoming a conduit for all identities, and for none at all.

The globalgothic body

To speak of butoh as a globalgothic phenomenon may make sense only if we suspend our definition of 'global' as a geographical, transnational register. For butoh philosophy and practice, the concept of the 'global' appears at a site other than the geographical, a site best captured by the word's medical, corporeal sense of encompassing or involving the entire body or psychosomatic organisation. I now want to consider how butoh relocates its venue of terror from the politico-geographical to the politico-corporeal. To begin, I draw on Juliette Crump's assertion that butoh dancers 'want to have the body itself contemplated as a small universe' (2006: 66). 'As in some meditative exercises', Crump contends, 'butoh philosophy claims that it is our muscles that retain memories, and that by creatively imagining the inside universe of the body we trigger those memories' (66). But while Crump, like Fraleigh, wants to tie that universal body back into a Zen Buddhist ethics of healing and compassion, I find its earlier articulations in Hijikata to be more terrifying and terrorising – to be, in other words, gothic. The concept of the universal is crucial to Buddhism, to be sure, but, as we will see, Hijikata's universal body is *not* a safe, homey space.

Let us return momentarily to Hijikata's vision of his body as quoted in his essay 'Wind Daruma': 'I would like to make the dead gestures inside my body die one more time and make the dead themselves dead again. I would like to have a person who has already died die over and over inside my body' (2000a: 77). In one way this definition of the butoh body renders it an open conduit for the past: its memory, its working through and its eternal return. It is something akin to what Toni Morrison calls 're-memory' in *Beloved*. Hijikata suggests as much in his homage to his dead sister. 'I often say that I have a sister living in my body . . . She's my teacher; a dead person is my butoh teacher. You've got to cherish the dead. Because we too, sooner or later, some day far or near, will be summoned, we must make extraordinary preparations while alive not to be panicked when that time comes. You must bring the dead close to yourself and live with them' (2000a: 77). But Hijikata's global body is not just an inviting nexus or a welcoming receptacle for the dead. Rather it is a body *in crisis*, by which Hijikata means that it must both actively suffer and actively cause suffering in others. Echoing his sources in Bataille, Sade and Artaud, Hijikata charges that the theatre has become a place where evil and suffering are meaningless; they are commodities to be consumed unless the butoh dancer intervenes:

> Audiences pay money to enjoy evil. We must make compensation for that. Both the 'rose-colored dance' and the 'dance of darkness' must spout blood in the name of the experience of evil. A body that has kept the tradition of mysterious crisis is prepared for that. Sacrifice is the source of all work and every dancer is an illegitimate child set free to experience that very quality. Because they bear that obligation, all dancers must first of all be pilloried. (2000c: 39)

And pillory he does, or worse. 'The method of murder has lost its seriousness. I do know how often I proposed the need for chopping heads with a hoe. Tragedy must be given precedence over production or it is just too frivolous' (2000c: 38). Tragedy, something Hijikata borrows wholesale from Artaud's full-bodied Theatre of Cruelty, is itself an attitude of the body. 'You have to pull your stomach up high in order to turn your solar plexus into a terrorist' (Hijikata, 2000c: 36).

What keeps this body-as-terrorist from enacting the simple subject–object positions of tyrant and victim that we so often see in the gothic is the degree to which the butoh body, in its quest for temporal and geographical connection, is also fragmented, discrete, seemingly at odds with itself. I argued in *Gothic Bodies* (1994) that the gothic ceaselessly stages for us the coherent, phallic body being rent to pieces as a way of engaging us, its spectators, in a complex relationship of sympathy and abjection. In this sense the 'gothic body' is constructed less as a thing than as a product of relations, relations to itself or to another body in pain. Much the same phenomenological strangeness motivates butoh. Consider, for example, two moments that Hijikata claims to be formative for his articulation of the butoh crisis, the body stretched into a fragmented relation to itself. The first invokes a childhood body, which is also a body in pieces. In the Tohoku district of Hijikata's childhood, most adults were farmers who had to leave their young children at home while they went out to work in the fields:

> In most families, the kids who were two or three were tied to posts in their homes. I would go to sneak at look at these kids, who are fascinating. They move in strange ways, like the ones who make their hands eat something. Being that age, they of course don't consider what strange things they are doing or even that they themselves are human . . . [Their mother] thought I was weird for going around so much to look at those kids, who treated their hands as if they were not their own hands. Their bodies were their own but their hands they treated like things. That's why they probably felt themselves to be 'other'. (Hijikata, 2000a: 74)

This fascination with the disembodied hand renders the body an uncanny site, strange precisely to the degree that one's feeling for one's body as a *whole* (or 'global') organism is haunted by the feeling that one's body is also 'other', in pieces or strange to the self. (Recall how the solar plexus terrorises the whole body.) Indeed, what Freud does for eyes in *The Uncanny*, Hijikata does for hands. 'The feeling somewhere inside your body that your arm is not really your arm', he says, 'conceals an important secret' (2000a: 75). Hijikata does not tell us exactly what that secret is, but we know it has something to do with the vicissitudes of the body in its global perception – and its proprioception – within the dancer. The butoh body in this reminiscence signifies most strongly in the fact that it knows itself to be separate, to be its own universe, yet to be fragmented at the same time. It is that space of fragmentation that butoh seeks to articulate – in both the verbal and gestural sense of the word 'articulate' – but which must, like any experience of gothic terror/ism, remain dis-articulate. That is why a common butoh trope is to have different parts of the body dance completely unrelated phenomena: your left foot is being eaten by ants while your right hand is foil crinkling in fire.[3] The body in butoh is a global constellation of dis-integrated parts.

It is in that dis-integration that we find the Japanese concept of *ma*, the 'space between' two objects or states of being through which the spirit must pass. The *ma* has religious connotations of spiritual transcendence, but it also suggested for Hijikata the material site of real terror. In a second childhood reminiscence which appears in an interview by Shibusawa Tatsuhiko, Hijikata presents a space of passage as being a state of terror worthy of gothic melodrama. 'My father used to recite old ballad-dramas, which he was lousy at, and beat my mother. To my child's eyes, he seemed to be measuring the length of each step he took before hitting her. Now that truly was terror. And, in effect, I played the role of a child actor in it, with the neighborhood watching from a distance' (Tatsuhiko, 2000: 50). What is important here is not the abusive father per se, so much as what renders the scene terrifying: that is, the well-tuned space the father is crossing to meet the mother in violence, the space she will watch him cross to violate her. In this *ma*-as-gothic-space, terror is not impending, it is enacted; it exists in that moment of the in-between. Truly this was terror, writes Hijikata, because for him the body-in-crisis is the body at the point where its status as distinct organism is on the brink of dissolution; it is the body of Sartre's criminal not dead but dead, preparing for the moment of death by being in the moment, having only desire and fear to assure him that he is not dead. And in the universe of the dancer's body, this fragmentation of self into *ma* is performed or passed through again and again. It is the space-time of imminent decomposition that consciousness can gesture to but cannot know. That it should happen for child-actor and neighbour-spectator, as it will happen again for dancer-actor and spectating audience, proliferates in time and space the gothic *ma* of Hijikata's butoh body. It renders butoh not a thing or style but a way of seeing and relating, a convergence of bodies in crisis.

Tracing the influence of Artaud's *The Theatre and Its Double* on Hijikata's butoh, Clark Lunberry suggests a fascination with violence and the grotesque that we can as readily apply to the West's ceaseless pleasures in gothic spectacle:

> With such an exhilarating vision of the theater, Hijikata perhaps saw in Artaud's writings the fervent demand that theater no longer present itself simply as a staged space for passive observation and casual entertainment, but, instead, as the site of trance-inducing, ritual impact of 'a whirlwind of higher forces,' of the devolution of language back into the glandular body, and of a frequently violent spectacle of cruelty constituted by a grotesque, monstrous kind of beauty. (2006: 83)

It is that 'devolution of language back into the glandular body', I am suggesting, that unites the aesthetic of butoh with the aesthetic of gothic, and that makes of each a 'global' enterprise in a way that an attention to cultural and national specificity may simply not account for. Seeking cultural determinism in butoh may ultimately be as unsatisfying as looking at one's hand to determine the whole of one's self, or at individual people to determine the quality of relationships. Butoh may in some ways be 'essentially Japanese', but the Japaneseness we might attempt to locate in it is the very Japaneseness it seeks to dis-articulate in its globalism of both nation and body. Butoh may be a product of the atomic aftermath, felt in Japan as in no other country in the mid-twentieth century, but its body establishes itself as a form of crisis that refuses placement in the local. Its body, rather, forces us to think the dis-articulations of the 'global' as within or against the 'universal', which is not the same thing. As Paula Marie Orlando writes, butoh is 'pre-Hiroshima or, more precisely, meta-Hiroshima – universal. The narrative told by the dance is without beginnings, and such pure gesture, as a form of articulation, seems uncontaminated by socio-historical realities. Or, at the very least, such signification seems to subvert and transgress socio-historical realities and, in Deleuzian terms, de-territorialize itself' (2001: 315). Much might be gained, then, if we de-territorialise the gothic and begin to ask questions of its bodily globalism: questions that the usual discourses of globalisation may not be equipped to answer.

Notes

1 In order to speak to the global aspect of the gothic and butoh, I am avoiding a discussion of the (perhaps too obvious) world of the Japanese gothic. Doubtless Japanese gothic and butoh would itself be a fruitful discussion, but it is outside the scope of this chapter.

2 May be less evident, but not necessarily. William Veeder argues that the gothic is a nurturing phenomenon to the degree that it liberates the reader's repressed passions but does so through the safe distantiation of representation (1998: 28). The degree to which such morphing is conscious is open for debate. For Crump 'the butoh performer's role is to set free his or her body, to transform it to a new body in all its old pain, authenticity, and vulnerability, to eliminate conventional habits and to expose the *unconscious* inner world of pain, doubt, and joy' (2006: 63, emphasis added). Ideally, one could see a conscious use of butoh dance in order to expose the unconscious in the dancer – and I know dancers who use butoh as therapy after a long day at the ballet barre – but I suspect what is more operative here is the kind of 'therapeutic' use that Veeder ascribes to the gothic, where we use representational tactics to hint at, if not exorcise, the demons we cannot deal with.

3 I am taking this example directly from a butoh workshop I took in the autumn of 2000, led by Jay Hirabayashi of Vancouver's Kokoro Dance.

References

Bruhm, Steven. 1994. *Gothic Bodies: The Politics of Pain in Romantic Fiction*. Philadelphia, PA: University of Pennsylvania Press.

Crump, Juliette. T. 2006. '"One who hears their cries": The Buddhist ethic of compassion in Japanese butoh'. *Dance Research Journal*, 38.1/2: 61–72.

Fraleigh, Sondra. 2010. *Butoh: Metaphoric Dance and Global Alchemy*. Urbana, IL: University of Illinois Press.

Hershkovitz, Meital, Hillary Raphael and Donald Richie. 2002. *Outcast Samurai Dancer: Japanese Avant-garde Dance*. London: Creation Books.

Hijikata, Tatsumi. 2000a. 'Wind Daruma'. *The Drama Review*, 44.1: 71–9.

——. 2000b. 'To Prison'. *The Drama Review*, 44.1: 43–8.

——. 2000c. 'Inner Material/Material'. *The Drama Review*, 44.1: 36–42.

Klein, Susan Blakely. 1988. *Ankuko Buto: The Premodern and Postmodern Influence on the Dance of Utter Darkness*. Ithaca, NY: Cornell East Asia Program.

Lunberry, Clark. 2006. 'East meets West meets East: Dreaming Japanese butoh'. In *The Avant-Garde and the Margin: New Territories of Modernism*, eds Sanja Bahun Radunovic and Marinos Pourgouris. Newcastle Upon Tyne: Cambridge Scholars, 74–87.

Morrison, Toni. 1987. *Beloved*. New York: Knopf.

Nanako, Kurihara. 2000. 'The words of butoh'. *The Drama Review*, 44.1: 12–28.

Orlando, Paula Marie. 2001. 'Cutting the surface of the water: Butoh as traumatic awakening'. *Social Semiotics*, 11.3: 307–24.

Sakamoto, Michael. 2009. 'Parallels of psycho-physiological and musical affect in trance ritual and butoh performance'. *Pacific Review of Ethnomusicology*, 14: 1–17.

Tatsuhiko, Shibusawa. 2000. 'Hijikata Tatsumi: Plucking off the darkness of the flesh'. *The Drama Review*, 44.1: 49–55.

Veeder, William. 1998. 'The nurture of the Gothic, or how can a text be both popular and subversive?' In *American Gothic: New Interventions in a National Narrative*, eds Robert K. Martin and Eric Savoy. Iowa City, IA: University of Iowa Press, 20–39.

3

Ian Conrich

Maori tales of the unexpected: The New Zealand television series *Mataku* as Indigenous gothic

Indigenous cultures, with their unfamiliar beliefs and practices, and their relationships to an earlier period of land settlement, are frequently appropriated by gothic fictions. In contrast, forms of the gothic created by Indigenous cultures are few. Within a consideration of this global issue, this chapter will explore the New Zealand television series *Mataku*, an example of Maori culture that adopts foreign approaches and acts as a transcultural form. The series reveals much about the global nature of the gothic, where contemporary culture and modern media practices present commercial arenas for Indigenous perspectives and superstitions to merge with more advanced horror traditions. Within the context of a developing television industry and an increasingly multicultural nation, this chapter will reflect on *Mataku* as an active engagement between non-Western and Western cultural practices.

Mataku (which translates as afraid or scared; the programme makers use the subtitle 'The Quivering') was made by South Pacific Pictures for TV3 (episodes 1–13) and by 4 Winds Films for TVNZ (episodes 14–20), and originally broadcast between 2002 and 2005.[1] The dramas foregrounded *Maoritanga* (Maori culture) and *taha Maori* (a Maori perspective), with Maori featured within the cast and presented within the crew, and the well-known actor Temuera Morrison appearing as the host. The stories conjoined Maori myths and beliefs with non-Maori gothic fiction to create transcultural dramas of the supernatural and the uncanny, human sacrifice, ghostly visitations and possession. Online publicity for the series promoted it as a 'trip into the unique and mystical world of supernatural tales, where ordinary characters encounter mysterious phenomena of Maori mythology' (qtd in Hardy, 2003/4: 94).

Gothic appropriations

American cinema has demonstrated the broadest and most explicit appropriations of Indigenous cultures for the creation of gothic screen fiction. It has been drawn mainly to its immediate Indigenous groups and stories of the Native American people, for gothic fantasies of alternative and ancient cultures that are commonly depicted threatening and assaulting the intruder or white settler. Examples appear in some of the genre's most celebrated and mainstream films, such as *Poltergeist* (1982), in which the source of the heightened supernatural activity is an ancient Native American burial ground, on top of which a modern residential suburb has been built. A Native American burial ground is capable of reviving the recently deceased in *Pet Sematary* (1989), whilst in another Stephen King adaptation, *The Shining* (1980), a desecrated Native American burial ground is presented as the cause of the terror at the isolated Overlook Hotel. This theme continues in the low-budget *Unseen Evil* (1999), and *The Dark Power* (1985), in which a sorority home for girls rests on top of a burial site for four Native American shamans. The association of avenging Native American spirits with the uncanny is in the remake of the *Amityville Horror* (2007), where a convenient explanation for a family's hauntings is revealed in the basement. The Amityville legend in this reinterpretation is twisted, with the uninhabitable home now imagined to be concealing deep within its foundations a series of cells, in which Native Americans in a period of white settler early contact were the subjects of torture and sadistic experimentation.

In many of the films a specific ancient tribal spirit or demon is awakened, the living are possessed and curses, legends, transformations and the acquiring of souls are common themes. In *The Cellar* (1989) a boy discovers the spirit of an ancient Comanche monster in the basement of his family home; reawakened ancient demons prowl the wilderness picking off unsuspecting travellers in *Eyes of Fire* (1983) and *It Waits* (2005); the city-bound werewolves that inhabit the derelict New York buildings in *Wolfen* (1981) are shapeshifters from Native American legends; in *Manitou* (1978), a possessed woman with a tumorous growth on the back of her neck gives birth to a demonic reincarnation of a sorcerer; and in the slasher film *Scalps* (1983) one of a group of college students digging at a sacred burial ground becomes possessed by the evil spirit of Black Claw and starts slaughtering his fellow pupils.

Similar narratives can be found in the films of neighbouring Canada. For instance, *Ghostkeeper* (1981) exploits the First Nations legends of the Wendigo, a cannibalistic spirit capable of possessing humans. In Australia the films *The Last Wave* (1977) and *Kadaicha* (1988) imagine the power of Aboriginal prophecies and curses affecting an invasive European culture. In the former an Aboriginal tribe warns of an apocalyptic great wave that will destroy the modern city of Sydney, whilst in *Kadaicha* (as with the film *Poltergeist*) ruthless property developers build over a sacred Aboriginal burial site. Both films demonstrate the distance that exists between cultures, with non-Indigenous Australians drawn into an Aboriginal world of superstitions, curses, disturbing dreamworlds and powerful stones. Significantly, many of these fictions are united by a view of the land as sacred and protected, with the Indigenous people depicted as greatly connected to their natural environment.[2] Moreover, across these post-settler and postcolonial nations a pattern is apparent that, in countries where Indigenous peoples are marginalised or subjugated, their culture and beliefs are rich sources for mining gothic tales of dark superstition and avenging supernatural forces.

Indigenous gothic

In contrast to these gothic appropriations, there are Indigenous forms of the gothic film. The Aborigine director Tracey Moffatt was the first Indigenous Australian filmmaker to make a feature-length fiction film. The production, *beDevil* (1993), a trilogy of ghost stories, is also notable for being the first Indigenous gothic film text. Whilst care, as will be discussed below, is required when labelling certain Indigenous texts as gothic, Moffatt's *beDevil* incorporates elements of European tales of the supernatural, alongside an Aboriginal perspective and cultural viewpoint. The supernatural tales in this film were inspired by the stories heard by Moffatt within the Aboriginal and adoptive white families in which she grew up. The tales are consequently presented with a mix of narrative strategies and a rich entanglement of stylistic and artistic forms. As Glen Masato Mimura argues, 'Against colonialism's representational "systems of classification", *beDevil* ingeniously orchestrates its three registers of discourse: highly stylised flashbacks of the past;

cinema verité of the present (mock-documentary film in its first story, amateur home movie in its second); and the antiseptic realism of tourist discourse. Yet for all its seeming formalism and abstraction, *beDevil* remains a worldly text' (1993: 112).

An initial challenge, though, when approaching related films has been not the extent of the gothic but whether the film is sufficiently Indigenous. With so few opportunities for Indigenous filmmakers to produce their own fiction films, issues of cultural identity and authenticity in regards to the production have become politicised. For the Maori filmmaker and theorist Barry Barclay, Moffatt's production is part of a small group of fiction feature films that were made with a clear Indigenous voice. He recognised such filmmaking, which he termed Fourth Cinema, as occurring in a place where that cultural group is 'an island within a modern state' (Barclay, 2003: 10), and therefore exists within a film system of representation that is controlled by outsiders. Fourth Cinema is seen as an act of empowerment, an essence outside the national orthodoxy, an Indigenous perspective able 'to look through the right pair of spectacles . . . to give vitality and richness to the way we conceive, develop, manufacture and present our films' (11). Barclay articulated the position in terms of Indigenous encounters, and ships and shores, with the orthodox camera position and gaze of First Cinema depicting the event from 'the ship's deck . . . owned and controlled by the people who own the ship' (10). In contrast, the position of the Indigenous filmmaker, the 'Camera Ashore, the Fourth Cinema Camera, is the one held by the people for whom "ashore" is their ancestral home' (10).[3]

Barclay's own feature, *Ngati* (1987), is regarded as the earliest example of Fourth Cinema. The problem with Barclay's definition is that its purism as to what constitutes Indigenous filmmaking removes important productions such as *Whale Rider* (2002). This film, in his view, cannot be seen as an Indigenous production, despite its strong Maori story, a story adapted from the novel *The Whale Rider* (1987) by the renowned Maori writer Witi Ihimaera, who gave the film his support. For Barclay the main issue is that the film was made beyond the Maori community, and the producer, South Pacific Pictures, and the director Niki Caro, are Pakeha (non-Maori), with this non-Indigenous background a crucial defining element in the film's credentials. Employing the international conventions of film, such as modes of genre – the coming of age film – and narrative expectations, *Whale Rider* is within this argument a representation of Maori culture as captured from 'the ship's deck'. As Kirsty Bennett writes, 'Pakeha can understand the story of *Whale Rider* precisely because it is no longer a Maori story – although it is masquerading as such' (2006: 21). If this position were to be accepted then the New Zealand film *The Strength of Water* (2009), directed by the Pakeha filmmaker Armagan Ballantyne, would not be regarded as Indigenous gothic, but, as I have written elsewhere, I consider the film as the first example of a transcultural Maori gothic film (Conrich, 2012: 405). Barclay's Fourth Cinema is quite exclusive, and is unable to accommodate contemporary media forms in which the vast interconnections of a globalised world are capable of creating a hybrid, a new Indigenous expression through the transcultural.

In *The Strength of Water,* a local tragedy occurs when a young asthmatic Maori girl dies after becoming trapped inside an abandoned freezer. Her young twin brother is traumatised by the loss, and he spends much of the rest of the film engaging with a sister whom only he can see or hear. This film, which features a strong Maori cast and a screenplay by the Maori writer Briar Grace-Smith, effectively combines elements of non-Maori gothic fiction with *Maoritanga.* This is definitely a Maori film, but it also contains many features, both in the story and in the film's design, that establish it as another example of New Zealand small-town gothic, which in itself is an appropriation of elements of American Southern gothic (see Conrich, 2012: 395–8). The film foregrounds *Maoritanga,* and it captures the wild landscape and crashing seascape of the Hokianga region in Northland, near the top of New Zealand, where many Maori reside. This is another isolated community within which some inhabitants feel trapped, and into which a young drifter, Tai (Isaac Barber), arrives and moves into an abandoned home, only to act as a catalyst for the tragedy. The cursed home, which belonged to his grandfather, is *tapu* (a forbidden place in Maori culture) and Tai, who says he is 'bad luck', is ostracised by the community.

Maoritanga

Maori culture (*Maoritanga*) may identify and recognise *tapu* spaces and buildings, sea monsters and dragons (*taniwha*), goblin-like sea creatures with vicious claws (*ponaturi*), forest spirits (*patupaiarehe*), evil tree humanoids (*maero/mohoao*), possessed souls, hauntings and spiritual visitations, but it would be inappropriate to label these creatures and events freely as gothic. The origins of these beliefs and their continued acceptance and reception within Maori culture are quite different from anything with which they may be compared within European and American values of the gothic. Maori beliefs, superstitions and legends are distinctly removed from the emergence of the gothic in the west. Maori culture in this context is not manufactured or the result of a commercial enterprise; instead its values are ingrained within the relationship this Indigenous culture has to *whenua* (the land) and the surrounding natural environment, which defines their identity in so many ways. *Whenua* is closely tied to the powerful concept of *turangawaewae* (a place to stand), which establishes the Maori as the *tangata whenua* (people of the land), with empowerment from connection to an environment that is forever home. For instance the placenta, which in Maori is also called *whenua,* is buried and gifted back to the earth when a child is born. The land is deeply ancestral, with many geographical features named and identified as genealogical markers. There is also a prevailing belief in *mauri* (lifeforce) and *wairua* (spirituality), as well as a continued telling of myths and legends, which do contain stories of *taniwha,* but these are all essential elements in an understanding of origins and an Indigenous cultural identity.

These are key reasons as to why there is a lack of Maori fiction, or culture, that could be regarded as gothic. The gothic is a term that does not sit comfortably with Maori spiritualism and beliefs, and therefore, whilst hauntings appear in novels such as Keri Hulme's *The Bone People* (1983) and Patricia Grace's *Baby No-eyes* (1998), to describe these texts as Maori gothic would be inappropriate. Any consideration of Maori fiction as gothic should consider the context and style in which the narrative is presented. Where Western themes and traditions are adopted, a transcultural Indigenous gothic can emerge. The Maori television series *Mataku* is therefore a significant programme. A modern and transcultural text, it clearly combines traditional Maori values, beliefs and mythologies with Western narratives of horror fiction, thereby demonstrating a rich example of the globalgothic. In what follows, the *Mataku* series will be considered as an Indigenous gothic form that reveals how the globalgothic is able to be observed within other cultures.

Maori television and *Mataku*

South Pacific Pictures made both *Whale Rider* and the first two series of *Mataku,* with the firm aim to attract a mainstream audience. The success of *Whale Rider,* and the earlier Maori film *Once Were Warriors*

(1994), helped to demonstrate that Maori stories had both local and international mainstream appeal, thereby weakening the belief of the television networks that audiences were not interested in Indigenous stories. The *Mataku* series was presold to three countries, including Canada, and subsequently sold to Russia, Finland, Malaysia, and Israel amongst others (Dunleavy, 2005: 323 n67).

Funding for *Mataku* was received from NZ On Air, the New Zealand Film Commission, TV3 and Te Mangai Paho, the latter established to facilitate funding for Maori-language broadcasting, including television, and which committed to the series only on the basis that approximately a third of the language content (subtitled in English) was in Maori. Only fourteen years earlier, in 1987, the Maori Language Act had been passed which officially recognised New Zealand as a bilingual nation. The year before in New Zealand, the Waitangi Tribunal had classified the Maori language as *taonga* (a cultural treasure), which needed active protection. The Waitangi Tribunal had been established to hear Indigenous grievances and apply compensation following the unfairness of the Treaty of Waitangi, signed between the British Crown and the Maori in 1840, and the subsequent widespread loss and theft of land in the nineteenth century. The Treaty had supposedly ensured the Maori of *tino rangatiratanga* (utmost chieftanship) or control of vital resources, and this was later viewed to cover the country's public broadcasting system. The Indigenous population, it was argued, should have equal access to this vital present-day resource, which at the time of *Mataku*'s initial transmission had heavily marginalised or stereotyped Maori content, programmes and representation on New Zealand television.[4]

In March 2004, just a year and a half after *Mataku*'s October 2002 first showing, Maori Television was launched, a channel broadcasting throughout the day predominantly in the Maori language with a wide range of Maori-produced programmes. The channel had been debated for some time, but had advanced as a result of the 2003 Maori Television Service Act, in which under Section 8 there is the stated need to 'promote te reo Maori me nga tikanga Maori [Maori language and Maori culture/customs and traditions] through the provision of a high quality, cost-effective Maori television service, in both Maori and English, that informs, educates, and entertains a broad viewing audience, and, in doing so, enriches New Zealand's society, culture, and heritage'.[5] A second Maori channel, *Te Reo* (the Maori language), launched in 2008, is broadcast entirely in Maori.

Mataku therefore has to be viewed within the context of New Zealand government policies and funding decisions regards the representation of Maori culture and language. Here there was a need for the series not only to satisfy funding requirements in terms of its Maori content but also for it to appeal to an audience that extended beyond Indigenous viewers. John Barnett, CEO of South Pacific Pictures, compared *Mataku* to *The X-Files*, the long-running American series of monsters and the paranormal which was then entering its ninth and final season. For Barnett the *Mataku* series was 'absolutely suited to a general audience, and I think that is what has excited the network. These are in exactly the same genre as all those other programmes you're used to seeing, all that is different is the faces are brown and they are Maori myths' (qtd in Revington, 2001: 34). Predictably, in maximising interest and awareness of the series, *The X-Files* was the contemporary text of reference within a globalgothic register, and the local media latched on to the association, dubbing *Mataku* 'the M-Files' (Cardno and Prebble, 2002: 74). Other writers, such as Fiona Rae in the *New Zealand Herald*, viewed the series as 'Our very own version of *The Twilight Zone*' (2002). The show's co-creator, Bradford Haami, has revealed that the television content they were being exposed to and influenced by included '*The Twilight Zone, Tales From the Crypt*, people like Vincent Price, *Doctor Phibes*' (Glynn and Tyson, 2007: 213). Haami continues: 'And then that program *The X-Files* came out. So we just thought we would write some stories associated with that genre of storytelling because no one else had done it' (Glynn and Tyson, 2007: 213).

Haami and the co-creator Carey Carter also drew on the stories, myths and legends that they had heard within their Maori families and communities: 'Haami's grandparents were *te reo* Maori (Maori language) speakers who often regaled him with stories grounded in traditional Maori cosmologies. Carter, by contrast, grew up hearing Maori stories in a [*marae*] traditional meeting house' (Glynn and Tyson, 2007: 207). Carter is quoted as saying that these old Maori stories 'belong to Maoridom . . . We're just the ones who had to find a way to tell our people's stories' (Schmidt, 2002: 13). It is this hybridity within the text, which mixes, reproduces and crosses cultures and networks, forms of storytelling, and the old and the new, that makes *Mataku* such a vibrant series. It is here through this Indigenous form of the gothic that the globalgothic emerges, functioning within a mainstream television series, popularising traditional narratives and with the unfamiliar need to educate, enrich and entertain.

Tales of the unexpected

Each episode of *Mataku* begins with the host Temuera Morrison presenting a brief and oblique introduction to the story that follows. In a style that is reminiscent of a group of television hosts of the uncanny and supernatural, from Alfred Hitchcock to Rod Serling or even the Cryptkeeper, Morrison repeats at the start that *Mataku* presents a 'supernatural world of the Maori', and 'chilling tales of the unexplained and unexpected'. What is unexpected within this series is the programme's use of the gothic to both entertain and educate. Western horror practices and styles of narrative and action are employed to convey Maori stories that instruct and advise in regards to specific Indigenous beliefs and cultural traditions.

Many of the episodes are set within a modern New Zealand, with the urban development of the metropolis a constant reminder that the land in some parts has been irrevocably altered. The city in *Mataku* appears to be forever Auckland, with Skytower, the southern hemisphere's tallest manufactured structure, visible in many shots even when the action is from a distance and beyond the urban limits. The rural is marked by abundant nature such as *ngahere* (forests), from which Maori journey into the city (a concrete jungle) as in the story *The Sisters: Nga Tuahine* (series 1, episode 4). The elder Maori sister in this story, Nola (Mamaengaroa Kerr-Bell), who is far from her home and community, has been displaced; the smoky nightclubs, strip-clubs, neon lights, gangs and drugs show the city to be a site of vice and danger that corrupts and damages *Maoritanga*. It is part of a wider theme within the series to which a number of episodes return, in which a contemporary Maori figure is shown to be troubled or disadvantaged for having ignored Maori traditions.

Significant necklaces of jade (*hei pounamu*) or bone (*hei matau*), which seem omnipresent throughout the *Mataku* series, and are often worn by righteous characters, act as signs of *mana* (importance) and a connection to *tipuna* (ancestors). In the city they are lost, and Nola, who cleans toilets, gets drunk, attempts suicide and is forced into sexual favours in order to pay her rent, is noticeably missing the protection that would be provided by her carving. Photographs and flashbacks are reminders of the distant *whanau* (family) and community, whilst the ghostly visit of a younger sister Naera (Nari Guthrie), who was taken by the *patupaiarehe* (forest spirits) at the start of the story, introduces an uncanny figure who has failed to age and is there to rescue Nola from the ‘bad place’. Naera is a connection to the past and she often clutches her *hei pounamu,* as she guides her sister back to her *turangawaewae* (standing place, or home), where she is culturally reconnected and reunited with her family. The journey back is achieved through Nola jumping to her death from a high-rise balcony, hand-in-hand with Naera. This is a leap of faith which sees her returning to happier times when her family was together, prior to the death of her parents and the loss of her sister to the forest, a space to which she has greater cultural attachment than the city.

Ancestral links to the land are emphasised in *The Blue Line: Kahurangi* (series 1, episode 1), in which an old wooden hut is to be bulldozed in order to make way for a casino. A young BMW-driving female executive, Sandra Edmonton (Cherie James), who works for the developer, has an office in an Auckland skyscraper, a space where she is high up from the land, and removed from her ancestry and Maori spiritual identity. The bulldozer twice breaks down on its way towards the demolition, whilst Sandra becomes possessed by the spirit of an old woman who in the nineteenth century lived in the home and who was murdered in the process of her land being stolen.

This episode demonstrates the ways in which the globalgothic has a political (as well as a cultural, historical and spiritual) dimension within the series. The loss of land is equated with a loss of identity: ‘we believe we are one with the land’, says one character. And whilst the protestors trying to stop the demolition are politicised, united under the *tino rangatiratanga* Maori nation flag which they fly, Sandra is on the other side of the metal fence in charge of land issues – but only those that will see the project through in favour of the Pakeha developer. As the spirit of the old woman possesses her, Sandra becomes increasingly distressed at the growth of a *moko* (facial tattoo) that is being tapped out in a traditional manner on her chin, and which only she can see. The *moko* is a statement of her identity and her increasing spiritual rediscovery that unites her back with the power in this ancestral land.

Mataku repeatedly addresses relationships between the present and the past, modernity and tradition, contemporary Maori values and ancestral beliefs. Values associated with home, community and belonging are asserted throughout the series through Maori cultural and political concepts such as *tangata whenua* and *turangawaewae.* The land is alive and filled with spirits and forces from the past. Consequently some places are *tapu,* and in the story *The Sands of Time: Te One Tahua* (series 2, episode 6) the forces that are locked into a Northland site of ancient death are disturbed and transplanted when the sand on this beach (the place of a tribal battle) is scooped up and made into bricks. These are used to build a high-quality home in which a modern Maori family reside, and in which the past and present meet, with piles and leakages of sand revealing the spirit's presence as it moves through the home.

Physical items and elements are depicted carrying *mauri* (a lifeforce) that binds and animates *taonga* and *tapu* objects to places, individuals and communities. The *mana* that flows as a result of the *mauri* is a force that should not be broken. In *The Heirloom: Te Kura Paraoa* (series 2, episode 7) a Maori conman associated with modern society and greed, who steals from a local tribe and duplicates their precious *patu* (Maori club-like weapon), is cursed and killed in a visit from a ghostly *tamatoa* (warrior). Similarly, in *The Rocks: Nga Kohatu* (series 1, episode 5) a striking rock formation on a hill is the site where an ancient warrior had been executed. Many years later, in a period around the Second World War, a settler who farms the surrounding land tries to dynamite the rocks out of anger at the loss of his wife. But the power of these rocks leads to him accidentally dynamiting the remainder of his family, and in distress he turns his gun on himself and commits suicide. The storyteller in this tale, who advises that the settler 'can't clear the land of its memories', and that 'the land in which we live can sometimes possess many secrets', is revealed at the end to be in fact the ghost of the farmer who committed suicide. The modern-day Pakeha geologist to whom he had been telling the tale, as a warning against taking rock samples, is revealed in a second twist at the story's end to have also become a ghost.

For these Maori tales of the unexpected there is a distinct *taha Maori*, with the Maori culture displayed not just through the storytelling. It is there flowing through the production itself, with its many Maori directors and writers, the performances of the actors and the presence of Maori practices such as *karakia* (prayers), *kapa haka* (structured song and dance) and *te toi whakairo* (the art of Maori carving). The episodes function within a Maori *mise en scéne* of *marae* (meeting houses), *tangi* (funerals), traditional woven cloths and paintings. They also were constructed following extensive research, consultation with *kaumatua* (elders) and *tohunga* (priests), with further guidance from special Maori cultural advisers (at least one on each episode) and a soundtrack employing traditional Maori instruments, which were often performed by the celebrated Maori musician and composer Hirini Melbourne.

This concern for authenticity was combined with the pressure that Carter and Haami felt in conveying to the world Maori traditional stories and culture. As Carter stated, 'We have a responsibility to our culture and our spirituality' (qtd in Schmidt, 2002).

Yet in these stories that aim to educate and inspire there is also the need to entertain and reach a wide audience through the modern medium of television. The international reach of the gothic and the televisual image results in the globalgothic form that is *Mataku* combining Western horror devices and conventions within the programmes. These include the low-held rushing camera effect suggestive of an unleashed unearthly force that is used in *The Sisters: Nga Tuahine,* and which is reminiscent of *The Evil Dead* (1981). In *The Blue Line: Kahurangi,* the property developer who kisses Sandra, followed by a spinning around in the embrace, who then discovers that he is actually kissing an old ghostly woman, reproduces a famous moment of the uncanny from *The Shining*. More generally, the creaking doors, billowing curtains and thunder and lightning at the start of *The Heirloom: Te Kura Paraoa,* are a convention of gothic fiction which nowadays borders on parody.

Glynn and Tyson employ Faye D. Ginsburg's theory of 'border crossers' (2003: 311), a term which she introduced 'to designate indigenous mediamakers who routinely move between different cultural worlds because they recognise a need to "speak effectively to (at least) two kinds of" communities: native and settler' (Glynn and Tyson, 2007: 207). *Mataku* as an example of the globalgothic makes these connections and more, conjoining the local and the global, the educational narrative and the world of entertainment, and the spiritual and the oral with the televisual and the transmitted. The globalgothic consumes, reproduces and repackages, with the cultural impact of *Mataku* even reaching popular animation in 2006 when series three of the highly popular *Simpsons*-styled New Zealand television animation series *bro'Town,* parodied *Mataku* in the episode 'Know Me Before You Haunt Me', in which Temuera Morrison appears as himself, and guest stars as the host of *Scary Maori Stories.*

Notes

1 The first series of *Mataku* (five episodes) was made in 2001, but for reasons unknown was not broadcast for another year, by which time a second series (of eight episodes) had been added. The first episode was shown on Thursday 3 October 2002.

The series is discussed by John Barnett, CEO of South Pacific Pictures, in the New Zealand *Listener*. See Revington, 2001: 34.
2 For a discussion of the uncanny in relation to the sacred in Aboriginal culture see Gelder and Jacobs, 1998.
3 For further discussions of Fourth Cinema see Bennett, 2006; Murray, 2008; and Columpar, 2010.
4 For further discussion see Fox, 2002: 260–9. Famously, in 1995, Maori protestors interrupted the TVNZ evening news demonstrating at the poor level of Maori representation on television.
5 For commentary on the launch of Maori Television see McCurdy and Kiriona, 2004.

References

Barclay, Barry. 2003. 'Celebrating Fourth Cinema'. *Illusions*, 35: 7–11.

Bennett, Kirsty. 2006. 'Fourth Cinema and the politics of staring'. *Illusions*, 38: 19–23.

Cardno, James, and Amy Prebble. 2002. 'The M-Files'. New Zealand *Listener*, 28 September, 74.

Columpar, Corinn. 2010. *Unsettling Sights: The Fourth World on Film*. Carbondale: Southern Illinois University Press.

Conrich, Ian. 2012. 'New Zealand gothic'. In *A New Companion to the Gothic*, ed. David Punter. Oxford: Wiley-Blackwell, 393–408.

Dunleavy, Trisha. 2005. *Ourselves in Primetime: A History of New Zealand Television Drama*. Auckland: Auckland University Press.

Fox, Derek Tini. 2002. 'Honouring the treaty: Indigenous television in Aotearoa'. In *New Zealand Television: A Reader*, eds John Farnsworth and Ian Hutchison. Palmerston North: Dunmore Press, 260–9.

Gelder, Ken, and Jane M. Jacobs. 1998. *Uncanny Australia: Sacredness and Identity in a Postcolonial Nation*. Melbourne: Melbourne University Press.

Ginsburg, Faye D. 2003. 'Embedded aesthetics: Creating a discursive space for Indigenous media'. In *Planet TV: A Global Television Reader*, eds Lisa Parks and Shanti Kumar. New York: New York University Press, 303–19.

Glynn, Kevin, and A.F. Tyson. 2007. 'Indigeneity, media and cultural globalization'. *International Journal of Cultural Studies*, 10.2: 205–24.

Grace, Patricia. 1998. *Baby No-eyes*. Honolulu: University of Hawaii Press.

Hardy, Ann. 2003/4. 'Return of the Taniwha: The re-spiritualisation of land and film in Aotearoa'. *British Review of New Zealand Studies*, 14: 87–104.

Hulme, Keri. 1983. *The Bone People*. Wellington: Spiral Press.

Ihimaera, Witi. 1987. *The Whale Rider*. New York: Harcourt.

McCurdy, Diana, and Renee Kiriona. 2004. 'On air at last'. *Weekend Herald*, 27–8 March, B1-2.

Mimura, Glen Masato. 1993. 'Black memories: Allegorizing the colonial encounter in Tracey Moffatt's *beDevil* (1993)'. *Quarterly Review of Film and Video*, 20.2: 111–23.

Murray, Stuart. 2008. *Images of Dignity: Barry Barclay and Fourth Cinema*. Wellington: Huia.

Revington, Mark. 2001. 'Maori Mirror'. New Zealand *Listener*, 15 September, 33–4.

Schmidt, Veronica. 2002. 'Bradford Haami and Carey Carter: Storytellers'. New Zealand *Listener*, 5 October, 13.

Internet source

Rae, Fiona. 2002. '*Mataku*: The Phantom Mana'. *New Zealand Herald*, 25 September. www.nzherald.co.nz/lifestyle/news/article.cfm?c_id=6&objectid=2848710. Accessed 19 February 2012.

Filmography

Amityville Horror. 2007. Andrew Douglas, dir. Metro-Goldwyn-Mayer.
beDevil. 1993. Tracey Moffatt, dir. Southern Star.
The Cellar. 1989. Kevin Tenney, dir. Southgate Video.
The Dark Power. 1985. Phil Smoot, dir. New Visions.
The Evil Dead. 1981. Sam Raimi, dir. New Line Cinema.
Eyes of Fire. 1983. Avery Crounse, dir. Elysian Pictures.
Ghostkeeper. 1981. Jim Makichuk, dir. Badland Pictures.
It Waits. 2005. Stephen Monroe, dir. Anchor Bay.
Kadaicha. 1988. James Bogle, dir. David Hannay Productions.
The Last Wave. 1977. Peter Weir, dir. United Artists.
Manitou. 1978. William Girdler, dir. Avco Embassy.
Mataku. 2002–5. South Pacific Pictures / 4 Winds Films.
Ngati. 1987. Barry Barclay, dir. New Zealand Film Commission.
Once Were Warriors. 1994. Lee Tamahori, dir. First Line Features.
Pet Sematary. 1989. Mary Lambert, dir. Paramount.
Poltergeist. 1982. Tobe Hooper, dir. Metro-Goldwyn-Mayer.
Scalps. 1983. Fred Olen Ray, dir. American Partnership.
The Shining. 1980. Stanley Kubrick, dir. Warner Bros.
The Strength of Water. 2009. Armagan Ballantyne, dir. Filmwork Ltd.
Unseen Evil. 1999. Jay Woelfel, dir. Monarch.
Whale Rider. 2002. Niki Caro, dir. South Pacific Pictures.
Wolfen. 1981. Michael Wadleigh, dir. Warner Bros.
The X-Files. 1993–2002. Ten Thirteen Productions / Twentieth-Century Fox.

4

Justin D. Edwards

'She saw a soucouyant': Locating the globalgothic

As we see throughout this volume, different cultures across the globe have depicted and continue to represent a shared sense of spectrality, uncanniness, zombies, vampires and other supernatural phenomena. Such figures and tropes are repeated across time and space, but they also shift and change according to the specificities of historical contexts, cultural legacies and ideologies. Yet we must also recognise that gothic tropes are not always static, fixed in one particular site, but travel across the globe in the movements of people and the global flows of cultural production disseminated widely in film, television, visual culture, new media. In this the globalgothic is not just about representations of the borders separating life and death, real and unreal, self and other; it is also about depictions of the liminal spaces that blur the boundaries between the local and the global, here and there, nation and migration. A strand of the globalgothic, then, appears in the dissolution of clear-cut jurisdictions where the law might provide order to chaos. And another related strand might arise out of the socially induced traumas that haunt the deferral of borders. In both cases globalgothic texts are concerned not only with individual subjectivity (gender, ethnicity, religion, racial identity) but also with the relations between individuality and the spectral movements of global forces that are uncontrollable and unpredictable.

One of the ways of thinking about globalgothic, then, is in relation to migrations or displacements that can, in some cases, engender social dislocations, cultural changes, travelling ideas and narrative shifts. The genealogy of zombie narratives, for example, is often traced from an

African diaspora and the forced movement of people from West Africa to the Caribbean and then, later, to the United States where they were adapted for such films as *I Walked with a Zombie* (1943) and *Dawn of the Dead* (1978).[1] Such deterritorialisations can help us to reflect historically on the pressure of monumental transnationalist and global shifts (economically, politically, geographically) and how gothic narratives have migrated and transformed aesthetic, ideological and political landscapes. Theorising these narrative movements in the unique historical moment of globalisation offers insights into how different gothic tropes intersect and overlap. In addition such migrations and displacements offer myriad dislocated sites of contestation to the hegemonic, homogenising forces of globalisation. For these movements can help us to rethink the rubrics of nation and nationalism, while also refiguring the relations of citizens and nation states.

To focus my discussion and remain sensitive to historical specificity, I situate my analyses of textual dislocations and oral transformations of gothic narratives within a Canadian diasporic novel, David Chariandy's *Soucouyant* (2007), which employs transnational gothic tropes from the vampire to the soucouyant. Specifically, I examine how *Soucouyant* reterritorialises boundaries by displacing the national narrative of subjectivity into the diaspora of identifications across culture, race, ethnicity, gender and ontology. It is at these crossroads that the gothic intersects with, transforms (and is possibly transformed by) the diasporic Canadian-Caribbean narrative of *Soucouyant*: the liminal and contested spaces represented by Chariandy have the potential to combine *Nosferatu* with French vampire myths and West African narratives of spirit possession. Thus, although it draws on Trinidadian folklore, *Soucouyant* differs from those Caribbean works that represent spirit possessions, disembodied voices and spectrality without invoking the language of monstrosity or terror. What I seek to interrogate is how a globalgothic novel like *Soucouyant* can point to the paradoxical continuity of the self within a temporality of resistance, while always addressing national and transnational experiences in historically defined representational forms through a multivalent combination of gothic Canadian *and* Caribbean modes and tropes.

Globalgothic locations

It is in the context of paradoxical continuity, multidirectionality and multivalence that we can begin to speak about the globalgothic in Canadian-Caribbean writing. For a non-synchronous politics of location can detour the pitfalls of the gothic's 'Europeanness', while simultaneously using the fruitful gothic paradigm offered by Glennis Byron and David Punter: the gothic as 'embroil[ed] in shifting boundaries' and 'migratory flights' where 'points of order' and the 'strongholds of reason' fall away (2004: 54). The diasporic shifts in boundaries and the migratory flights found in *Soucouyant* invoke a politics of location that disrupts points of order and invades the strongholds of reason. Like the gothic, this diasporic narrative turns away from any recognisable master-trajectory or coherent sense of imaginary origin.

In *Soucouyant* oral narratives and folklore are distant and hardly understood relations to a lost past that are rewritten in a new context. By reframing imagined localised stories and cultural memories, Chariandy reinvokes the past and, in so doing, inscribes complex ties to regions, nations and territories that are simultaneously inhabited yet remain distant. However, this turn to folklore might also be read as a response to the threatening blankness of deterritorialised forms of globalisation. From this perspective the globalgothic of *Soucouyant* attempts to circumvent the fears and anxieties of a breakdown in local communities and personal subjectivity. I do not want to suggest that a writer like Chariandy is searching for a lost origin or trying to recuperate a 'pure' or 'native' cultural legacy. Rather I argue that he invokes fragments of orality and folklore alongside a multiplicity of other narrative forms to represent anxieties about the collapse of material and conceptual boundaries.

Globalgothic dislocations

Smaro Kamboureli writes that diasporic subjectivity in Canada 'is constantly under revision in a *mise en abîme* fashion', and the identity of the Canadian writer, as a diasporic subject, constantly hovers on the edge of an abyss (2000: 22). Kamboureli sees the 'edge' as both a threat *and* a possibility: it includes the threat of non-being and the possibility of speaking from a politics of location that is outside the dominant discourse, dislocated from the centre. We might consider this link between diaspora and *mise en abîme* as just another mapping in which the abyss is a border or a margin by another name. But this link can be read also as a desire to speak from a heterotopic space where one can express the reterritorialisation of the shifting boundaries of identity

– the paradoxical continuity of the self – that characterises a politics of location as multidirectional and multivalent.

Dislocation from one context, then, becomes relocation in another. Yet, in the context of a competitive publishing industry, novels without master trajectories are more difficult to market and sell. Chariandy has, in fact, discussed the 'risky' side to writing multidirectional and multivalent narratives. 'Non-linear' and 'associative techniques', he writes, can be misunderstood as 'seemingly random evocations of feeling, touch, memory and history'; but to structure *Soucouyant* differently, he maintains, 'would have missed the point entirely, for the novel attempts to capture the processes of remembering and forgetting in the context of a character whose "spirit" is possessed by dementia' (Demers, 2007). Here Chariandy's comments are consistent with the unique structure of the novel. Still, the paratext of *Soucouyant* tries to provide a clear frame of reference, a stable ground upon which to tread. According to the paragraph printed on the French flaps (presumably added by the publisher), a 'soucouyant is an evil spirit in Caribbean folklore, and a symbol here of the distant and dimly remembered legacies that continue to haunt the Americas. This extraordinary first novel set in Ontario, in a house near the Scarborough Bluffs, focuses on a Canadian-born son who despairingly abandons his Caribbean-born mother suffering from dementia.' This description suggests that the novel is a seamless story linking a coherent symbol to a collective memory in the context of a Canadian-Caribbean family living in a Toronto suburb. By packaging *Soucouyant* in this way the publisher tries to offer an answer to the question: what is this novel about? And in terms of sales, a clear response to this question is crucial, for the single-word title might not be familiar to readers outside of Trinidad.

My own reading of *Soucouyant* is so far from the publisher's synopsis that I might as well be dead. The blurb promises smooth surfaces and rational teleologies; it offers assurances about clear-cut definitions and lucid trajectories, uncomplicated by intricate intersections or paradoxical juxtapositions. The novel, though, does not adhere to these borders. For the narrator struggles (and fails) to articulate a stable definition of the word 'soucouyant', what the paratext unproblematically defines as 'an evil spirit of Caribbean folklore'. Even the chapter headings riff on several variations of the word: soacawyoon, ssooouccooo, souuoyawnn, including the erasure of crossed-out versions, ~~souku~~, ~~so Su~~, ~~sookey~~. Here Chariandy picks up on the diverse spellings of the word, with some sources using 'soucouyant' and others preferring 'soucriant'.[2] But, regardless of variant spellings, the narrator finds sources that identify the figure as part of a Trinidadian narrative: the soucouyant is a creature who lives by day as an old woman on the edge of a village and who, by night, strips her wrinkled skin and puts it on a mortar. She then flies in the shape of a fireball through the darkness in search of a victim, seeking out someone whose blood she can suck. A soucouyant, the story goes, can be killed only when coarse salt is placed on the mortar containing her skin; then she cannot return to her skin and she, in turn, dies. Here the unity of this narrative ends. Some accounts of soucouyants suggest that the victim dies and transforms into another blood-sucking creature; others state that the victim simply dies and that the existing soucouyant takes over the victim's skin.

'What do a boy', the Trinidadian mother of the narrator asks, 'who grow up in Canada know about soucouyants?' (Chariandy, 2007: 135). What indeed. He knows that a soucouyant – whatever that might be – was once seen in Trinidad by his mother, although she never adequately describes or elucidates the experience. 'She saw a soucouyant', he tells us, 'but she never explained or deciphered. She never put the stories together. She never could or wanted to do so' (136). In fact, the ambiguously named narrator – 'homeboy'? 'Eyestache'? '*Me*'? (30, 92, 43) – is so far removed from the subject of soucouyants that his mother, Adele, dismisses his attempts to fill in the gaps of her experience: '*Child?*' she shouts, 'Is *I* telling the story or *you*?' (45). Nevertheless the narrator longs to tell of soucouyants and he yearns to know; so much so, in fact, that he becomes haunted by the word he can never fully grasp. This haunting arises out of the soucouyant's liminality: it belongs to a point of consciousness he cannot experience or feel and a place where external sources are of little use to him. At the local library he finds the word in a glossy Caribbean tourist book published for Canadians, the cover bearing 'a picture of a black man playing a steel pan, an impossibly huge smile on his face. Impossibly cheerful colours. A white family looking on, cameras around their necks' (136–7). Instead of offering him answers to questions and shedding light on the past, he finds that his 'history is a travel guidebook' and 'a creature nobody believes in. My history', he concludes, 'is a foreign word' (137).

What does it mean to locate one's history in a foreign word? It is a sign of dislocation, but it is also a recognition that one's history is not part of the land or soil one inhabits. Rather it is located on the page and, as such, it must be read, deciphered and interpreted. This act of reading is foregrounded throughout the novel and the narrator's perusal of the guidebook echoes his examination of the Canadian medical pamphlets. In fact his research into soucouyants begins to merge with his investigation of dementia – a condition from which his mother is diagnosed as suffering – and, as a result, the novel hybridises the vampiric imagery of Caribbean spirit possession with the Canadian medical definitions of dementia. In this *Soucouyant* blurs belief systems and ontologies by linking the shape-shifting trope of spirit possession in Caribbean narratives to the discourses of dementia in Canada.

Given that dementia includes memory loss, the novel's subtitle, 'A novel of forgetting', gestures to the personal narrative of a woman whose first symptom of presenile dementia is impaired memory, which is followed by impaired thought and speech. As if possessed by a spirit, she utters disjointed sentences that might or might not correspond to repeated attempts to find lost memories. In the language of medical diagnosis Adele suffers from the degeneration of the frontal and temporal lobes with loss of memory, intellectual ability and transitory aphasia. But her forgetting is not the only memory loss of the novel. For the representation of dementia is just one way of exploring the fragility of cultural memory and the frustrations that arise from trying to rearticulate the past. After all, the narrator foregrounds a struggle for the past, and this struggle does not identify history as a blank page, for events such as the Middle Passage or the institutionalisation of slavery cannot be dismissed. Rather the struggle is a thinking through of what the past means, a past that is both elsewhere and here, as well as an attempt to read that which has been forgotten through omissions in official records by those who stand to benefit from such amnesia. This is, in part, what the narrator faces. He is interested in establishing a connection to the past, but his attempts foreground the very difficult process of establishing such connections within a diasporic context.

The narrator, born and raised in the Toronto suburb of Scarborough, finds himself in a liminal space: he is 'from here' and yet shares complex forms of social allegiances to other places, pasts and cultures. The figures of home and belonging, then, return to haunt *Soucouyant* and, in fact, the east-end suburban house at the end of a cul-de-sac in a 'good part' of Scarborough is a central feature of the text. But what is important is not so much the dead end or its centre–periphery relation to the city. What is important is the fact that the house is quite literally on the edge: the old house was built 'on the edge of the bluffs', teetering on an enormous 'slope of clay' beside 'the great lake with its unmarred horizon' (13, 16). The history of the house, which is part of a more general history of forgetting, is identified by Miss Cameron, librarian and local historian; constructed in the mid-nineteenth century, it was the first house in the area. Over time, erosion has pushed the edge of the Scarborough Bluffs closer to the house, so close, in fact, that one visitor to the house discreetly bounces on the floor near the wall closest to the bluffs to test its stability. Adele and the narrator are part of an unstable geography that reflects other transnational dislocations.

Enter the gothic. For in the context of the haunted suburban house on the eastern fringes of Toronto the narrator struggles to articulate those memories that have been lost through amnesia. Late in the text, for instance, he draws on gothic language in yet another attempt to define and explain the figure of the soucouyant. He states,

> A soucouyant is something like a female vampire. She lives a reclusive but fairly ordinary life on the edge of town. She disguises herself by dressing up in the skin of an old woman, but at night she'll shed her disguise and travel across the sky as a ball of fire. She'll hunt out a victim and suck his blood as he sleeps, leaving him with little sign of her work except increasing fatigue, a certain paleness, and perhaps, if he were to look closely on his body, a tell-tale bruise or mark on his skin. (135)

Here the phrase 'something like' and the conditional words 'if' and 'perhaps' signal the tentative nature of his definition. Yet the gothic discourses of vampirism, cannibalism, flaying, monstrosity and victimisation combine in his attempt to articulate and recapture those stories lost by migration, displacement and forgetting. The simile that begins this definition offers a comparative frame of reference, indicating how gothic discourse travels and migrates by way of a dislocation from a specific region or place. Simultaneously, though, new globalgothic expressions emerge and extend outwards to connect with other narratives, forming new regional or transnational alliances.

The narrator's vampiric Canadian-Caribbean definition also emerges out of a European tradition, for the Trinidadian word 'soucouyant' derives from Creole versions of French. A word and a folkloric tale that are themselves hybridised forms that link West Africa, the Caribbean and Europe, the first two syllables of the Creole word 'soucouyant' are homonymous with 'succubus', which is the Latin word for 'vampire' and derives from the fourteenth-century word 'succuba', meaning 'someone who lies under'. A succubus is also, like a soucouyant, always specifically gendered and refers to a female demon who copulates with a man while he is asleep. A succubus, then, is the female form of the 'incubus', which in medieval Latin referred to a sexually threatening male demon or something causing mental distress, confusion or disorientation, such as a nightmare. Such references to mental distress and disorientation are significant for *Soucouyant* because they relate directly to the novel's depiction of dementia. Confused and bewildered, Adele's illness causes her to wander the neighbourhood half-naked, mumbling incoherent phrases and urinating in inflatable swimming pools. Just as the text asks 'what is a soucouyant?' the narrator questions definitions of dementia, suggesting that it escapes definition, existing as it does beyond the fringes of the knowable, the clear-cut, the definable. Perhaps dementia is spirit possession by another name. Or perhaps spirit possession is another name for dementia.

At home in one's skin

In the narrator's description of the soucouyant, skin plays a central role. The victim's skin is marked by the creature's teeth and the victimiser uses skin to conceal herself by day, shedding her flesh by night. This, then, speaks to the conceptions and rhetorical patterns that see skin as boundary and surface contact, while also capturing the phantasms of removing the skin. Here skin functions as the other of the self: the soucouyant's skin is her cover or mask, a façade that she projects out to the world. In this the skin is an enveloping layer in which the figure lies hidden, a conception diametrically opposed to the notion that skin is a source of identity that reveals individuation. The skin of the soucouyant is like a cloth garment, a concealing veil, that hides the vampiric figure and functions as a separating layer surrounding her inner body space. Thus the 'flaying' of the soucouyant, the removal of her veil, does not only reveal what is inside but also displaces her from what we would generally recognise as human. Yet because the flaying is done by the soucouyant herself, it moves from a singular act of destroying the individual to a conscious and transforming act of will: it is semantically recoded from a final act into a transitory moment. This transitory moment rests on the metaphor of the naked truth, which rests on the mechanism of a moment of complete uncovering that must end in another veiling. For, after marking the skin of her victims, the soucouyant returns to her fleshy garment and her place on the edge of town. She must return to living in the house of her skin.[3]

Images of being simultaneously at home and not at home in one's skin are palimsestically evoked throughout the novel. And at times it seems as if Chariandy is invoking the novel *In the Castle of My Skin* (1953), by the Afro-Caribbean writer Georg Lamming, where dark skin, in the image of the 'castle', is identified not only as a refuge but also as an inescapable prison. For in *Soucouyant* the dementia that restricts and contains Adele's life also forces her to confront memories of her life in Trinidad and, more specifically, the city of Carenage. Although she has tried to forget, her traumatic past cannot be repressed. It returns in the memory of a childhood experience during the US occupation of Trinidad in the Second World War: her mother is doused in petrol and set on fire, the flesh consumed by the blaze. 'There was only a thin creeping of a flame', he says, 'and inside this, visible now for the first time to Adele, a human form . . . She senses more now, and begins to beat at her body, fanning the flames and transferring them to herself. Adele herself feels a pain assaulting her, a sheet of pain on her back and shoulders. A hat of orange light. A halo. She sees her mother in a dress of fire' (193). Engulfed by fire, Adele's mother is effaced. Her face is burned and she is no longer at home in her skin, displaced from the homely site of her body. 'There's a plastic look to the woman's face', says the narrator, looking at a photo of his grandmother years later, 'her face is a mask and her skin has buckled with heat' (115). As in Stephen Crane's *The Monster* (1899) in which Henry Johnson, Dr Trescott's black servant, suffers from hideous facial burns that disfigure his skin, the burning of Adele's mother's flesh transforms her into a monstrous figure who haunts Carenage. The 'impossible face' makes her into 'a monster' (116).

In the analogy linking the house and the human body, the skin is the façade, the surface that contains and protects the homely site of identity. But the grotesque site of Adele's traumatic memory bears witness to a destruction of the homely space that is related to her experiences of movement and migration. This experience, I suggest, moves from the soucouyant's flayed skin to the burning flesh of Adele's mother to the text's epigraph, the verse fragment from a Caribbean tale that is repeated in the middle of the novel: '*Old skin, 'kin, 'kin, / You na know me, / You na know me*' (134, emphasis in text).

Here the '*Old skin*' begins by gesturing to its surface as a possible site of enunciation: a surface upon which the past has been inscribed and can be read by the observer. However, the rest of the fragment resists the notion of the body's surface as a place where knowledge about identity is formed or assigned. For the fragment refuses to equate the surface of the '*Old skin*' with a source of knowing, thus negating the notion that skin itself stands metonymically for the whole person. Instead, the fragment insists on *not knowing* through its repetitive assertion: '*You na know me, / You na know me.*' But who or what is denied knowledge? The skin itself? Or perhaps the Other who gazes on the subject who speaks these words?

These questions are not mutually exclusive. For one way of understanding this fragmented verse is in its movement from 'skin' to ''kin'. While the apostrophe identifies the latter as a fragment of skin, ''kin' is also a homonym of 'kin', which can refer to someone related by blood, as in family relations, or a member of a group that shares characteristics with another group. One's kin, then, might share a similar skin colour or other physical features that are akin and, quite often, a person's kin is familiar. By extension, the familiar is that which is recognisable or known, and in this sense skin and kin might be conceived of as related to epistemology. What is the nature of knowledge? And, in particular, what are its foundations, scope and validity? However, if we read the speaker of this verse as addressing the Other's gaze, then knowledge for the speaker has nothing to do with the factual age or colour of the skin. Instead, it has to do only with those who look at him and project an identity on to the individual. The voice, though, resists the projected ascription as cast and distorted reflections in the following ways: one sees only the outer shell of the person, imaginary ideas about him or the reflected observer himself. The gaze bounces off the body and is reflected back in a distorted manner. The skin is non-transparent, a mere empty shell offering no insight of any kind into the person's state of being.

Yet Chariandy's text also depicts the very real racism that is directed at those who are non-white kin, those who have darker skin than the Euro-Canadians who appear in the novel. For instance Meera and the narrator's brother are abused in a racially motivated attack by a group of Euro-Canadian kids; they are forced to kiss and grope, fulfilling a false 'notion of what a black boy and girl should be willing to do' (159). In another section, the narrator describes being verbally attacked by racist abuse: the words 'nigger' and 'paki' are flung at the narrator on the street and in the schoolyard (157–9). Here the racist practice of othering, the demarcation and devaluation of the other, and its attendant value judgements become tied to one's flesh: skin implies a way of both seeing and being seen, both of which contribute to the reinterpretation of the status of identity. As a result Chariandy's use of the skin motif is original and multilayered: in a nation that espouses an official policy of multiculturalism, in which all conceivable skin tones appear side by side, the demonisation of dark skin challenges the mythic harmony of the Canadian mosaic.

Unbecomings

In *Skin Shows*, Judith Halberstam reflects on the historical shifts in discourses of monstrosity and the dissemination of the gothic. In so doing she highlights the dichotomy between surface and depth or inside and outside, which the monster embodies through the visible layer of its skin and the secret depths underneath. On the basis of this central trope, Halberstam argues that gothic monsters are overdetermined signifiers, figures of excess that organise the interplay of several discourses, inviting the audience to suppress some strands of discourse while foregrounding others. If, as she suggests, gothic monsters make the very process of interpretation visible, then any articulation of monstrosity would reveal more about the interpreter than about themselves (Halberstam, 1995: 175–7). As such my act of interpretation is at once revealing and concealing: my attempts to read Chariandy's text might simultaneously mask and unveil my own subject position, political agendas and institutional affiliations. Nevertheless, in *Soucouyant* the narrator's diasporic context engenders a struggle for articulation that exposes the stitches, the artifice, the seams of what his Canadian-Caribbean frame of reference can utter as whole, organic and seamless. Ultimately, what he says about the soucouyant will always mean too much, and therefore too little.

Why is this the case? One reason is that the narrator is simultaneously part of and not part of – inside and outside – the ontology upon which the soucouyant rests. Indeed the dislocated subjectivity that this produces is highlighted in Chariandy's critical essay 'Postcolonial Diasporas', in which he explores the multiconscious state of the migrant who experiences a sense of dislocation alongside the hope of a new identity that can transcend the restrictive borders of the nation (Chariandy, 2006: 9). In this the search for a sense of belonging is, then, vital in the process of becoming. Such a process is, for Gilles Deleuze and Félix Guattari, part of the concept of 'Schizoanalysis' in which 'the unconscious is an accentuated system', 'a mechanical network of finite automata (a rhizome)' (1988: 18). Here it might be tempting to identify the rhizomic as offering a model of becoming within the context of a transnational experience. In fact Deleuze and Guattari situate displaced figures and their narratives – zombies, spirits, vampires – within a rubric of stories about 'becomings':

> Man does not become wolf, or vampire, as if he changed molar species; the vampire and the werewolf are *becomings* of man, in other words, proximities between molecules in composition, relations of movement and rest, speed and slowness between emitted particles. Of course there are werewolves and vampires, we say this with all our heart; but do not look for a resemblance or analogy to the animal, for this is *becoming*-animal in action. (1988: 249, my emphasis)

Theorising vampires and werewolves as 'becomings' is, I would suggest, appropriate in the context of a European ontology and the sway of modernity. Yet Chariandy's narrative does not conflate the rhizomic with the diasporic, nor does the text position such displaced figures on the terrain of 'becoming'. On the contrary *Soucouyant* moves fluidly from spirit possession and vampirism to the suffering caused by the overdetermined signifier known as presenile dementia. By linking such figures to the degenerative illness, Chariandy is primarily interested in an incapacitating state of *unbecoming*. In fact, in an interview with Charles Demers, Chariandy used the term 'unbecoming' to describe his novel. '*Soucouyant* began', he recounts, 'with my personal effort to imagine a woman suffering with pre-senile dementia; and . . . the dementia itself, as a medical condition, awed, terrified, and humbled me in ways that I still find difficult to express. I have developed such enormous respect for those who experience or have to witness, in intimate terms, this particularly devastating process of *unbecoming*' (Demers, 2007, my emphasis).

In this context, then, the globalgothic is about being both inside and outside, part of and not part of, the ontology upon which the soucouyant is based. This in-between situation arises out of the flows, movements and travels of the gothic in a culture of globalisation whereby new time-space circumstances for cultural expression emerge and extend outwards to connect with regional or transnational alliances. But a sense of rootlessness can also surface here, resulting in expressions of anxiety – even terror – through narratives of displaced subjectivity. One response to these fears is the production of locality in the rewriting, resuscitation and re-energising of an imagined past. Thus, globalgothic might draw on the folklore of a particular region (or place) just as transnational narratives sometimes articulate the story of displacement through a reconnection to a distant past and place. Globalgothic, then, stresses the resulting alienation and disconnection, the breakdown of community, the emptying out of the human subject.

But how can one find an adequate symbolic language to account for this sense of fractured and plural identities in the context of globalisation? Chariandy also addresses this question as the figure of the soucouyant gestures toward new spaces for considering multivalent identities through transnational gothic narratives. By writing this figure, which transgresses the spaces, borders and boundaries separating Canada and the Caribbean, Chariandy seeks an adequate way to articulate the past (folklore) and reinvigorate history in the present (globalised North America). While he recognises that we should not neglect the painful realities of displacement in pursuit of the figurative, he also writes that neither can we neglect the fact that the figurative aspects of the gothic can offer 'something else': irrepressible desires, imagined pasts, projected futures. And it is precisely this 'something else' which cannot *but* be articulated 'figuratively' or 'metaphorically'.

What I want to call attention to here is how a narrative of Trinidadian spirit possession is translated in the diasporic context into a global-gothic narrative: the reference to the 'female vampire', the sleeping victim consumed and the marks left on the sleeping man's skin. This is a gothic migration *par excellence*. For the narrator's attempts to understand the figure of the soucouyant lead to this passage and indicate a frame of reference that is linked to his mother's house in suburban Toronto and his Jimi Hendrix T-shirt. For he finds himself in a liminal space – he is 'from here' and yet shares complex forms of social allegiances to other places, pasts and cultures – but the gothic provides an adequate symbolic language to account for his sense of fractured and plural identities. It is within the multivalence of this diasporic experience, then, that the gothic becomes a way for the narrator to conjugate difference into manners of being and belonging. This is, I think, significant not only because it offers a way of articulating a sense of 'outside belonging', a longing to be, but also because it lies in sharp contrast to representations of spirit possession, hoodoo, conjure, obeah and myalism in contemporary fictions located specifically within a Caribbean context. Jamaican fiction such as Erna Brodber's *Myal* (1988) and *Louisiana* (1994), for instance, depict disembodied voices, spirit possessions and spectres not in gothic terms but as part of Caribbean ontologies related to the magico-religious traditions of the archipelago.

Notes

1 See, for example, Judie Newman's *The Ballistic Bard: Postcolonial Fictions* (1995), Zora Neale Hurston's *Tell My Horse: Voodoo and Life in Haiti and Jamaica* (1938) and Juliet Lauro and Karen Embry's 'A Zombie Manifesto' (2008).

2 Jean Rhys, for instance, uses the spelling 'soucriant' in 'The Day they Burned the Books': 'her eyes had gone wicked', the narrator says, 'like a soucriant's' (1996: 238).

3 The salt on the skin that is meant to kill the soucouyant conjures up images of embalming or the curing of flesh. But salt is also linked to other Caribbean narratives and contemporary writing: Édouard Glissant's *Le Sel Noir* (1960), Earl Lovelace's *Salt: A Novel* (1996) and Nalo Hopkinson's *The Salt Roads* (2003). Moreover, in Dionne Brand's *In Another Place, Not Here* (1996) the image of salt is closely connected to the Middle Passage and the sense of abandonment.

References

Bissoondath, Neil. 1994. *Selling Illusions: The Cult of Multiculturalism in Canada*. Toronto: Penguin.

Brand, Dionne. 1990. 'The language of resistance'. Interview with Beverly Daurio. *Books in Canada*, 19.7: 13–16.

——. 1996. *In Another Place, Not Here*. Toronto: Knopf.

——. 2001. *A Map to the Door of No Return: Notes to Belonging*. Toronto: Doubleday.

Brodber, Erna. 1988. *Myal*. London: New Beacon.

——. 1994. *Louisiana*. London: New Beacon.

Byron, Glennis, and David Punter. 2004. *The Gothic*. Oxford: Blackwell.

Chariandy, David. 2007. *Soucouyant*. Vancouver: Arsenal Pulp Press.

Crane, Stephen. 1899. *The Monster and Other Stories*. New York: Harper.

Deleuze, Gilles, and Félix Guattari. 1988. *A Thousand Plateaus*, trans. Brian Massumi. London: Athlone Press.

Dickinson, Peter. 1999. *Here Is Queer: Nationalisms, Sexualities, and the Literatures of Canada*. Toronto: University of Toronto Press.

Edwards, Justin D. 2005. *Gothic Canada: Reading the Spectre of a National Literature*. Edmonton: University of Alberta Press.

Gibbon, John Murray. 1938. *The Canadian Mosaic*. Toronto: McClelland and Stewart.

Glissant, Édouard. 1960. *Le Sel Noir*. Paris: Seuil.

Halberstam, Judith. 1995. *Skin Shows: Gothic Horror and the Technology of Monsters*. Durham, NC: Duke University Press.

Hopkinson, Nalo. 2003. *The Salt Roads*. New York: Warner.

Hurston, Zora Neale. 1938. *Tell My Horse: Voodoo and Life in Haiti and Jamaica*. Philadelphia: Lippincott.

Jacobs, Jane M. 1996. *The Edge of Empire: Postcolonialism and the City*. London: Routledge.

Kamboureli, Smaro. 2000. *Scandalous Bodies: Diasporic Literature in English Canada*. Toronto: Oxford University Press.

Lamming, George. 1953. *In the Castle of My Skin*. New York: McGraw Hill.

Lauro, Juliet and Karen Embry. 2008. 'A zombie manifesto' *boundary 2*, 35.1: 85–108.
Lovelace, Earl. 1996. *Salt: A Novel*. London: Faber and Faber.
Morrell, Carol. 1994. Introduction. In *Grammar of Dissent: Poetry and Prose by Claire Harris, M. Nourbese Philip, Dionne Brand*, ed. Carol Morrell. Fredericton: Goose Lane, 9–24.
Newman, Judie. 1995. *The Ballistic Bard: Postcolonial Fictions*. London: Arnold.
Porter, John. 1965. *The Vertical Mosaic: An Analysis of Social Class and Power in Canada*. Toronto: University of Toronto Press.
Rhys, Jean. 1996 (1960). 'The Day They Burned the Books'. In *The Routledge Reader in Caribbean Literature*, eds Alison Donnell and Sarah Lawson Welsh. London: Routledge, 237–42.

Online sources

Chariandy, David. 2006. 'Postcolonial diasporas'. *Postcolonial Text*, 2.1. http://journals.sfu.ca/pocol/index.php/pct. Accessed 2 December 2008.
Demers, Charles. 2007. 'Forgotten son: David Chariandy on *Soucouyant*'. http://thetyee.ca/. October 17. Accessed 5 September 2009.

Filmography

Dawn of the Dead. 1978. George Romero, dir. United Artists.
I Walked with a Zombie. 1943. Jacques Tournier, dir. RKO Radio Pictures.

5

Sue Zlosnik

Globalgothic at the top of the world: Michel Faber's 'The Fahrenheit Twins'

Since its inception in the eighteenth century, gothic has represented anxieties about time, space and mortality in a secularising world. In the dimension of space, gothic can be claustrophobic, as in the dungeons and other enclosed spaces in the fiction of writers such as Lewis and Poe, or, conversely, agoraphobic, as in the sinister wildernesses of American gothic. Time too presents itself as disturbingly unstable, with a primitive past all too likely to irrupt into a present that is also haunted by intimations of a menacing future. Poised in an unstable present, the body is a vulnerable entity in the world of gothic, where the boundaries between life and death are often rendered permeable.

In the two and a half centuries since the emergence of Western gothic, popular perceptions of time and space have changed, a process that has accelerated in recent decades with the phenomenon of globalisation. As Paul Virilio claims, 'What coincides with us in real time . . . is no longer some house or architecture but the *oikumen*, the whole of the inhabited earth' (2000a: 77). And as Andrew Herod points out, there is some debate about the origins of a planetary consciousness: it has been variously related to the growth of the slave trade – and hence contemporaneous with the rise of the gothic – to the invention of telescopes in the sixteenth century and to earlier pre-Christian beliefs. Undoubtedly, he claims, the developments in modern communications through inventions such the telegraph in the nineteenth century enabled a sense of 'panoptical time' (2009: 43). Moreover, the developments of the last two and a half centuries have, according to Robert Markley, rendered the world a more threatening, non-human and more sublime place.

'In the 1790s', Markley notes, 'the nebular hypothesis of planetary formation advanced by Pierre Simon de Laplace, the "discovery" of geological time by James Hutton, and the argument for species extinction put forth by Georges Cuvier transformed the conception of climate by decoupling history from human experience and memory' (2011: 67). Paradoxically, as we have moved into the twentieth and twenty-first centuries, the polar regions have become less potent as sublime landscapes. The Arctic is now a charted territory 'on top' (conventionally) of a planet that the twenty-first-century reader can comprehend as an entity and see in its entirety through images from space. It was not always so. The far north was for many centuries an unexplored place of wonder and folklore. As Joanna Kavenna explains, ever since the ancient Greek explorer Pytheas claimed to have found and then lost a mysterious frozen land beyond the known world which he named Thule, it became 'entwined with thousands of years of fantasies about what might lie beyond the edges of the maps' (2005: 5). This legacy of the image of the polar regions allowed them to be envisaged as a site of the sublime. This found expression, for example, in nineteenth-century painting, perhaps most famously Caspar David Friedrich's *The Wreck of the Hope*, also known as *The Polar Sea* or *The Sea of Ice*, which was completed in 1824 and depicted a shipwreck in the Arctic Ocean. In gothic fiction the most famous example is the framing location of the Arctic wastes in Mary Shelley's *Frankenstein* (1818), but the Antarctic also provided a sublime setting, as in Coleridge's poem 'The Rime of the Ancient Mariner' (1798) and Edgar Allan Poe's strange tale *The Narrative of Arthur Gordon Pym of Nantucket* (1838). Alluding to the early twentieth-century explorations of the north and south poles, Andrew Herod points out that 'for some this closure of the Earth's last two geographic frontiers was viewed as marking the end not of geography but of history' (2009: 38), a sentiment echoed in 1989 by Francis Fukuyama in his analysis of the end of the Cold War and the spread of global capitalism, 'The end of history?' (1989). Yet it would seem that the technology accompanying global capitalism has effected the annihilation of space by time rather than vice versa. Indeed this effect is seen to be one of the key features of the modern global condition. In the words of Paul Virilio, we are 'not seeing an "end of history", but . . . an end of geography' (2000b: 9).

Michel Faber's 'The Fahrenheit Twins' is the title story in a collection of weird tales published in 2006. It is a story that has fired imaginations, leading to an adaptation for the stage (in London in 2009) and the appropriation of its title for the name of a Dutch indie rock band. Faber sets it where Mary Shelley left *Frankenstein,* in the frozen wastes of the Arctic, at 'the icy zenith of the world' (Faber, 2006: 231). It is the tale of a quest for origin and anxiety about destination. Its twenty-first-century wilderness provides the setting for a mythopoeic tale about the moribund nature of Western culture. Writing of eighteenth-century gothic fictions, Fred Botting suggests, 'The wild social and natural landscapes of the fictions . . . present worlds that have abandoned principles of morality and propriety, places outside the rule of law, that is, without proper paternal regulation' (2008: 201). In Faber's landscape, the now-charted Arctic, the gothic father has intruded but his authority is undermined by the events that develop. It is the death of the mother figure, so often absent or disempowered in gothic fiction, which sets these events in train, events that symbolise the inexorable passage of time.

Described in a recent essay as 'a globe-trotting allegorist from The Hague, reared in Melbourne, Australia and now residing forty miles north of Inverness, Scotland' (Snodgrass, 2011: 111), Faber may be considered to have a more personal global perspective than many other writers. Although much of his writing succeeds in sustaining a sense of the uncanny, 'a strangeness of framing and borders, an experience of liminality' to use Nicholas Royle's words (2003: 2), Faber cannot be easily categorised as a gothic writer. Most of his work avoids the conventional tropes of gothic although he has an enduring preoccupation with the abject, and in *The Fire Gospel* (2008) myth and history are subjected to a darkly comic satiric treatment. Gothic intertexts are clearly visible in such novels as *The Hundred and Ninety-nine Steps* (2001), a story of haunting and violence set in Whitby, and Mary Ellen Snodgrass characterises his 2002 neo-Victorian novel *The Crimson Petal and the White,* probably his best-known work, as subverting various conventions of the female gothic tradition. The short story 'The Fahrenheit Twins' provides a new twist to the parodic gothic of Angela Carter in her rewriting of European fairy stories, *The Bloody Chamber* (1979). Like Carter, Faber draws attention to the similarities between gothic narratives following the mid-eighteenth century and tales derived from earlier folk myths, and, like Carter, he offers a critical change in perspective. Carter famously claimed in 1974 that 'we live in Gothic times' (1974: 122) and contemporary scholars continue to explore the implications of such an assertion. For Fred Botting, 'To live in Gothic times means that the genre loses its specific intensity, shedding the allure of darkness, danger and mystery' (2008: 39–40). Those who seek horror, according to Botting, must look elsewhere (2008: 162). The familiarity and popularity of gothic monsters such as the zombie and vampire suggest that they may have other cultural work to do.

In 'Gothic times', many reworkings of the traditional tropes of gothic are parodic, an interrogation of the already written as in Carter's *The Bloody Chamber*. Such parodic reworkings often demonstrate what Horner and Zlosnik have called 'the comic turn', with 'parody . . . as a literary mode that, while engaging with a target text or genre, exhibits a keen sense of the comic, an acute awareness of intertextuality and an engagement with the idea of metafiction' (2005: 12). The parodic engagement of 'The Fahrenheit Twins' with some of the traditional tropes of the gothic is frequently comic in effect while at the same time freighted with allegorical import.

The eponymous twins, a latter-day Hansel and Gretel, are the only children of two anthropologists, Boris and Una Fahrenheit, who are undertaking permanent fieldwork studying the fictional indigenous Guhiynui (a name chosen for comic effect if pronounced phonetically) on a remote island in the Arctic tundra. This, according to their mother, is a 'little paradise' in which mother and father are 'monarchs' and 'their two children prince and princess' (Faber, 2006: 232). The names of the twins, Tainto'lilith and Marko'cain, signify an outcast status of which they are innocent: the former refers to Lilith, the banished first wife of Adam according to Jewish folklore, and the latter to Cain, the first born of Adam and Eve according to Genesis, who killed his brother Abel and became the first murderer. The twins have been born on this remote island and their existence is 'a secret from anyone in the green parts of the world' (234). Already alarmed by the prospect of the passage of time and the changes it will bring, they attempt to make it stand still through ritual communion with the universe. Confronted by the traumatic event of their mother's death, they set off with her body into the wilderness in the expectation that a signal will come from the universe to tell them how to dispose of it. Ill equipped by their father (wilfully, in all likelihood), they survive a gruelling journey, experience unexpected revelations and return to find that a new woman has taken their mother's place. They then determine to leave their father's house and go south into the 'green' parts of the world.

This bare synopsis gives an indication of the mythopoeic quality of Faber's tale, which, while resistant to easy categorisation, locates itself in relation to the folktales and religion of Western culture and their manifestation in the gothic tradition. It succeeds at one and the same time in creating uncanny effects and working through a dark parodic humour in a recognition that these traditions are of the past. Living beyond the bounds of civil society, Faber's twins believe they commune with the universe yet their ritual attempts to stop time are doomed to failure and the emptiness and stasis of their world are shown to be illusory. They can be in this place only through modern technology: a helicopter, a generator and other devices are their lifeline. Their journey takes them to the edge of the island, a coastline beside a raging sea, where they encounter the signs of a different culture and learn something about their maternal origins, although this is not something they are able to articulate.

Already rendered potentially uncanny because of their doubling, the twins are possessed of 'uncannily' keen vision (232). They are gothic children whose apparent innocence is the slate upon which a narrative of cultural rupture, dispossession and exile will be written. Steven Bruhm notes in a recent essay that 'Gothic literature in general and Gothic children in particular have monstrously proliferated since the 1950s. Most interesting are the ways the Gothic deploys a putative childhood blankness to serve specific cultural ends' (2006: 100). The interplay between innocence and experience is enacted through Marko'cain and Tainto'lilith, as events are focalised through them with a third-person narrative voice reporting their perceptions in a dispassionate tone. With 'virtually unlimited space' for play, 'time was no problem' for them (231). There is a hint of corruption in the 'scattering of tiny puckered scars from a mysterious disease' on their cheeks; the significance of the fact that, 'black-maned, seal-eyed' (235), 'they resembled neither their father nor mother' only becomes apparent as the story progresses (233). Their innocence itself is terrible. Like Iain Banks's Francis Cauldhame in *The Wasp Factory* (1984), they sustain a primitive belief in magic and their own capacity to affect the workings of the universe through acts of ritual cruelty. Most significant of these is the annual ritual of blinding an Arctic fox as the summer sun rises above the horizon, an attempt to stay the passage of time. They have been told by their mother that their bodies will change in the future, that Marko'cain will 'sprout a beard' and Tainto'lilith will 'grow teats' (234). Masculine certainty of the efficacy of the ritual is expressed by Marko'cain, who claims, 'I feel it in my testaments' (236), an unwitting comic evocation of religious belief.

In contrast with the blankness of the Arctic landscape, the Fahrenheits' home, a 'domed monstrosity of concrete, steel and double-glazed glass' which stands out 'from the landscape like an abandoned spaceship on the moon' (236), is filled with the kitsch that Una has brought from her former life. The twins' sense of their European heritage is derived from 'careful study of these things – the little wooden horses with real manes and tails, the crystal baubles with cherubs inside, the music boxes that played Alpine melodies, the stuffed mouse with the Tyroler hat, green velvet jacket and lederhosen' (237). As if to mock the twins' fear of the passage of time, multiple cuckoo clocks strike the hour, offering a reminder of the famous meditation on European culture by Orson Welles as Harry Lime in the film *The Third Man* (1949). One of these has unaccountably gone missing, however.

In this symbolic tale the search for origins is represented in various ways. 'The Fahrenheits' house was infested with paper' (238). Told by their mother that all the books and papers had once been trees, the twins, who have never seen a tree, attempt to reverse the process and grow a tree 'by pulping a book into paste and burying it in a compost of excrement and yeast' (238). Needless to say, this is a failure. Meanwhile, they are making their own book, a 'Book of Knowledge' in which they record the fragments of information that their taciturn and distracted mother imparts to them. It is her death, however, that leads them to discover their own origin, even though they can barely comprehend its meaning. It is here that the gothic plot is at its most apparent. For the gothic father, Boris Fahrenheit, a 'tall thin German, grey of face and silver of hair' (232), the twins are 'an indulgence of their mother's which he tolerated so long as it didn't interfere with his research' (233). When one day the parents return from an expedition, it is apparent that Una is ill and there is a hint that he may be responsible for her condition, a suspicion strengthened for the reader by subsequent events. In spite of the twins' devoted nursing, she dies and is contemplated by them in her bed with 'her flesh . . . the colour of a peeled apple', a description carrying echoes of the original sin of Genesis. For the twins her death is a turning point, not least because, believing in their own primitive magic, they think they 'would certainly have done something to stop it' (241) had they known that death was a likely outcome of her illness. Confronted by the abject prospect of their mother's corpse, they are presented with a decision by their father, who appears to abdicate all manner of responsibility in this matter. Moreover they seem to think that their father is now likely to desert them, and Tainto'lilith reflects that they are now orphans 'like in the storybook of *Little Helmut and Marlene*' (241), a traditional-sounding tale that appears to be an invention of Faber's, like several others mentioned by the twins.

It is a measure of their lack of socialisation that Marko'cain suggests they might eat their mother's body to dispose of it; cannibalism is apparently not taboo for them. Rejecting this as impractical, they decide to 'take their mother away with them into the wilderness. Once they were far enough out there, they would wait for a signal from the universe as to the best thing to do with the body' (246). What they might regard as a signal is entirely intuitive; what they discover allows the reader to construct a coherent narrative of their origins and subsequent dispossession. Setting off with dogs and a sledge, they are equipped by their father but, either through incompetence or malice, the endowment of this gothic father is useless: the bag of provisions turns out to contain only 'some big crumpled-up papers . . . and a heavy book called . . . *Principia Anthropologica*' (258). What should have been dog food is tinned tomato, ominously described as 'a globulous pool of gore enriched with pale seeds' (253), and, abjectly, as 'chilly, snot-textured fruit' (259) when they have to resort to eating it. Cooking fuel is revealed as cooking oil, emitting when ignited, in one of the story's frequent comic turns, 'a faint aroma of singed fried food, familiar to the twins from their mother's meals' (254). Not surprisingly, Tainto'lilith asks, 'Do you think perhaps our father is trying to kill us?' (258).

A powerful symbol of the redundancy of Western culture is to be found in the twins' discovery of a 'monumental steel crucifix' (255), standing alone in the wilderness when they eventually reach the barren coastline with its 'tortured rock formations – volcanic froth frozen in time' (253). They briefly consider the possibility of resurrection but then dismiss this idea as frightening and decide to wait for a different message. In fact the cross is a relic of death in technology, the blades of a crashed helicopter in which 'complex skeins of blood [pattern] the upholstery' (256). The only succour it can offer is a dislodged family of voles that provides food for the famished dogs. The modern mechanical means of transport, the means relied upon by the Fahrenheit parents, has been destroyed by 'the universe', and nature in its primitive form, red in tooth and claw, is in the ascendancy. In the midst of a storm, listening to the 'fearsome and relentless' hubbub of the sea, and as the summer sun begins to show itself as a 'pearly glow' on the horizon (259), the twins debate their sameness and difference and face the possibility that their father has murdered their mother. They also see him as helpless without a woman and decide to return to him. Their burning of the *Principia Anthropologica* is done out of the need to keep warm, yet it provides a crucial symbolic prelude to the 'message from the universe' (263) that they have been confidently awaiting.

Still some distance from the Guhiynui village, they hear the sound of a cuckoo clock and are brought face to face with their own origins – although what they find appears enigmatic to them. The sound comes from a single Guhiynui dwelling, framed by whalebone and clad with whaleskin, 'in all respects identical to the drawings their mother had made of such dwellings in her notebook' (265). They find it deserted and 'from the moment they stepped inside' they are 'intoxicated by the mysterious potency of the place' (266). The traditional Guhiynui interior is decorated with paintings bearing images of adventure and hunting as well as intimations of immortality in the form of birds carrying 'tiny sleeping humans towards the sun' (267). Yet it is also imbued with traces of their mother and the aura of the status she had enjoyed with the tribe, especially the artist, as they are confronted by her image itself: 'directly above the bed, there was the largest painting of all, a dynamic full-length portrait of a dark-skinned male and a slender creamy-white female. From her stylized hairdo and the blush on her cheek, it was quite obvious that this woman was meant to be Una Fahrenheit' (267). This image is defamiliarised by the artistic conventions of another culture and the twins' naive inability to interpret the representation: 'The man had some kind of extra limb growing from between his legs, and Una had two mouths, one on her face and another, much larger one, on her belly' (267). Their discovery of this maternal place and their acceptance of its significance, in spite of their inability to read the signs that are so clear for the reader, tempts a psychoanalytic reading. Their almost overwhelming need to return to the mother's bed – 'Both twins felt sick with desire to sleep in that bed, knowing very well that it was not intended for them' (268) – is an overdetermined gesture at the universalising narrative of psychoanalysis. Yet another kind of reading is more persuasive: there are also clear signs that this is a place of cultural hybridity. The mother's bed is 'a big nest of seal skins, all different kinds . . . It looked supremely comfortable, especially with two fluffy pillows at the far end, each covered in a pastel-coloured pillow case embroidered with tiny edelweiss' (268). The mystery of the twins' appearance is solved for the reader here: they are the product of two very different cultures, and it would seem that the gothic father Boris is not their true father. Here too time intrudes, its strange and relative quality emphasised, with 'the missing cuckoo clock, defiantly keeping its exotic brand of time with its delicate pendulum' (266), a portent of the inevitable changes that have come upon them and the uncertainty of their future. Once they have 'reverently' placed their mother's body in the bed, the cuckoo clock calls again: 'it had used twelve of its cries to call them here, and must begin again' (269). And so must the twins is the implication here.

They are torn between the Guhiynui village, which Marko'cain favours, and a return to 'our Father's house', which is Tainto'lilith's choice, because 'The Book of Knowledge is there', although her brother states flatly that 'we know everything now . . . there is nothing more to know' (269). Waiting in vain for a message from the universe, they must now make their own decision, a symbolic turning away from the primitive belief in magic that had been their guide so far. The capitalisation of 'Father', with its Biblical overtones, freights the word with a symbolic significance and the reader is reminded, on their return, that this is also the gothic father. They arrive half dead 'like a couple of imperfectly defrosted fish' (270), but, instead of rejoicing at their return as if they were like the prodigal son, Boris is 'thunderstruck' (271). His sinister quality here is comically expressed as he 'exposed all his teeth in a startlingly unbecoming smile' (272).

In an adaptation of a classic trope from folk tales, the twins find a stepmother installed in the paternal home, one who appears to have been unaware of their existence. Miss Kristensen represents a startling intrusion from the 'civilized world', her very name suggestive of Western culture and her appearance 'uncannily similar to one of the many dolls their mother had given them over the years, an impish Scandinavian poppet' (272). Plying them with food and 'milk . . . from colourful little cartons manufactured in Canada', she 'radiated nurture' (272). She may be regarded, like Boris, as a symbolic figure, although she appears to be an inversion of the wicked stepmother. Instead she represents the seductive comforts of the 'developed world', which the twins instinctively reject. Indeed the feast induces a prolonged bout of vomiting. Their unintended pilgrimage to their own origins has made them resistant to the symbolic mothering of Western culture, expressed through a burgeoning awareness of their own incipient sexuality: 'unspoken between them was a bewildering new anxiety: the possibility of Miss Kristensen volunteering to bathe them. The thought was more terrifying – more taboo, somehow, than anything else they had yet encountered' (273). Their experiences have destroyed their innocence, and their suspicions about Boris's intentions now extend to the newcomer. It is Marko'cain who suggests that Miss Kristensen might have told their father to get rid of them, in spite of the fact that, as his sister points out, she seemed genuinely surprised to see them. In a distinctly gothic turn Marko'cain suggests killing their father but his less 'cocky' and more compassionate sister tries to think of a way to save him, 'that poor old baby who was, after all, helpless without a woman' (274). Thus the gothic family dynamic is played out with Tainto'lilith showing signs of accepting the role of victimised gothic heroine. She proposes flight rather than fight and they agree to run away. By this point in the story the gendered differences between the two initially androgynous twins are becoming very pronounced, Marko'cain's masculine bravado contrasting with his sister's sensitivity and propensity for tears in what he envisages as 'a lifetime . . . of secret sorrows' (276).

The ending of the story is ambiguous. It appears to conclude on an optimistic note as Tainto'lilith reflects, 'And yes, her brother was right, they had much to look forward to, in the big wide world down below. The Book of Knowledge had a lot of blank pages' (276). This optimism is undermined, however, in a number of ways. They have decided this time to reject sledge and huskies in favour of the modern means of transport, the helicopter. Marko'cain's masculine hubris, his 'swagger of purpose' (275), is reflected in his conviction that he can fly the aircraft because he and his sister have 'read the book', in other words, the pilot's manual. The reader is inevitably aware of the fate of the crashed helicopter they had encountered in the wilderness, although neither makes reference to it at this point. It could be, therefore, that their elected exile from the 'little paradise' will result in premature death. If this is not the case, their exile will take them to places they have only heard and read about but in their new state, it is suggested, there will be no sublime discovery, no revelation. The circularity of the globe itself is imaged in the description of their clothes in the washing machine. 'Behind the big glass porthole . . . their clothing had begun to spin, an inextricable, mesmerising ring of embroidered pelts. Soon they would be able to put it on again, and cover their nakedness' (276).

In this gruesomely comic new version of exile from Eden, the twins will, in their dispossession, become what Zygmunt Bauman calls the 'vagabonds' of the modern world. For Bauman, 'modernity is the impossibility of staying put. To be modern means to be on the move' (1997: 77). The story's subtext indicates an ecological turn in a world where trees are legend and time cannot be reversed to grow them from the books they have become. The family name, 'Fahrenheit', evokes the temperature scale devised in the early eighteenth century and once in general use throughout the Western world. It is now retained primarily by the United States, while other countries have moved on to Celsius; the reluctance of the United States to ratify the Kyoto protocol on climate change remains a significant factor in threatening the polar ice caps through global warming. Another likely source for Michel Faber's choice of name is the widely distributed film by Michael Moore about false values and paranoia in American society in the twenty-first century, *Fahrenheit 9/11* (2004), released two years before the publication of Faber's story. Another resonance of the name is that of Ray Bradbury's 1953 novel *Fahrenheit 451*, alluded to in Moore's title, in which the role of the fireman in the dystopian society it depicts is to burn books. It may be pure coincidence or allegorist's luck that Faber is the name of the former English teacher in Bradbury's novel who articulates what is lost through the destruction of books and the freedom of knowledge they imply. Certainly, 'The Fahrenheit twins' provides much food for thought about the relationship between culture and environment and prompts the reader at the beginning of the twenty-first century to consider the global future. It is an allegory that parodies the well-worn tropes of a Western tradition, gothic, in order to imagine the world in a state of profound change.

References

Banks, Iain. 1984. *The Wasp Factory*. London: Macmillan.

Bauman, Zygmunt. 1997. *Postmodernity and Its Discontents*. Cambridge: Polity.

Botting, Fred. 2008. *Limits of Horror: Technology, Bodies, Gothic*. Manchester: Manchester University Press.

Bradbury, Ray. 1953. *Fahrenheit 451*. New York: Ballantine.

Bruhm, Steven. 2006. 'Nightmare on Sesame Street: or, the self-possessed child'. *Gothic Studies*, 8.2: 98–210.

Carter, Angela. 1974. 'Afterword'. *Fireworks: Nine Stories in Various Disguises*. Cambridge: Harper and Row, 132–3.

——. 1979. *The Bloody Chamber and Other Stories*. London: Gollancz.

Coleridge, Samuel Taylor. 2006 (1798). 'The rime of the ancyent marinere'. *Lyrical Ballads*, by Samuel Coleridge and William Wordsworth, ed. Michael Schmidt. London: Penguin Classics, 1–25.

Faber, Michel. 2001. *The Hundred and Ninety-nine Steps*. Edinburgh: Canongate.

——. 2002. *The Courage Consort*. Edinburgh: Canongate.

——. 2002. *The Crimson Petal and the White*. Edinburgh: Canongate.

——. 2006. *The Fahrenheit Twins*. Edinburgh: Canongate.
——. 2008. *The Fire Gospel*. Edinburgh: Canongate.
Friedrich, Caspar David. 1824. *The Wreck of the Hope / The Polar Sea / The Sea of Ice*. Hamburg: Kunsthalle Hamburg.
Fukuyama, Francis. 1989. 'The end of history?' *The National Interest*, 16: 3–18.
Herod, Andrew. 2009. *Geographies of Globalization*. Oxford: Wiley-Blackwell.
Horner, Avril, and Sue Zlosnik. 2005. *Gothic and the Comic Turn*. Basingstoke: Palgrave Macmillan.
Kavenna, Joanna. 2005. *The Ice Museum: In Search of the Lost Land of Thule*. Harmondsworth: Viking/Penguin.
Markley, Robert. 2011. 'Climate science'. In *The Routledge Companion to Literature and Science*, ed. Bruce Clarke with Manuela Rossini. Oxford: Routledge, 63–76.
Poe, Edgar Allan. 1838. *The Narrative of Arthur Gordon Pym of Nantucket*. New York: Harper.
Royle, Nicholas. 2003. *The Uncanny: An Introduction*. Manchester: Manchester University Press: An Introduction.
Shelley, Mary. 1818. *Frankenstein, or The Modern Prometheus*. 3 vols. London: Lackington, Hughes, Harding, Mavor and Jones.
Snodgrass, Mary Ellen. 2011. 'Michel Faber, feminism and the neo-gothic novel: *The Crimson Petal and the White*'. In *21st Century Gothic: Great Gothic Novels Since 2000*, ed. Danel Olson. Lanham: Scarecrow Press, 111–23.
Virilio, Paul. 2000a. *Polar Inertia*, trans. Patrick Camiller. London: Sage.
——. 2000b. *The Information Bomb*, trans. Chris Turner. London: Verso.

Filmography

Fahrenheit 9/11. 2004. Michael Moore, dir. Lion's Gate Films.
The Third Man. 1949. Carol Reed, dir. Lion Films/Selznick International.

6

Aspasia Stephanou

Online vampire communities: Towards a globalised notion of vampire identity

> Even people who don't like vampires know what one is. The vampire is as common as a Big Mac.
>
> A vampire fan, qtd in Dresser

> if we celebrate hybridity and heterogeneity, we must remember that they are also privileged terms of advanced capitalism, that social multiculturalism coexists with economic multinationalism.
>
> Hal Foster, *The Return of the Real*

New technologies such as the internet have facilitated the globalisation of cultural exchanges and the creation of online or cyber-communities. In a globalised culture, global flows of ideas, people, images, commodities, technologies and money are moving speedily across the geographical perimeters of the world, travelling from one place to another in intricate ways (Appadurai 1996) and impacting on the individual's experience of the world. Online communities are similarly developing beyond national frontiers and promising the construction of a globalised society and culture. As David Bell argues, globalisation opens up 'the whole world as a potential source of community' (2001: 96) and because we are *disembedded*, no longer confined by place, we can 'choose our communities', 'play with our identities' and 're-imagine the very notion of community' (97). 'In the face of all this disembedding, detraditionalizing, globalizing uncertainty', Bell writes, 'we need to find new way to belong – and the internet is on hand to provide exactly that' (97). While the vampire communities existed before the rise of new technologies of communication, the internet has facilitated and propagated the number of online vampire communities and accelerated the processes of constructing or structuring the culture of vampirism and its definitions. The new virtual networks have also created the idea of closeness and social communion in what William Mitchell has described as an 'incorporeal world', transgressing both corporeal and geographical boundaries (qtd in Robins 2007: 229). While these imagined new possibilities, where distance becomes meaningless and the subject leaves the meat behind, are enthusiastically embraced, they also expel otherness in the pursuit of a 'generalised and globalised intimacy' (Robins, 2007: 229). This illusory sense of intimacy, accompanied by a detachment from reality and its chaotic complexity, nullifies the experience of the other, his/her difference and distance.

This raises the problematic of a global cultural homogenisation or uniformity, through the cultural imperialism of Western forms. According to David Bell, when we think about cyber-communities we need to be 'mindful of the ways communities deal with difference, rather than merely celebrating their inclusivity' (2001: 110). Similarly, global media's control of cultural flows has created the hegemony of global celebrities, such as in the case of the US vampire Don Henrie representing the global vampire community on SciFi's reality television series *Mad Mad House* (2004). An Asian American, Don became a vampire icon, glamorous and sexually appealing; his ethnicity gave way to a lustrous commodified image of Hollywoodised vampires: false blue contact lenses, false fangs, long, artificial nails, and the ubiquitous gothic, Victorian-era attire: a hyperreal transnational vampire for our times.

While on the one hand it can be argued that the globalisation of the vampire figure produces a unitary vampire culture propagated by the vampire community, media and advertising industry, on the other hand the globalisation of various cultural elements creates hybridisation and a melange of cultures. For Paul Hopper it is 'debatable whether capitalism, American power, or some other influence, is producing a unitary global culture' (2007: 5). Although there might not be 'a dominant homogenizing cultural power at work', he suggests, there are definitely 'homogenizing forces' experienced by people globally (109). Because 'cultural globalization is complex, heterogeneous and plural' (186), we should be talking about global cultures instead of *a* global culture, and consequently globalgothics instead of a unitary globalgothic culture.

If the vampire of literature used to be a malign migrant, carrying pestilence and infecting the West with Eastern influence, the vampire has become a cultural icon, adapted to the self-acclaimed real vampires' beliefs: a global melange of Eastern and Western influences. As Joseph Laycock points out, self-identified vampires have emerged through a four-stage process: '1. Discourse creates a category – the vampire. 2. Individuals come to identify themselves in the category. 3. Individuals redefine the category and de-otherize it. 4. The category becomes a source of identity and a "technology of the self"' (2009: 28). The use of such concepts such as 'de-otherizing' the vampire is problematic, given that it is vampire literature and film that facilitated the humanisation of the vampire and not the self-identified vampires. In addition the fact that vampires have redefined vampirism through Eastern spiritualities and other Eastern religious symbols raises further questions. For the religious scholar Christopher Partridge, who has observed the re-enchantment of the West through Eastern spiritualities, the cyber-spirituality of certain online vampire organisations and houses is a characteristic example of this Western re-sacralisation. Despite celebrations of the East, this Western re-enchantment is entrenched in an increasingly orientated New Age capitalist market that supplies the spiritual needs of its Western consumers.

The idea of an online vampire *community* reveals a desire and nostalgia for an old sense of community which has been eclipsed in contemporary societies, a concept that is, however, regressive and utopian. While the terms *community* and *subculture* are both used to describe the vampire groups and organisations, the self-proclaimed vampires seem to prefer the concept of community, which pertains to the ideal experience of meaningful 'virtual togetherness' (Bakardjieva, 2007: 236) and conjures up the ideal of a local connection of shared values and kinship. The idea of a subculture, however, does not necessitate participation or a shared sense of identity and orientation toward the world (Todd, 2001: 59). For Nancy Baym an online community exists as long as the 'participants *imagine* themselves as a community' (qtd in Bell, 2001: 102), while for David Bell it is technology that gives 'a silicon-induced *illusion* of community' (2001: 102). The interactivity of online communities suggests that 'the global can become as manageable and familiar as your local community (the community that you have, nostalgically, lost)' (Willson, 2007: 217). In the Voices of the Vampire Community (VVC) global vampire discussion, one of the main issues is the description of the global vampire groups as a subculture or a community. Valens, a member of the global vampire community, notes that 'I personally like the idea of community. In some cases, it may bring us closer' (Valens, 10 July 2009: 22). Indeed, online vampire groups have helped bring together vampires from isolated localities and provide information about their condition. As Kevin Robins explains, 'Solidarity in cyberspace seems to be a matter of extending the security of small-town *Gemeinschaft* to the transnational scale of the global village. There is, however, something deceptive in this sense of continuity and fulfilment' (2007: 150). Although, he explains, there is 'the invocation of community', there is no 'production of society' (150). There exists a 'simulation of the old forms of solidarity and community' but that only produces 'an alternative to society' and not an alternative society (150), the artificiality of community and not the material and local reality of difference, conflict and disorder that characterise real social life (151). Online vampire communities are perhaps examples of 'the age-old ideal of a communications utopia' (151). As Sorkin notes, 'the highly regulated, completely synthetic vision provides a simplified, sanitized experience that stands in for the more undisciplined complexities of the city' (1992: 208).

The sanitised and conservative character of online vampire communities is exemplified by the application of rules in order to create a traditional sense of community or family. The real vampire community consists of individuals who need to consume blood (sanguine vampires), energy (psychic or tantric vampires) or both (hybrid vampires) in order to function mentally and physically. Some view vampirism as a medical condition or deficiency; others see it as a state of being. Some of the vampire groups, such as The Temple of the Vampire, Ordo Strigoi Vii and The Order of the Vampire, forbid any consumption of blood and support the idea that vampires are made instead of awakened. Both The Temple of the Vampire and Ordo Strigoi Vii refer to their members as 'born to the Blood', despite their belief in the initiatory model of vampirism which is based on the idea of becoming a vampire. Some vampire organisations bestow titles on their members such as 'Azralim' to refer to older vampires (Laycock, 2009: 88) or refer to their makers as 'Fathers'. The symbolic reference to blood is of course here operating as a marker of familial bonds and the heritage of the Family (Sebastiaan, 2010: 14). As Laycock notes, Ordo Strigoi Vii 'harbors elements of the awakened model' since 'potential members must have a certain quality that Sebastiaan has compared to a genetic marker' (2009: 81).[1] There is a fetishisation of the ideals of community here: a family sharing something that is even perhaps ingrained in their DNA: an obsessive simulation of a traditional community based on a certain kind of 'vampiric blood' that invokes fantasies of pure bloodlines. Such encounters in cyberspace are not about transformation of identity based on the distance and difference between strangers (Robins, 2007: 234) but about confirmation of identity and of certain vampiric characteristics that people can emulate in order to feed on the illusion of intimacy and belonging. There is an evident preoccupation with narcissistic feelings of grandiose superiority, but also fascination with fictionalised universes such as those of White Wolf's roleplaying game *Vampire: the Masquerade* (1991).

The online vampire communities adopt the Western notion of the vampire as a positive and transformative self-identity. However, as Jan Nederveen Pieterse and other hybridity theorists of globalisation argue, cultures are a melange of influences. For example, US culture's 'acceptance of the vampire', according to Norine Dresser, 'has evolved over time, built upon a foundation of prior beliefs in the supernatural brought here by immigrants from all parts of the world' (1989: 47). It is not only the imported folklore that needs to be accounted for but also Native American beliefs in vampire creatures, such as the Ojibwa legend of the ghostly man-eater (Dresser, 1989: 47). Vampirism may be a melange of different beliefs from around the world, but, nonetheless, the dominant influence on real vampires today comes from European and US vampire representations and should not be underestimated.

The dominant Western model of vampirism, offered by various online real vampire groups, is ordered according to the desires of individual vampires, who generally remain anonymous. These disembodied others can claim and justify any vampiric history they can imagine without any limits. As Kevin Robins notes, 'there are no Others (no other bodies) to impose restrictions and inhibitions on what is imagined or done . . . Virtual empowerment is a solipsistic affair, encouraging a sense of self-containment and self-sufficiency, and involving denial of the need for external objects' (1995: 144). This infantilism and narcissism of disembodied others is a characteristic of some of the virtual vampire groups where the myth of the vampire is exalted and the individual's physical embodiment is discarded as unnecessary. As one self-defined real vampire notes, 'Personal accountability and responsibility is unfortunately sorely lacking with some participants in this community' (Merticus, 6 December 2008, 62). Lady CG, a sanguine vampire and the moderator of the vampire forum *Smoke & Mirrors*, claims that vampiric blood drinking is not only a Western phenomenon but has also been witnessed in the Maasai tribe (Lady CG, 2011). Similarly, Brad, a sanguine vampire, cites the Maasai tribes as a justification for blood drinking in Norine Dresser's *American Vampires* (1989) (21). Such generalisations seem predominantly to erase the difference of civilisations that have their own history and specific local practices. The drinking of blood from living cattle is evident, of course, in the Maasai and Samburu, but only under specific circumstances. It is still practised in contemporary African communities, but generally as part of the ritualistic initiation of boys, or blood is given to women after childbirth to regain their strength and replenish their loss (Askew, 2004: 45). In Samburu raw blood is consumed after an animal is killed, but is mixed with fat and milk (Askew, 2004: 45). Kelly Askew has commented on the way such tribes are depicted by Hollywood, often creating the negative dichotomy between them as 'savages' and us as 'civilised' Westerners (2004: 54). Although the vampire community has interpreted such images in a positive light in order to justify and explain the sanguine thirst for blood, it seems that their knowledge is confined to the stereotypical Western depictions perpetuated by the media, and the 'delimited set of images circulating globally' of the Maasai warriors consuming raw blood (Askew, 2004: 54). While Western vampiric blood drinking is argued to be closer to African blood drinking than to the European fictional vampiric practices, this gesture is reductive, revealing little understanding of African blood rituals and ignoring the wider cultural and historical meanings of these practices.

While virtually everyone can participate in the simulated vampiric communities of cyberia, there are certain limitations. First, one needs to fulfil the requirements set out and disseminated online by the vampire communities. These communities were formed by Americans, who were the first to access and utilise the internet. Consequently, there are material concerns relating to what kind of subjects can access online communities in general. As the sociologist Susan Leigh Star explains, people need money to buy computers, a house with a telecommunications infrastructure for connecting to the internet, access to maintenance people to plug you in, education, time and ability to make and sustain membership (qtd in Bell, 2001: 108–9). In addition, vampire definitions apply to global subjects that experience the conditions of postmodernity: the search for self, disenchantment, alienation and displacement. The Western bourgeois subject, entrenched in the processes of capitalist society, is perhaps the most probable candidate for online communities in general. The global vampire community is then inextricably connected to the workings of global capitalism and the domination of Western culture, where the popularity of vampire symbols and gothic images, of the occult and Eastern spiritualities, are generally the basic ingredients of vampiric identity online or offline. Even if US online vampire communities appeal to global vampires, beyond national borders, English is still used as the primary language for communication.

The fact that specific identities are preferred, such as fetishised versions of vampiric stereotypical hyper-genderings or clichéd vampiric images that tend to erase real-life differences, is another problematic aspect of virtual vampire communities. Although real vampires are sometimes against such conservative imagery, they cannot disengage from the fantastical depictions of cinematic and glamorous vampires. Despite their concern with gothicised imagery, most online images of vampires, from websites such as the US LesVampires.Org and House Crimson Blade, to the British Countess Elizabeth's Vampire Coven, perpetuate the look of gothic: Victorian clothing and white makeup. Western media propagate a global vampire image, and many vampires have expressed their concern about the specific vampire image favoured by media. Real vampires are excluded from documentaries if they do not fall into a certain category of vampire, for example, the predictable global image of Hollywood glamour. While online vampire communities argue that they want to be more believable online and do not tolerate the sexualisation of vampiric imagery, they very often court media attention, flaunting and celebrating their stereotyped exoticism through simulated vampire imagery. They become mere figures in a media show that serves the economic interests of corporate television.

While it can be said that the US vampire community has tried to create a globalised notion of vampire identity that is less fictional and applies to all individuals from around the world, it has in fact facilitated the uniform spread of a Westernised version of the vampire. Apart from international vampire organisations located in the US, there are a growing number of vampire groups from other countries. There are, for example, now British, French, German, Brazilian, Russian, Czech and Armenian vampire forums online, all presenting their own ideology in their own languages. While the British and US online communities are significantly more developed in terms of their large number of members, their division into different houses and organisations, and their circulation of various online articles, new websites from other countries are appearing online and elaborating upon vampire ideas derived from the Anglo-American models. For example, the German online vampire group Vampyrs refers to the vampire as 'shadow', a concept used by Frater Mordor in his book on real vampirism, *Das Buch Noctemeron: Vom Wesen des Vampirismus* (*Noctemeron: On the Nature of Vampirism*, 2003).

Nevertheless, despite the use of different names, the influences from the US online vampire groups are obvious. The use of the Ankh as a symbol of vampiric identity, utilised by Father Sebastiaan's Ordo Strigoi Vii and other vampire houses that belong to his Sanguinarium network of vampire families, has become a clichéd symbol of vampirism used in both the German and the Brazilian sites. The Brazilian resource site *Vampyrismo* offers links to the Círculo Strigoi: Officina Vampyrica. This group, as it notes, follows the US online vampire group House Sahjaza and in general adheres to the Western model of vampirism, especially the ethics set out by Father Sebastiaan and Michelle Belanger in 'The Black Veil v2.0' and his Ordo Strigoi Vii (Círculo Strigoi, 'History'). Círculo Strigoi offers an 'Introduction to Vampirism' which takes the form of a paid subscription for a course of thirteen online or face to face meetings (Círculo Strigoi, 'Introduction to Vampirism'). Apart from being introduced to aspects of vampirism and vampiric practices, the participants are given a letter of confirmation and a silver pendant, the Moonlight Black Ankh. Another Brazilian vampire group, Artemis Mortis Lux, offers affiliation through the purchase of their book *Vampirus Draco Nocturnus: Vampiric Path*. The Russian resource site Vampirizm.ru mainly advertises vampire balls, events and video games, while the Armenian website RealVampires offers an online 'vampshop' which sells vampire T-shirts, bags and gothic jewellery. Although these countries do not offer the same wealth of online vampire communities, their groups reflect the dominant Western approach through shared vampire terminology and the familiar marketing of vampiric goods. The proliferation of global vampire communities resembles a 'digital commoditocracy' (Land, 1995: 200), a cyberspace supermarket where vampire organisations advertise their vampiric products to online consumers shopping for identities at the comfort of their own house. Delocalised, they participate in a 'KAPITAL UTOPIA' (Land, 1995: 201), where ethnicity, local cultures and histories are less important than the exchange of money for esoteric knowledge and prized artefacts.

However, in a public meeting of real vampires held on 6 December 2008 the US vampire community showed awareness of other vampires from around the world and their different cultural contexts. The vampires found that the 'normalization of resources and information-sharing' 'between U.S./Canadian and European/South American/etc. vampires' could be achieved by producing 'multi-lingual translations of documents and culturally diverse forums' (VVC, 2008: 3). It is obvious that US vampires want to make their ideas more accessible by translating them into other languages. However, this can also lead to a sameness that threatens diversity. The Armenian resource site RealVampires now has translations of articles and links to US websites, such as Sphynxcat's page, Sanguinarius.org and Darknessembraced.com. To a certain degree, US groups' interest in spreading their message is a paternalistic gesture that seeks to control vampiric identity without actually taking into consideration the cultures and traditions of geographically different localities. By translating articles that define vampirism in relation to Western folklore and literature, the US vampires encourage Armenian vampires to mimic the fictitious nature of their own pseudo-knowledge, while ignoring Armenia's own mythological creatures, such as the vampire sea-monster *Nhang* that can transform into a woman and drink the blood of its victim (Ananikian, 2010: 93–4). At the same time, however, any discussion that wants to acknowledge the so-called differences of vampire communities from other countries needs also to acknowledge that these non-US online groups have been adopting and imitating the Western concept of vampirism of their own volition. Many of these, like the Armenian RealVampires, appropriate English names or use the alien term *vampire* to define their groups. Vampirism as a predominantly Western phenomenon relies on fictional histories and, consequently, any attempt to form a vampire community in cyberspace or offline will result in the dissemination of endless simulations of the same.

US vampires also presume that the vampire condition is a global phenomenon and that the vampire should be changed according to each country's 'cultural context – mystic religion, scientific research, or some other "hobby"' as most places in the world 'are not free enough to come out of the coffin' (Zero, 2008: 47). Characteristics of contemporary Western subjects, such as religious individualism, search for self and spirituality, are considered to express similarly the needs of all global individuals. For example, the vampire Zero refers to Latin America and Africa where 'gangs, criminals, and warlords have used aggressive supernatural iconography for intimidation and to cover up heinous crimes' (Zero, 2008: 47), which he sees as a hindrance to the global expansion of a vampire community. He completely ignores the ruthless and inhuman conditions, political turbulence and class inequalities evident in these countries, whose subjects have other priorities than online self-fashioning.

While it can be said that there are homogenising tendencies influencing online vampire communities from around the world, there are also heterogenising forces that counteract the idea of Westernisation or Americanisation. The view that globalisation is homogenisation or Westernisation ignores the cultural counter-flows travelling from other countries to the West (Hopper, 2007: 102), and is, according to Pieterse, 'empirically narrow and historically flat' (Pieterse, 2009: 87). For Pieterse globalisation should be viewed 'as a process of hybridization that gives rise to a global mélange' (2009: 65). Hybridisation and what Negri and Hardt refer to as nomadism and miscegenation are 'figures of virtue' and 'the first ethical practices on the terrain of Empire' (Hardt and Negri, 2000: 362). As Hardt and Negri argue, 'celebrations of the local can be regressive and even fascistic when they oppose circulations and mixture, and thus reinforce the walls of nation, ethnicity, race, people, and the like' (362). It is then, through circulation and mixing and not local isolation and purity, that 'the human community is constituted', 'a multicolored Orpheus of infinite power' (362).

The use of the Egyptian ankh by members of the global vampire community is exemplary of the travelling symbols and myths from other cultures that have been adopted by contemporary vampires. The use of the ankh, in its many guises and shapes, by various vampire houses, 'symbolizes the House and its ideals' (Belanger, 2003). In *The Vampire Ritual Book* (2003) Michelle Belanger explains that the rituals of the vampire community, which function as bonds within the community, are mainly 'syncretic, integrating elements from a variety of other systems and adding concepts relevant to vampires' (Belanger, 2003: n.p.). Vampires can find inspiration in pagan and Wiccan rituals she writes, but also 'will feel free to draw material from the rituals of ancient Egypt, from Hinduism, Persian traditions, Japanese Shinto, shamanism, and even LaVeyan Satanism' (Belanger, 2003: n.p.) in order to create their own vampire rituals. Religious practice becomes a global melange with the vampire self at the centre, a diluted concoction served according to the appetites of the vampire cosmopolitan.

Many online vampire communities cultivate and utilise the Eastern concepts of subtle energies, the Indian *prana*, Chinese *chi* or Japanese *ki* (lifeforce or universal energy) to refer to the energy flows in the blood or within the body. For example, while in Chinese thinking *chi* is an abstract term that refers to the vital energy within all living things, it has been colonised by the vampires in order to express their own specific ideas. According to Partridge, Western societies turn to ancient and Eastern cultures for their spiritual guidance, and cyberspirituality is an ordinary experience now, 'attractive to those seeking some form of detraditionalized alternative spirituality' (Partridge, 2005: 148). Indeed Eastern spirituality is an everyday phenomenon because it is nurtured by a growing market economy for all things Eastern. Partridge mistakes this turn for an innocent search for alternative spirituality and guidance and fails to recognise that this is a trend toward the inner self that facilitates the global system of capitalist accumulation, conditioning a subject, no longer concerned with political action or resistance, but increasingly withdrawing from the world. For Žižek the New Age 'Asiatic' thought has become the 'hegemonic ideology of global capitalism' (2001: 12) for exactly this reason: 'it enables you to fully participate in the frantic pace of the capitalist game while sustaining the perception that you are not really in it . . . what really matters to you is the peace of the inner Self' (2001: 15).

For Partridge such alternative spiritualities are characterised by their turn to the East for their self-spirituality and West for their demonology. The vampire, for example is celebrated as 'both demonic and iconic' in contemporary culture (2005: 208). The reason for choosing the demonic from Christian demonology for the construction of the dark side is simply its 'familiarity and accessibility', especially its predominance in popular culture (Partridge, 2005: 278). While there are demonologies in the East, these 'are complex, not well known, and are not prominent' in western occult systems (278). Although this seems an interesting turn, given that the vampire in literature always originates and travels from the East, it also reveals the problematic nature of his argument. Partridge overlooks the fact that the vampire is more attractive to Western subjects than Eastern demonologies are. While individuals do use complex concepts from Eastern spiritualities, they prefer to identify with vampires rather than with 'primitive' or unfashionable Eastern demons. The hybrid experience is then a controlled encounter with the East that helps only to shape an individual's self-image.

Despite the fact that the blending of the East and West evident in the practices of the vampire community can be considered as a positive hybrid experience, such an experience remains superficial, a fleeting encounter that follows the dictates of a western consumerist logic and embraces the new and exotic as a fashionable accessory to the bourgeois lifestyle. For Hopper, despite Western people's hybrid experiences, it is still their national or Western culture that exerts more influence upon them. For many in the West 'it is arguably their individual freedom that they especially value, as it is this that provides them with the opportunity to "mix-and-match", culturally speaking' (Hopper, 2007: 129). While Pieterse believes hybridisation to be a common experience and not 'a plaything of bourgeois or bohemian elites' (2009: 120), it is also necessary to consider what Zygmunt Bauman refers to as 'a global hierarchy of mobility' (1998: 69). The online vampire community, like any other cyber-community, predominantly consists of global mobile elites, whereas the poor are struggling to partake in globalising practices (Hopper, 2007: 189). Real vampires are not born, as they claim, with the vampiric condition. Rather, they are nurtured within a capitalist network of vampire products and are children of a society that has schooled them to enjoy their difference, individualism and spirituality, all products sold to them every day in real life and the fleeting paradises of cyberia.

Note

1 Sebastiaan Van Houten, or Father Sebastiaan Todd, is the founder of the vampire network of houses, organisations and clubs The Sanguinarium and the left-hand path vampire group Ordo Strigoi Vii. From 2002 The Sanguinarium has no longer been in existence but its concepts, rituals and network of houses are still in operation. In addition Father Sebastiaan's Ordo Strigoi Vii practises and disseminates those ideas.

References

Ananikian, Mardiros H. 2010. *Armenian Mythology: Stories of Armenian Gods and Goddesses, Heroes and Heroines, Hells and Heavens, Folklore and Fairy Tales*. Los Angeles: Indo-European Publishing.

Appadurai, Arjun. 1996. *Modernity at Large: Cultural Dimensions of Globalization*. Minneapolis: University of Minnesota Press.

Askew, Kelly M. 2004. 'Striking Samburu and a mad cow: Adventures in Anthropollywood'. In *Off Stage/On Display: Intimacy and Ethnography in the Age of Public Culture*, ed. Andrew Shryock. Stanford: Stanford University Press, 31–68.

Bakardjieva, Maria. 2007. 'Virtual togetherness: An everyday-life perspective'. In *The Cybercultures Reader*, eds David Bell and Barbara M. Kennedy. London: Routledge, 236–53.

Bauman, Zygmunt. 1998. *Globalization: The Human Consequences*. Cambridge: Polity.
Bell, David. 2001. *An Introduction to Cybercultures*. London: Routledge.
Dresser, Norine. 1989. *American Vampires: Fans, Victims, and Practitioners*. London: Norton.
Foster, Hal. 1996. *The Return of the Real: The Avant-Garde at the End of the Century*. Cambridge, MA: MIT Press.
Frater Mordor. 2003. *Das Buch Noctemeron. Vom Wesen des Vampirisonus*. Lübeck: Bohmeier Verlag.
Hardt, Michael, and Antonio Negri. 2000. *Empire*. Cambridge, MA: Harvard University Press.
Hopper, Paul. 2007. *Understanding Cultural Globalization*. Cambridge: Polity.
Land, Nick. 1995. 'Meat (or how to kill Oedipus in cyberspace)'. In *Cyberspace, Cyber Bodies, Cyberpunk*, eds Mike Featherstone and Roger Burrows. London: Sage, 191–204.
Laycock, Joseph. 2009. *Vampires Today: The Truth about Modern Vampirism*. Santa Barbara, CA: Praeger.
Partridge, Christopher. 2005. *The Re-enchantment of the West*. Vol. II. New York: T. & T. Clark.
Pieterse, Jan Nederveen. 2009. *Globalization and Culture: Global Mélange*. Lanham, MD: Rowman and Littlefield.
Robins, Kevin. 1995. 'Cyberspace and the world we live in'. In *Cyberspace, Cyber Bodies, Cyberpunk*, eds Mike Featherstone and Roger Burrows. London: Sage, 135–55.
——. 2007. 'Against virtual community: For a politics of distance'. In *The Cybercultures Reader*, eds David Bell and Barbara M. Kennedy. London: Routledge, 227–35.
Russo, Arlene. 2005. *Vampire Nation*. London: John Blake.
Sebastiaan, Father. 2010. *Vampyre Sanguinomicon: The Lexicon of the Living Vampire*. San Francisco: Red Wheel.
Sorkin, Michael. 1992. 'See you in Disneyland'. In *Variations on a Theme Park*, ed. Michael Sorkin. New York: Hill and Wang, 205–32.
Todd, May. 2001. *Our Practices, Ourselves, Or, What It Means to Be Human*. University Park, PA: Pennsylvania State University Press.
Willson, Michelle. 2007. 'Community in the abstract: A political and ethical dilemma?'. In *The Cybercultures Reader*, eds David Bell and Barbara M. Kennedy. London: Routledge, 213–26.
Žižek, Slavoj. 2001. *On Belief: Thinking in Action*. London: Routledge.

Internet sources

Belanger, Michelle. 2003. *The Vampire Ritual Book*. www.sacred-texts.com/goth/vrb/index.htm. Accessed 24 April 2011.
Círculo Strigoi. 'History'. *Vampyrismo.org*. www.vampyrismo.org/officinavampyrica/historia.html. Accessed 12 May 2011.
——. 'Introduction to Vampirism'. *Vampyrismo.org*. www.vampyrismo.org/officina-vampyrica/historia.html. Accessed 12 May 2011.
Lady CG. 2011. 'Re: A sanguinarian treatise: An argument for partition from the vampire community by CJ'. 23 February. *Smoke & Mirrors Forum*. http://

smokeandmirrors34981 . yuku . com / topic / 26500 / Sanguinarian-Treatise--Argu ment--Partition---Vampire-Commun?page=3. Accessed 24 April 2011.

Merticus. 2008. 'Public meeting', 6 December. Voices of the Vampire Community (VVC). www.veritasvosliberabit.com/images/VVCPublicMeeting12.06.08.pdf. Accessed 24 April 2011.

Valens. 2009. 'Global vampire community discussion (Public)'. 10 July. Voices of the Vampire Community (VVC). www.veritasvosliberabit.com/images/VVCGlobalVampireCommunityDiscussion07.10.09.pdf. Accessed 24 April 2011.

Voices of the Vampire Community (VVC). 2008. 'Public meeting', 6 December. www.veritasvos liberabit.com/images/VVCPublicMeeting12.06.08.pdf. Accessed 24 April 2011.

Zero. 2008. 'Public meeting', 6 December. www.veritasvosliberabit.com/images/VVCPublicMeeting12.06.08.pdf. Accessed 24 April 2011.

7

Isabella van Elferen

Globalgoth? Unlocatedness in the musical home

Globalisation has given rise to two new gothic modes. Globalised gothic, on the one hand, can be defined as the circulation of gothic themes and styles in worldwide locations, through a range of media, and embedded in the capitalist structures of market and consumption. Globalgothic, on the other hand, offers a gothic critique of globalisation, exposing the anxieties and excesses that sift through the carefully laid out safety nets of international culture. The Goth scene would seem to represent both gothic modes. Firstly, the scene, its style and its music are globally spread, and Goths from all over the world connect with one another via websites and social media. Secondly, as Goth self-fashions itself as the dark side of global consumer culture, it subverts the globalised commerce and media it employs. Music is a crucial factor in the local and global identification strategies operative in the scene; moreover, Goth music presents a spatio-temporal unlocatedness and subjective disrootedness that challenge dichotomies such as local/global and underground/mainstream. Yet Goth is a predominantly Western affair, and it is thoroughly imbued in commercial and medial structures; Goth music, subversive as it may be, depends on these structures for its dissemination. How globalised is Goth, to what extent can it criticise globalisation and what role does music play in these processes?

Goth unlocation

Large internet communities like *VampireFreaks* illustrate that Goth has become an international scene with participants in a variety of countries from North America to Australia and Europe. As well as enabling Goths to connect with one another, these internet communities are an important means of (self)education, providing lists of recommended literature, films and bands, philosophical and social debates and participants' poetry, stories and videos. Goth has become a prime example of what Pierre Lévy (1999) has called 'collective intelligence', the shared knowledge emerging in networked groups of individuals. Some communities are exclusively dedicated to single aspects of Gothdom, such as gothic history, absinthe or dark art.

The broad internet presence and usage of Goth seems indicative of the scene's globalisation. But the internet is not as global as it would seem: rather than engendering the 'global village' that Marshall McLuhan envisioned in 1964, online communication has also strengthened existing local ties, and the personalisation of already existing communities into networks (Wellmann, 2004: 29). Online Goth communities often similarly reinforce location-based communities. In spite of the existence of seemingly international websites such as *VampireFreaks*, the demographic of these sites still shows a strong dominance of the country of origin (in the case of *VampireFreaks*, the US). Like other web communities, online Goth communities often function not only as an intensification of personal interest but also as an extension of offline social ties. There are Goth communities focused on North America or on Western European countries, from the *American Goth* to *Blackweb België*; moreover, there is a plethora of even more localised communities aimed at specific regions or towns, from *The Neitherland*'s guide to Philadelphia Goth to *Gothic City*, the 'black site' of Dresden. A special place within these location-oriented Goth communities is taken by Goth dating sites, which need to be somewhat geographically limited for practical reasons.

In its offline manifestation the scene operates on remarkably local scales. Goth club nights mostly attract local visitors and show notable regional differences. Within the small area of the Netherlands alone, for instance, two highly distinctive Goth sub-subcultures with their own preferred venues occur: Utrecht, with the Cyberia parties in club Tivoli, is a centre of Cybergoth, while Amsterdam, with the Medusa and Gothique Classique parties, is home to neoromantic Goths. Festivals such as the Wave Gotik Treffen in Leipzig (Germany), M'era Luna in Hildesheim (Germany) and Whitby gothic Weekend (UK) are internationally orientated and attract visitors from a number of countries. The demographics show, however, that these international festival visitors all come from a restricted part of the world: the nationality of festival visitors is limited to a small number of Western European countries, most notably England, Germany, Italy, France, Benelux and Scandinavian countries. Within these geographical confinements, the scene is ethnically confined also: the overwhelming majority of scene members are Caucasian.

This Eurocentrism can partly be explained by the scene's own origins in late 1970s England. Moreover, the gothic genre at large, from which the scene derives its name and style, is also commonly understood as British in origin. The scene flaunts its historical heritage in musical lyrics, in the screening of gothic films at club nights and festivals and in fashion. Goth clothing is often geared towards the embodiment of gothic ghosts: outfits may reference vampire stories, Byronic gentlemen, Victorian ladies or Wildean dandies. The alleged British origins of Goth lead one of Paul Hodkinson's respondents to claim that all 'foreign Goth is shit. It was invented in Northampton in 1979 by Bauhaus and no one else knows how to do it apart from us lot' (Hodkinson, 2002: 69). The statement raises interesting questions. Bauhaus named themselves after a German school of architecture; their most famous hero, Bela Lugosi, was a Hungarian actor working for one of Goth's arch-enemies, the Hollywood mainstream. So how British *were* Bauhaus? The Britishness of Goth, in fact, is as much a product of selective retrospection as that of gothic itself: since the gothic novel was heavily influenced and inspired by German and French literature and culture, the roots of the genre have been argued by such critics as Terry Hale (2002) to lie in those countries as much as in England. Goth has thus made its own origin the subject of that nostalgic backward glance which characterises gothic storytelling: swept in veils and surrounded by mystery, it signifies the fantasy of an origin rather than an objective fact (if such a thing exists).

A second geographical fantasy pervading the scene is that of the alleged Gothness of all things German. Germanic orientation has been a firm Goth signifier pervading the scene since its inception. Bauhaus's German band name was mentioned above; the immensely popular first vampire film, Murnau's *Nosferatu eine Symphonie des Grauens* (1922) was made in Germany; scene icons like Nina Hagen and Velvet Underground's Nico were German; others, like David Bowie and Nick Cave, lived in Berlin; Siouxsie Sioux and others insert German lines in their lyrics. Germany, moreover, has become a locus of Goth culture and festivals that is at least as important as England, and many of the scene's most popular artists are German. The *Neue Deutsche Todeskunst* in the 1990s included German Goth bands ranging in style from heavily neoromantic (Lacrimosa) to darkwave (Deine Lakaien), industrial (Das Ich), medieval (In Extremo) to EBM (:wumpscut:). These styles shared a preference for the German language and themes pertaining to darkness and melancholy, death and pain, religious and sexual deviation. The reasons for this Goth appropriation of German culture may be a combination of the country's cultural heritage, its relation to the gothic genre and Germany's military history. Bands like Feindflug exploit this latter aspect: the performances of this percussion-only, aggrotech band are laden with Nazi symbolism and samples from fascist speeches. Without mentioning the war, bands like this – Rammstein follows similar strategies – create the effect of an absent presence, the return of a globally recognised repressed. In this sense Goth's German fantasy is a more poignant example of globalgothic than its mythologised Britishness.

In its negotiations of local connectedness and global boundlessness, Goth lacks and evades the geographical spread implied in globalisation. Goth operates outside the global/local dichotomy, and therefore qualifications like glocal or translocal do not convincingly apply. While these concepts reflect the conflation of the global and the local in one cultural phenomenon, I would argue that Goth itself negates the possibility of geographical location: it is *unlocated*. This is nothing more and nothing less than an effect of the gothic nostalgia for and transgression of a home, an origin that the genre rewrites and clothes in mystery. Goth, like gothic, expresses the unfamiliar familiarity of the home, and this can lead to any identification pattern based on un/locatedness: the teenager not belonging in her local school community, the 'dislocated national subject',[1] affective kinships with fantasised British or German cultures. Like gothic, Goth does not reside here, but there: and 'there' must simultaneously be as mythologised and as spectral as possible. The unlocation performed by Goth thus often takes the curious disguise of fantasised parochialism. The fantasy location of Goth, moreover, is removed not only in space but also in time: the gothic glance is a nostalgic one. The Goth idealisation of London is aimed specifically at the late 1970s, and is paired with similar nostalgic fantasies regarding Victorian dandyism and medieval Celtic cultures. Goth does not dwell in now but in back then; and, just like its place, its time must be hazy too. It is from those hazily nostalgic unlocations that globalgoth is at times able to address the uncanny presences in globalisation such as the ghost of fascism. That Goth does not always venture the step from practical globalisation to global cultural critique is illustrated by its self-entrapment in Britishness; similar tensions between globalised Goth and globalgoth occur in the subculture's negotiation of commerce and media.

Unlocated self-fashioning

The historically developed style and themes of gothic function as Goth subcultural capital, an immaterial currency of knowledge and attitude that identifies subcultural belonging (Thornton, 1995: 98–104). This subcultural capital is key to the scene's geographical and historical unlocation: it is in gothic books and films that Goths find the nostalgia for the long-gone times and places through which they self-identify. The same capital determines the fashion style of the scene, which is aimed at the embodiment of gothic fantasies. Valerie Steele has noted that 'gothic fashion, like the gothic novel, tends to be obsessed with the past, often a theatrical, highly artificial version of the past that contrasts dramatically with the perceived banality of contemporary life' (2008: 104–5). In this practice of nostalgic self-fashioning, outward appearance has an interesting relation to the evasion of place and time that characterises the subculture. The detailed outfits in Goth milieu – including clothes, makeup, jewellery, hair extensions, handbags, gloves, hats and fans – are put on to a self and displayed in the observing gaze of an other. While the Goth style itself is very noticeable and recognisable, however, the observing other is not to identify too readily who is beneath the makeup. Goth gear is at once a means of self-expression and a mask: it is not for nothing that masked balls are popular in the scene. Goth self-fashioning is a subjective reflection of the subculture's unlocatedness: their wearer hidden in the veils of romanticised melancholy, the Victorian corsets, Celtic jewellery and androgynous cross-dressing reveal nothing except gothic fantasies of 'then and there'.

Goth fashion is but one part of the representation of a world of subcultural capital, and is not regarded as being possible without the other. For these reasons Catherine Spooner notes that within gothic discourse 'the clothes are the life: Gothic chic is not a full surface with a Gothic psyche, but an intrinsic part of it' (2004: 197). Goth self-fashioning happens on the inside as well as on the outside: being Goth requires a close alignment of looks, attitude and knowledge. Goth subcultural capital is to be flaunted, which leads to a dismissive attitude towards those who do not know their gothic history. Goths do not just read about melancholy, they live and aestheticise it. On this principle 'fake' Goths are mercilessly unmasked. The following comments on the Australian Goth Forum are telling of the snobbish attitudes regarding 'fake' Goths: 'no one (outside of our limited-at-best circles) seems to be aware of the difference between "true Goth" and "oh I'm so trendy because i wear emily the strange". black clothes do not a Goth make' (gothic.org.au Forum).

Another exponent of the entanglement of style and subjectivity in Goth is the fierce rebuking of Marilyn Manson. Manson's self-presentation as shock rocker has gained him the reputation of an attention seeker, separating him far from the introversion and melancholy through which Goth identifies. His omnipresence in mainstream media is interpreted as bending for mass entertainment, which opposes the underground authenticity that Goth seeks. Some of Hodkinson's interviewees even complained that the superficiality of 'baby Goths' is 'Marilyn Manson's fault'; being Goth, they emphasise, requires more than just 'a little bit of eyeliner' (Hodkinson, 2002: 79).

Scene participants who, conversely, overvalue the importance of gothic inheritance are not much appreciated either. Those who overstate their Gothness by too much flaunting of gothic heritage are considered to suffer from the 'Gother than thou syndrome' (Hodkinson, 2002: 80–2). Goth is characterised by a paradoxical 'ironic authenticity': Goth authenticity lies in the careful balance between the display of subcultural capital and self-irony. This ironic authenticity is the theme of the popular comic book *Oh my Goth!* Following the adventures of Goth alien Hieronymous Poshe, who flies around in a cathedral-shaped spaceship, the reader encounters the emblems of Goth capital: Nosferatu, the Batcave, Bram Stoker, Lord Byron, clove cigarettes and fake English accents. The story is interspersed with interludes such as 'Mommy, am I a Goth? (A simple checklist for those who aren't sure)':

> 2) If you go to great lengths to look like a vampire from the 18th-century . . .
> . . . you are probably a Goth.
> If you actually believe that you are a vampire from the 18th-century . . .
> . . . you are not a Goth! (you're psychotic!) (Voltaire, 2003: n.p.)

Another, more complex, counterpoint to the 'Gother than thou syndrome' is the denial of subcultural belonging. Goth icons such as The

Sisters of Mercy, Siouxsie Sioux and Bauhaus all claimed they had nothing to do with Goth. Within the subculture itself the situation is no different: any self-respecting scene participant will firmly deny being Goth. Such declarations of not belonging to a group, of course, reflect the speaker's own feelings of individuality rather than the question of whether or not they are representative of the cultural phenomenon that is Goth. Agnes Jasper argues that these denials are part of a subcultural tactic that 'wards off classificatory strategies of dominant, non-subcultural culture' which ensures that mainstream culture remains unable to pigeonhole or imitate the hidden secrets of underground authenticity (2004: 90). Through the denial of group belonging, one's own as well as Goth's 'true' identity remains clad in mystery, and both are safely protected against what are perceived as the malevolent forces of mass, media and money.

Like other underground scenes, Goth is haunted by these three 'm's constituting the unspeakable nemesis: the mainstream. But the scene's practical relation to these forces is rather more ambivalent than the ideological rejections of Manson or baby Goths suggest. Goth has relied on its own media and economies since its early distribution of (self-made) fanzines and trade of (vintage) clothing.[2] The rise of the internet facilitates a huge online economy of subcultural goods, and has thereby expanded the existing economic and medial structures within the scene. The vast majority of Goth clothing is bought online, either through specialised webshops or on second-hand websites (Hodkinson, 2002: chapter 7). Goth music, too, is often purchased or downloaded from the internet, and discussions about music take up a significant portion of online communication among Goths. Both for clothing and for music, Goths are relatively dependent on internet economies. Because Goth clothing shops are rare, most scene members cannot simply go out shopping for gear. As the number of record stores worldwide has dramatically decreased since the advent of download culture, it is hard to find Goth music in physical shops also; as a consequence both lines of trade flourish on the internet.

While the scene is thus thoroughly imbued in mediated communication and economic exchange, it also still claims to be 'underground', and therefore could claim to subvert globalisation. But this claim to globalgoth critique is not always justified. As in the case of Goth's global/local spread, there is no unambivalent distinction between 'mainstream' and 'underground' media and markets on the internet. The grassroots media, alternative clothing sellers and independent record labels that Goths are dedicated to can be found in corners of the internet, and, however specialised and hidden these corners may be, anyone inside or outside the scene has access to them. Goth clothes, shoes and accessories are surprisingly expensive, and the fact that Goth is such an expensive hobby resolves all doubt with regards to the scene's relation to commerce and money. Similarly, the DIY ideology of Goth has evolved from underground to commonplace in the participatory age of Wikipedia and MySpace (Schaefer, 2011). Online communities such as Darkstarlings.com, which advertises itself with the tagline 'the Anti-Social Network', confirm rather than subvert awareness that Goth is a thoroughly mediatised subculture – albeit one that wishes to remain 'underground'.

Stylised but invisible, capitalist but underground, mediated but antisocial: Goth self-fashioning is obsessed with the evasion of globalised commercialism and mediatisation, even if that evasion requires the half-lies of 'niche' online communities and webshops. With its location, time and subjectivity difficult to pinpoint, Goth aspires to critique the forces of globalisation from behind a number of elaborate veils. The subculture's entanglement in locality, trade and media shows that this globalgoth critique is not always convincing; the ephemeral sound of Goth music may mark the closest that the scene can come to the shadow sides of globalisation.

Goth's unlocated musical home

Music is one of the most important components of Goth subculture. Goth music expresses the melancholic not-belonging, the nostalgic glance and the evasive subjectivity that characterises the subcultural capital. While Goth lyrics speak of loneliness and faraway realms, the music accompanying them offers subtle glimpses of other times and places. Music's ephemeral phenomenology, however, ensures that these fantasy realms will never fully be reached: as deeply as any listener can be engrossed in the realities that music suggests, they evaporate with the dying sound of the closing chord. Musical experience is perhaps the most powerful form of immersion, tying itself irresistibly and irreparably to the listener's heart and thereby moulding individual or collective identities, but in addition musical experience is also profoundly and fundamentally nostalgic. Music is always-already on its way to its own demise: every experience it engenders is temporary, and listening always signifies the birth of nostalgia. It is for these reasons that music is able to accompany Goth discourses of unlocation, nostalgia and evasion: musical experience itself negates location and temporal situatedness; its meanings are subjective and changeable rather than objective and fixed, and its flow is as inescapable as inherently finite (Nancy, 2007: 13–19, 67–8). Because of its inevitable immersive forces, Goth music can take listeners along on its journeys across spaces and times, moulding their subjectivity by every passing chord.

The disrooting of local boundedness is expressed in Sol Invictus's 'English Garden' (*In the Rain*, 1995). The lyrics sketch a Victorian country home whose idyllic atmosphere is turned bit by bit into one of literal *unheimlichkeit* through insistent and unanswered questions:

(verse)
Why was the governess sent away?
Why won't any of the servants stay?
Is that thunder overhead?
And who's that standing by my bed?

(chorus)
An English garden in the rain
Something hidden, something strange
Don't go walking in the woods
Yes Father dear, you're understood.

(25–32)

The gradual destabilisation of the home is musically underlined through the deceptive simplicity of Sol Invictus's 'folk noir'. The song opens with a gentle acoustic guitar joined by a harpsichord. The harpsichord's timbre evokes mixed connotations, wavering between cultured concert evenings for the middle classes and the dark inversion of that culturedness found in such horror films as *The Hunger* (Scott, 1983) and *Interview with the Vampire* (Jordan, 1994). The ambivalence of these connotations is intensified by the compositional technique in this opening section: both instruments create a 'lamento bass', a repeated descending bass line often used in classical funerary music. Sol Invictus's lamento bass descends in minor from tonic E to dominant B. Throughout the verses this pattern is repeated, thus emphasising the harmonic 'tension chord', the dominant, more than the 'home' chord, the tonic; this musical destabilisation is increased through the consistent use of inverted (six-four) chords. Only in the choruses is the musical home confirmed through repeated cadences, low celli and on-beat percussion; but this affirmation seems unsure, as the stumbling grace notes in the high strings (C–B and A–B) keep suggesting we *only just* made it to the cadence. Meanwhile the harpsichord has made way for an even more eerie timbre, that of the organ.[3] It is clear that 'something hidden, something strange' pervades the familiar. The idealised British home of Goth is thus musically disclosed as the locus of nothing less than the uncanny itself.

Various Goth musical subgenres thematise the gothic dislodging of time. Medieval Goth expresses nostalgia for the medieval and pagan past, a past hidden deep in history and veiled by such mysterious cloaks as obscure languages and pagan rituals. This romantic nostalgia for the irrational, dark Middle Ages is historically analogous to that shaping the gothic novel. Like gothic medievalism, the medieval fantasy of Goth is as much a nostalgic perversion as Goth Britishness or Germanness; of course, the fact that medieval Goth is mostly a German subgenre only confirms the latter fantasy. Not shy of crass anachronisms, Goth medievalism juxtaposes medieval and self-concocted Latin texts, medieval (bagpipes, tin whistle, fiddle), classical (harpsichord, organ), folk (guitar, harp) and electronic instruments. Medieval bands often have classically trained singers, mostly sopranos; they are sometimes nicknamed 'the heavenly voices', stressing the escapist component of the genre. These serene classical voices are contrasted by heavy male grunts that draw the listener back into the metal age of the present. Electro-medieval bands such as Helium Vola and Qntal render audible the gothic nostalgic glance from the 'here and now' into the 'then and there' by assigning a significant role to music technology throughout their work. Invoking a musical dialogue between the Middle Ages and the present through the conflation, for instance, of trance beats with medieval troubadour songs, these bands invite their medieval nostalgia to invade the realities it mirrors. While Goth web communities seem to confirm the scene's appropriation of technological globalisation, electro-medieval Goth music thus conversely emphasises that technology can create a space and time rather *outside* globalisation and media: technology's function here is that of a sonic time machine reinforcing Goth unlocatedness through music.

As in the subculture's online and offline negotiations of location and temporal situatedness, the musical distortions of space and time in Goth reflect the scene's veiled subjectivity. This convergence of gothic strategies characterises the German act Sopor Æternus and the Ensemble of Shadows, a project of 'intersexual' singer Anna-Varney Cantodea. Cantodea embodies Goth shrouded subjectivity: born male, she rejects fixed gender and regards herself as simultaneously both and neither male and/nor female: album covers portray her naked without genitals or breasts. Moreover, she explicitly presents herself as a gothic author. The band name means 'eternal sleep', and Cantodea's pseudonym refers to Rymer's vampire penny dreadful and a Latin composite that can be translated as 'I sing the goddess'. She is reluctant to give interviews and 'refuses to perform her magic(k)al work live in front of a human audience'; instead she lets her unusual music videos speak a ghostly message of haunting and transgression, which are 'intended as a spiritual healing-process for the wounded soul' ('About Sopor Æternus and the Ensemble of Shadows'). If Marilyn Manson is regarded as fake Goth, then Cantodea's self-fashioning verges on the Gother than thou syndrome.

Musically Sopor Æternus blends medieval, baroque, folk, dark wave and cabaret styles in her expression of themes ranging from gothic isolation to necrophilia, (self-) mutilation and transcendent rituals. 'Time stands still . . . (but stops for no-one)' appears on her debut album: '. . . *Ich töte mich jedesmal aufs Neue, doch ich bin unsterblich, und ich erstehe wieder auf; in einer Vision des Untergangs . . .*' (1994).[4] The track starts with an unusually long opening section. For nearly three minutes all that is heard is syncopated percussion and, consecutively, low strings, acoustic guitar, synthesiser and high strings stating the harmonic basis of the song. Later on an alto recorder reinforces the ostinato in the manner of Jacob van Eyck's medieval virtuosic variations. Like Sol Invictus's 'English Garden' – and quite a large number of other Goth songs – this composition is harmonically organised by a lamento bass, in this case descending from E to B. On and on it goes, down and down, making the listener wonder whether this endless descent represents the only home that Goth has. When the lyrics finally come in they stress merely the irrelevance of chronology: 'Time is fleeting, time stands still / It stops for no one and we're trapped within' (33–4). With the help of multiple tracking, the vocal part of the song is shaped as an auto-duet, Cantodea's dialogue with her veiled, hidden self: her voice itself a veil between male and female timbres, the low overtones filtered out by a raised larynx. Trapped for nine minutes in seemingly never-ending musical and lyrical time, all that remains is the question of when, where and how the self can exist.

A possible answer appears in 'The dreadful mirror' from 2003 album *Es Reiten Die Toten So Schnell . . . (or: the Vampyre sucking at his own Vein)*,[5] an album whose special edition included communion wafers and graveyard soil: 'At times it seems that I'm existing only / Within some fading memory / But dreams are all sacred, dreams are all holy / And by far still the safest place for my poor soul to be' (5–8). The self, according to Cantodea, exists only within memory, the trustworthy mirror of the mind. The uncanniness pervading Sol Invictus's English home here turns even further inward, ruling the mind also. Its dreadful mirror twists and disfigures, like a distorting mirror at some dark fairground, and the musical setting of these words is clearly meant to trigger that connotation. Amidst a rolling triple metre and up-tempo percussion, the F minor key presents itself in repeated descending synthesiser chords. Its minor gloom is underlined not only by the lyrics but also by the timbres of a harpsichord and the occasional church bell. Echoing samples of high female voices in wordless glissandos resonate high up in the soundscape of this eerie carnival; a sampled choir speaksings in the background of Cantodea's words, voicing, it seems, the living corpses mentioned in the lyrics. Within these parameters the painfully florid motifs of the xylophone moving up and down through the musical texture only reinforce the grind of the song's ghostly triple metre. The song is composed like a horror soundtrack, with its warped funfair idiom, its disembodied voices and its doom-laden lyrics. The most discomforting aspect of this soundtrack is that it inevitably drags the listener through the distorted mirror sketched in the lyrics: in recognition of the image it casts, the Goth self can only 'danc[e] in circles with the dear living dead' (10).

In Goth music endless repetitions leave the downward fall of the funerary bass or the circular sweep of the musical mirror the sole indicators of place, time and self. Goth music activates a gothic undoing of location, time and subjectivity, moving listeners beyond such mundane planes as globalisation, commerce or media. Wherever it is listened to – at home, in a local Goth venue, through globalised internet radio or on a glocal mobile device – it dislodges time, space and self. This music offers Goths a musical counter-site to the globalised mainstream it despises so much, even if they have discovered the music through MySpace, 'liked' it on Facebook and downloaded it through iTunes. The globalised logistics of Goth musical culture do not necessarily interfere with its globalgoth strategy of unlocation, as the two operate on wholly different planes. Sol Invictus and especially Sopor Æternus could not have existed without the internet; but musical inversion can turn globalised media into sites of gothic unlocation, and invites listeners on a nostalgic journey to nowhere led by unfamiliar voices. Globalgoth's only home, thus, appears through a musical glass darkly.

Notes

1 Ken Gelder's assessment of Australian Goth (2007).
2 See Hodkinson, 2002, chapters 6 and 8; Spooner, 2004, chapter 4.
3 On the organ timbre see Julie Brown, 2010.
4 Usually translated as '. . . I kill myself every time anew, but I am immortal, and I rise again; in a vision of doom . . .'.
5 Usually translated as 'The dead ride so fast'.

References

Brown, Julie. 2010. 'Carnival of souls and the organs of horror'. In *Music in the Horror Film: Listening to Fear*, ed. Neil Lerner. London: Routledge, 1–20.

Gelder, Ken. 2007. 'The (un)Australian Goth: notes towards a dislocated national subject'. In *Goth: Undead Subculture*, eds Lauren M. E. Goodlad and Michael Bibby. Durham, NC: Duke University Press, 217–30.

Hale, Terry. 2002. 'French and German gothic: The beginnings'. In *The Cambridge Companion to Gothic Fiction*, ed. Jerrold E. Hogle. Cambridge: Cambridge University Press, 63–84.

Hodkinson, Paul. 2002. *Goth: Identity, Style and Subculture*. London: Berg.

——. 2007. '"We are all individuals, but we've all got the same boots on!" Traces of individualism within a subcultural community'. In *Goth: Undead Subculture*, eds Lauren M. E. Goodlad and Michael Bibby. Durham, NC: Duke University Press, 322–31.

Jasper, Agnes. 2004. '"I am not a Goth!" The unspoken morale of authenticity within the Dutch gothic subculture'. *Etnofoor*, 17.1/2: 90–115.

Lévy. Pierre. 1999. *Collective Intelligence: Mankind's Emerging World in Cyberspace*, trans. Robert Bononno. Cambridge, MA: Perseus.

McLuhan, Marshall. 1964. *Understanding Media: The Extensions of Man*. New York: McGraw Hill.

Nancy, Jean-Luc. 2007. *Listening*. New York: Fordham University Press.

Schaefer, Mirko Tobias. 2011. *Bastard Culture! How User Participation Transforms Cultural Production*. Amsterdam: Amsterdam University Press.

Sol Invictus. 1995. 'English Garden'. *In the Rain*. CD. London: Tursa.

Sopor Æternus. 1994. 'Time stands still . . . (but stops for no-one)' . . . *Ich töte mich jedesmal aufs Neue, doch ich bin unsterblich, und ich erstehe wieder auf; in einer Vision des Untergangs* . . . CD. Dieburg: Trisol – Apocalyptic Vision.

——. 2003. 'The dreadful mirror'. *Es Reiten Die Toten So Schnell . . . (or: the Vampyre sucking at his own Vein*. CD. Dieburg: Trisol – Apocalyptic Vision.

Spooner, Catherine. 2004. *Fashioning Gothic Bodies*. Manchester: Manchester University Press.

Steele, Valerie. 2008. *Gothic: Dark Glamour*. New Haven: Yale University Press.

Thornton, Sarah. 1995. *Club Cultures: Music Media and Subcultural Capital*. Cambridge: Polity Press.

Voltaire. 2003. *Oh My Goth! Version 2.0*. New York: Sirius.

Wellmann, Barry. 2004. 'The glocal village: Internet and community'. *The Arts and Science Review*, 1.1: 26–30.

Internet sources

'About Sopor Æternus and the Ensemble of Shadows'. www.soporaeternus.de/Info.html. Accessed 18 August 2011.

American Goth. http://americangoth.com/. Accessed 25 September 2011.

Australian gothic Forum. Posting 2 July 2011. www.gothic.org.au/Brisbane/viewthreat.php?tid=4426&page=3. Accessed 24 August 2011.

Blackweb België. www.blackweb.be/. Accessed 12 September 2011.

DarkStarlings.com. www.darkstarlings.com/fp.php. Accessed 19 October 2011.

Gothic City: Dresdens Schwarze Seiten. www.gothic-city.de/index.php. Accessed 20 August 2011.

The Neitherland. www.neitherland.com/hyperballad/clubs/philly_other.shtml. Accessed 26 October 2011.

VampireFreaks. http://vampirefreaks.com/. Accessed 24 August 2011.

Filmography

The Hunger. 1983. Tony Scott, dir. Metro-Goldwyn-Mayer.

Interview with the Vampire. 1994. Neil Jordan, dir. Warner Bros.

Nosferatu eine Symphonie des Grauens. 1922. F.W. Murnau, dir. Prana Film.

8

Barry Murnane

Uncanny games: Michael Haneke's *Funny Games* and globalisation's new uncanny

Since its release in 1997 critics have interpreted Michael Haneke's *Funny Games* in terms of European counter-cinema's deconstruction of Hollywood genre film. Such accounts have drawn on a range of provocative statements by the Austrian director, who has gone on record to state that his intention in making the film was to 'rape the viewer into independence' and thus disrupt the uncritical consumption of violent images at the heart of Hollywood horror and thriller genres (Urs and Weingarten, 1997: 147).[1] Both *Funny Games* and Haneke's subsequent US remake, *Funny Games U.S.* (2008), aim to disrupt such patterns of passive reception, teasing viewers with seemingly endless suspense in the face of impending violence, only to cut away from the depiction of the actual act at the crucial moment. Haneke thus denies the viewer the moment of catharsis and relief from tension of the traditional horror film in order to alert attention to the scandal of a form of popular culture that sanctions the aestheticisation of violence. On the face of it these films seem, then, to offer little scope for a traditional reading in terms of horror, terror and the uncanny of the gothic.

This chapter begins with a warning issued by Fred Botting, that 'beyond transgression, all the paraphernalia of gothic modernity change: the uncanny is not where it used to be' (2007: 200). The implication here is that the transgressive role previously attributed to the gothic has become redundant in a society which no longer requires fictional ghosts, doubles, monsters and vampires because, firstly, the technical, medial and globally capitalised economic networks of postmodernity produce copious amounts of such figures themselves, and, secondly, because they too have become infinitely marketable categories in the popular culture industry. If we understand 'Hollywood' as shorthand for a form of popular cinema of horror and thriller genres which is globally present and which Haneke identifies as having a colonising effect on the spectator's mind (hence the need to awaken the viewer), then Haneke's film has much in common with Botting here. This chapter argues that *Funny Games*'s reaction to genre film may be located within such discourses of globalised/transnational cultural production in order to ascertain where the uncanny (paraphrasing Botting) may be located today. Not only does the film depict disruptions to domestic refuge whilst simultaneously creating a disturbing viewing experience, it does so, I argue, by drawing on concepts of the uncanny which have become central components in recent theories of globalisation.

If critics thought they had Haneke safely compartmentalised as 'counter-cineaste', his decision to make an almost shot-by-shot US remake of the 1997 German-language original in 2008 came as something of a surprise. This is not a mainstream Hollywood film, not least because it was not managed by a Hollywood major (the smaller Halcyon, Tartan and Celluloid Nightmares backed the film); it is, however, a notable example of the 'Hollywoodisation' of European, Asian and other cinemas that has played such a prominent role in recent film history. *Funny Games* joins an illustrious group of films from Alfred Hitchcock to John Carpenter to Hideo Nakata that have produced, in essence, uncanny doubles of themselves. In Haneke's case, this filmic doppelganger proves to be an even more uncanny experience as it actually repeats the thematic concerns and diegetic practices of the original film on the level of production and distribution: it becomes, in a sense, the uncanny double of an uncanny film.

Haneke's stated aim with the first *Funny Games* film was, as we have seen, to challenge the role of spectators who consume images of violence as a matter of enjoyment. With its story of a family being terrorised in what becomes an unhomely home by two cold-blooded killers, 'Peter' and 'Paul',[2] who repeatedly comment extradiegetically on their hackneyed roles as slasher-figures straight out of popular horror films, *Funny Games* actually tells two stories. Close attention to Paul's repeated comments on such issues as the proper length of feature films shows that Haneke essentially projects two figures straight out of Hollywood into a diegetic space that cannot contain them. In so doing he couples a narrative based on uncanny disturbances of domestic space with a metafilmic discourse on globally successful film genres, suggesting that the global presence of Hollywood is in some way responsible for the murderous action in the film. Peter and Paul are best understood as embodiments of what Haneke identifies as Hollywood's neocolonial, homogenising grasp on global film consumption; they even suggest how this expansive colonisation works by identifying themselves as the disturbing agents of the viewers' own desire for pleasure through violence in the frequent extradiegetic pieces to camera (Morrow, 2001: 11). They are murderers because Haneke has simply lifted them straight out of Hollywood and projected them into a space that they proceed to colonise.

The identical story in both films is as simple as it is remorseless. The Schober family[3] travel to their holiday retreat by a lake where two young men previously shown in conversation with their neighbours arrive at their house looking for eggs for dinner. The situation inexplicably and without motivation quickly descends into violence; the father George slaps Paul in the face for being brazen before Peter retaliates by breaking his leg with a golf-club. The two intruders terrorise and torture the family before introducing a 'game' they wish to play – seemingly not for the first time, something later confirmed when the corpse of the neighbours' daughter is discovered by the boy Georgie. They bet that the family will be dead within twelve hours unless they manage to win a series of (impossible) competitions. This torture is interrupted only by the most famous sequence in the film, when the wife, Ann, manages to shoot Peter only for Paul to grab a remote control, leave the diegetic level and 'rewind' the film to before Peter's death: the most obvious instance of disruption to the generic laws of the slasher movie. Having finally killed Ann, Peter and Paul disembark from a boat at a neighbour's house, suggesting that the 'funny game' of filmic violence will be repeated here once more.

Even leaving aside the shot-by-shot remake for the moment, it is possible to see *Funny Games* as two movies in one, creating an intensely uncanny and shocking viewing experience. While Peter and Paul torturing and murdering the family in their holiday home can be watched as an unsettling slasher movie, albeit in self-reflective form, the instances in which Paul in particular departs from the diegetic level of torture to reflect on his own role as a stereotypical slasher as well as on the audience's expectations and desires create an entirely different film. In showing his awareness of his role as a murderer, Paul effectively reveals the space of the film that we as spectators are watching to be doubly signifying: firstly, as a home under threat, and, secondly, as a space in which a reflection on the global reach of horror films becomes manifest.

On the first level of this double signification, the Schobers' house is invaded by their violent tormentors dressed in strangely American frat-boy clothing already suggestive of a confrontation between Alpine locality and global consumerism. In narrating a transmutation of the family home into a site of inexplicable torture, *Funny Games* most obviously draws on one of the mainstays of Hollywood horror. As David Sfora points out, in *Funny Games* the 'very house that should afford them protection traps the family that is terrorized' (1996: 98). Two sequences in particular connote this clear demarcation of domestic space in the film. Firstly, when the family pull into the driveway of the house, they pass through a large automatic gate marking a clear distinction between inside and outside the family home. Secondly, the prolonged neo-realist 'kitchen story'-like shot in which Ann sets about preparing dinner for the family sets up an astonishingly traditional sense of domesticity inside the home.[4] In both scenes the domestic calm is obviously rather fragile from the start: the need for protective fences and gates makes this clear, and Ann's role as domestic goddess is undone by the massive knife she wields while on the phone.

Haneke underlines this reading in his explanation of the unavoidable fatalism of the film: 'The fact that the family can't escape is due to the way they've tried to insulate themselves from the world with their money, they've locked themselves in' (cited in Falcon, 1998: 12). The act of creating the home, Haneke suggests, is in itself based on extreme fear and uncertainty; the homely is founded by an aggressive act of imposing one's own contingent meanings on space in order to create a sense of safe place, demonstrated here, for example, in the demarcation of the home through the gated gardens.[5] But the borders between inside and outside are already long-since disrupted: when Georgie later slips through a gap in the fence in order to escape, complete insulation of the home is shown to be patently unmanageable. The concept of home is thus both founded *and* confounded by a sinister sense of disturbance from the outset; it is always already a place under threat.

As a place of sanctuary that is simultaneously under threat, this home is an ideal example of Freud's uncanny, which Nicholas Royle has interpreted as being a disturbance of the very idea of *property* (2003: 1, 6). The uncanny is a paradoxical feeling in which the subject experiences something not belonging to *its self* but in *itself*; it is the experience of the foreign in one's own self, of a subject which is not the master in/of its own house. Freud's metaphorical link to space and the mastery over space relies, of course, on the central spatial connotations of the German word *unheimlich,* which plays with questions of the properness of place, of the home and unhomely. It also relies on a logic of secrecy and repression in which the repressed, the secret, comes back into full view (Freud, 1955: 220–2, 226).

The spatial relations in *Funny Games* draw on precisely this model of the uncanny: when George, the father, strikes the first blow against Peter and Paul, making him a potential origin of violence against the family in the film, there is a suggestion that the young men are little more than the return of repressed violent tendencies in the family itself.[6] The musical guessing-game in the car at the start of the movie, the first 'game' Haneke shows us, likewise serves as a formative sign of a competitive streak and a general mistrust running through the family. Once the piece of music has been identified, Ann and George eject the disc abruptly in order to continue the game of one-upmanship, while there is some concern that the opponent may have been cheating. This interaction is interrupted by the extradiagetic explosion of John Zorn's aggressive cacophony of industrial-punk while blood-red letters spell the title of the film: the games played by the family are complexly linked as latent forms of the violence and murder at the heart of familial domesticity. Haneke presents a materialisation of repressed, im*proper* aggression inherent to the Schobers' familial *propriety,* and he does so by unpacking the spatial contexts of Freud's uncanny to reveal their domesticity and homely *property* as an experience of literally losing the always already tenuous mastery over their own home. *Funny Games* is literally a discussion of the uncanny patterns of property.

In this regard Peter and Paul seem to be uncanny embodiments of repressed desires, tensions and aggressions within the bourgeois familial home. Two almost mirror-image shots in this sequence underline this reading. When Peter first introduces himself to Ann at the door of the house, the camera is positioned immediately behind her shoulder looking through the screen-door suggesting a clear distinction between her as insider and Peter as outsider. Barely five minutes later, the roles are reversed, with Peter and Paul showing their mastery both over the house and the Schobers as the camera is positioned behind them looking at the Schobers, pushed back out through the door of their own house and literally no longer masters of their own home. The portrayal of the uncanny on this level of signification remains remarkably traditional and allows the spectator easily to locate *Funny Games* in terms of generic horror and thrillers.

There are very good reasons as to why the house appears unhomely, not the least of which is that we never really learn where it is located. In the first film it is obviously the Alps, but where: Austria, Switzerland, Italy or Germany? Moreover, if Haneke can transfer the action to anywhere – a remarkably flat, American landscape in *Funny Games U.S.* for example – is it actually possible to solve the question of a distinct location at all? The very doubling of the earlier film suggests that this film is not just about making clearly identifiable spaces uncanny through their 'Hollywoodisation', but about the uncanny dislocatedness of space in global modernity itself (see below). This denial of clear location is underlined by non-diagetic aspects and contexts of the film: in the German-language original, for example, George and Ann are played by actors (Ulrich Mühe and Susanne Lothar) with obviously North German accents, making them outsiders in the Alpine region, undermining any claims to spatial belonging they may harbour.

The plot suggests that we need to think differently about space.[7] The Schober house is actually a home *away from home*: as a holiday-home, it is a transitory location for tourists on the move and is thus always-already unhomely. The opening sequence formally underlines this dislocatedness by providing only images of the family on the road. Neither the helicopter tracking-shot nor the various close-up shots of hands, faces or parts of the car provide sufficient information with which to identify the space, thus reproducing the thematic issue of dislocatedness in the spectators' own viewing experiences. On the macro-level this denial of location is achieved in one of contemporary horror film's most common strategies of *estranging* spatial strategies by focusing specifically on non-places such as the motorway and the holiday home. On a micro-level Haneke's use of camera positioning shows a persistent refusal to use genuine point-of-view or shot-counter-shot perspectives and establishing shots with which the spectator can gain a sense of position in the depicted diegetic world. Indeed the location of *Funny Games* appears to be completely *dis*-located.

Funny Games here enacts one of the more unsettling moments of contemporary global culture, namely the manner in which 'a high degree of human mobility, telecommunications, films, video and satellite TV and the Internet have contributed to the creation of trans-local understandings' (Vertovec, 2009: 12). As with the Schobers at the start of the film, global culture is something that is mobile, travelling, always on the move. Whether through cross-border transactions in economics, movements of people or amalgamations of cultures in globalised cities, contemporary societies are increasingly defined by their varying positions in global and transnational orders of space. The Schobers' holiday home is a tourist destination and as such can only ever be a temporary domicile, a momentary point on a network of endless movements.

Arjun Appadurai underlines the 'complex, overlapping disjunctive order' of 'diverse *local* experiences of taste, pleasure and politics' as a result of these far-reaching processes (1996: 32; my emphasis). Rather than functioning as an intact relationship to one's immediate environment, the local is increasingly considered as simply one further interface in the global communication networks. Supposedly stable locations such as home, region or nation reveal themselves as embroiled in unceasing processes of global signification; they appear to be interpenetrated by processes (possibly) happening elsewhere (the here and the elsewhere are not all that separated) (see for example, Sassen, 2001). Such spatial relations appear to be inherently uncanny. If the local is merely a momentary position on a global network – what globalisation theory has wittily termed 'glocalisation' – and if momentary acts of identity-formation and cultural production are always conducted through global circuits and flows of cultural artefacts, then glocalisation describes a sense of place in which the home/the local is always already uncanny/unhomely/foreign. The globalised local is always already shot through by aspects of foreign cultural signification, economics and politics, meaning that one's surroundings seem to be constantly haunted by traces of familiar-unfamiliar meanings and signs (see, for example, Shohat and Stam, 1996; Polan, 1996).

This leads us directly to the second layer of signification in *Funny Games* mentioned above. Here Paul suggests that the space of the home/the local is always already uncanny, because as it is already overwritten with aspects of foreign cultural signification, namely with the generic signifiers of a Hollywood slasher movie. Haneke's complex diegetic and extradiegetic spatial forms thus reproduce the uncanny spatial relations of globalisation in that this Alpine locality seems to be constantly haunted by traces of familiar-unfamiliar meanings and signs, namely by freely circulating cultural signifiers of popular, globalised visual culture. Haneke has repeatedly addressed these issues in his films by linking socio-political processes of transnational migration, cultural transfer and mediatisation with visual media in general and with the perceived homogenising effects of Hollywood film in particular. This is most obviously visible in the opening sequence of *Caché* (2005), which employs security cameras instead of real streetscapes, meaning that viewers are faced with their own roles as spectators through an encounter with their spectatorial doubles in the film. Haneke's approach to capturing the complex overlapping of 'legal, political and cultural ramifications, not only for the practices and meanings, but for the places as well' in globalised society is to show how this impacts on experiences of space through a general mediatisation of everyday life (Vertovec, 2009: 12).

I would suggest that Peter and Paul in their double-film actually embody what *Caché* with its self-reflective use of frames of vision only suggests: namely the spectral, mediatised cultural imaginaries described by Paul Virilio in *The Vision Machine* which have unfolded themselves over our everyday interactions in space and time and which Haneke, in the case of *Funny Games* at least, has identified as emerging from Hollywood. The aggressive metafilmic reflexivity suggests that the only motivation for violence is the generic rules of slasher-horror and thriller movies and the expectations of the audience: 'We are still under feature length', objects Paul to an appeal for pity, and addresses the audience directly: 'You want a proper ending with plausible development, don't you?' Haneke is reacting here to a perceived creation of homogenised, uncritical consumers of violent cinema. Paul's disturbing set-pieces to camera repeatedly make viewers aware of their expectations of and complicity in how the film will progress. Such moments of self-reflexivity point towards a layer of medially omnipresent fictions and practices emerging from Hollywood cinema that have, Haneke urges us to consider, completely colonised filmgoers' minds. Scott Durham concludes that the 'media thus appear in this film as the ultimate perpetrators of its violence – a violence inflicted, as Paul's repeated winks and nods remind us, with the tacit consent of the consumers of its images' (2010: 248). I would merely amend this reading by suggesting that Peter and Paul are the manifestations of these globally circulating images, discourses and patterns of reception in a space which thereby becomes far more complex, far more unsettled or unsettling and thus: uncanny.

Funny Games can thus be seen as an instance of Fredric Jameson's 'geopolitical' analysis of cinema in postmodernity: both versions engage with the patterns of 'cognitive mapping' according to which our movements through the world are dominated by 'idea[s] that include

. . . an image, or an image that comes pre-packaged and already labelled with its ideational slogan' (Jameson, 1992: 2). Elsewhere Jameson has discussed how this ideational 'pre-packaging' of responses to the environment is related to a colonisation of the subject's unconscious. Under the conditions of globalisation individuals have become:

> submerged in [postmodernity's] henceforth filled and suffused volumes to the point where our now postmodern bodies are bereft of spatial coordinates and practically (let alone theoretically) incapable of distantiation; meanwhile, it has already been observed how the prodigious new expansion of multinational capital ends up penetrating and colonizing those pre-capitalist enclaves (Nature and the Unconscious) which offered extraterritorial and Archimedean footholds for critical effectivity. (Jameson, 1992: 48–9)

Whereas the final image of the two young men sailing their boat across the lake captures the general principle of placelessness shared by *Funny Games* and Jameson here (this would the first of the 'double' films referred to above), their earlier self-commentaries and ironic awareness of their own stereotypical mediatised identities as slashers (the topic of what I have termed the 'second' film) underlines how Hollywood generic film, as Haneke's foremost example of global media and culture, has 'penetrated' and 'colonised' even the remotest of Alpine regions.

Peter and Paul effectively appear out of thin air as artefacts of a globally mediatised culture of violence, thereby revealing the space of the family house to be a strange mixture of Alpine tranquillity and Hollywood mediascape. The culmination of Haneke's use of the two young men as a means of reflecting on the global mediatisation of the everyday sphere comes in a harrowing scene over twelve minutes in length following Georgie's murder as his corpse lies in front of the blood-splattered television in the living-room. Haneke here confronts the viewer with a palpable, and violent, making unhomely of a space more usually configured as the safe and clearly defined place of sanctuary signified as home. The central presence of the television, incidentally showing an American Nascar race, highlights once again the role of global media in making space unhomely and shows how medially transported images are able to suture themselves into the consciousness of subjects moving through, and interpreting, space and time.

In enacting complex patterns of transnational movements and disruptions, *Funny Games* thus identifies and plays out a new form of the uncanny in globalisation, and Haneke demands of his viewers that they too come to terms with these processes. This relies on a series of interfections of the local and global in contemporary transnational culture, for which Homi Bhabha has traced a series of derealisationary effects producing an unsettling, transitory space in which lines of demarcation, difference and exclusion fade into each other (Bhabha, 1992). What *Funny Games* suggests is that such interfections have produced patterns of social and cultural interaction which themselves seem inherently uncanny, even gothic. These translocal processes are, however, anything other than the liberating model suggested by Bhabha (1992: 151–2).[8]

As Steven Vertovec has pointed out, globalisation has not simply produced endless delimitation and flows of movement *á la* Bhabha; rather the experience of these flows and the translocal is 'nevertheless anchored in places' (2009: 12). Any experience of globalisation's procession of media images, consumer culture and so on always takes place in a specific locality. Globalisation is not entirely placeless; rather it always involves a localised moment of 'grounding'. It is this 'grounding' of global networks which does not run smoothly in *Funny Games* and which, in the form of unrelenting violence, renders the space of the family home uncanny. As a figure, *grounding* obviously refers to the electronic and medial conditions enabling globalisation; yet, whereas earthing or grounding circuits makes them safe, instances of a gothic grounding seem related to anxieties: here is there, then and now all at once and this experience of rapid displaced placement and confrontation with foreign culture is thoroughly brutal, necessitating collisions of horrific proportion. This is a production of locality that seems always already dangerously charged.

With *Funny Games* already an uncanny artefact, Haneke doubled his own film by making *Funny Games U.S.* ten years on. If the uncanny effect of the first *Funny Games* arose through a doubling of the film's diegesis in order to show how Hollywood genre film has begun to exert an undue control over our relationship to space, time and culture, then *Funny Games U.S.* essentially repeats this process all over again. The earlier portrayal of disrupted concepts and experiences of space/place, global/local, film/reality showed how global culture has created a signature phantasmagoric spatial experience which is uncanny. The remake, on the other hand, reproduces this process on an actual, material level of production, distribution and reception. It transfers a European film dealing self-reflexively with the Americanisation of cultural production, into a 'Hollywoodised' version which seems now to reproduce these uncanny effects at multiple levels. Haneke employs the *U.S.* of the remake's title as a form of shorthand for these effects, and Hollywood is little more than a screen on to which he projects and abjects – which, since Kristeva (1982), has become a defining category of the gothic – the negative effects of globalisation.

This critical relationship to Hollywood does raise the question, however, as to the legitimacy of considering Haneke's film as an example of globalgothic cultural production, a question that can be addressed in a number of ways. Firstly, distinguishing between *Funny Games* and horror ignores the need to reproduce a generic frame, or set of markers of horror, if the viewer is to recognise what mode the director wishes to critique (Speck, 2010: 5). Apart from the obvious slasher/horror storyline of home invasion, *Funny Games* reproduces formal features of this subgenre; Oliver Speck points to the opening bird's-eye view of a driving car as a reference to the classic beginning of Stanley Kubrick's *The Shining* (1980) (2010: 31); likewise extended close-ups of such objects as a knife left on the boat, the golf-clubs and the disturbed family dog barking function as genre markers. Catherine Wheatley has shown how Haneke draws on 'techniques for spectatorial manipulation familiar from both Hollywood cinema and counter-cinema' (2009: 45) to coax viewers with the cathartic emotional strategies of horror only to block this pleasure spectacularly when Paul 'rewinds' the film to undo Ann's temporary victory. I read this 'incorporation of commercial convention' (Wheatley, 2009: 27) as an uncanny act of mimicry of its own, an act so successful that one critic has christened Haneke the 'Master of Everyday Horror' (Jones, 2011) and Mark Kermode has compared *Funny Games* openly with Wes Craven's *Scream* series as a related example of self-reflexive horror (1998: 44–5).

Secondly, it is possible to identify Haneke's critique of commercial cinema as firmly located within contemporary cultural practices and globalgothic film. This becomes increasingly clear if one looks more closely at *Funny Games U.S.* The remake was not only a US/UK/France co-production, showing that Haneke is by no means immune to the transnational economics of global cinema (see Galt, 2010: 229–35), but was also distributed under the label 'Tartan Extreme', the marketing label under which such Asian horror films and their US remakes as Hideo Nakata's *Ringu* (1998) and Takashi Shimizu's *Ju-On/The Grudge* (2003) were released. While I would not go as far as suggesting that both *Funny Games* films are anything near 'mainstream' products, it is plausible to see both as a globalgothic artefact in terms of form, production and distribution/reception. Both films not only deal thematically with issues of globalised modernity and the challenges or threats of global culture, they also circulate as *actual* products involved in globalisation's uncanny structures. *Funny Games* is a sheep in wolf's clothing in that it sutures itself into globalised culture in order to correct what Haneke identifies as its inherent malaise; it is a homeopathic dose of Hollywood's gothic to cure a perceived Hollywoodisation of culture itself. Haneke seems to have created an almost universally deployable film in order to counter what he sees as the homogenising effects of universal, global culture, and there is no good reason as to why Peter and Paul should not appear in a *Funny Games Thailand, Japan, Brazil* or *Australia*. As Paul says to George following his brief escape in *Funny Games U.S.*: 'Player One, Next Level'.

Notes

1 My translation ('Meine Filme vergewaltigen den Zuschauer immerhin dazu, selbst nachzudenken'). On Haneke as art-house cineaste see, for example, Wheatley, 2009.
2 In keeping with common critical practice I refer to the young men by these names in this chapter, although it is important to underline that these names are completely random; they also refer to each other as 'Beavis' and 'Butthead' for example. There is no reason why Peter and Paul should be any less part of their performance; indeed, the lack of fixed names seems part of Haneke's project of disruption.
3 I refer to the characters by their English names only for ease of reference.
4 On Haneke's relation to Italian neo-realist cinema in particular see Rhodes, 2010.
5 On this postmodern concept of enforcing meanings on space see for example Cresswell, 2010.
6 Gail Hart, however, suggests that the subsequent retribution for this 'feminine slap' – Paul cripples George's leg with a golf-club – is out of all proportion to the original offence and is, as such, a deliberate act of misleading on Haneke's part (2006: 68).
7 In the following remarks I will be doing so mainly in relation to what Marc Augé has termed 'Non-places' (1995).
8 That this liberating movement of the uncanny is at the core of Bhabha's project becomes clear in his celebration of de-subjectivity through hybridity and mimicry (in Rutherford, 1990: 208–10, 212).

References

Appadurai, Arjun. 1996. *Modernity at Large: Cultural Dimensions of Globalization*, Minneapolis: University of Minnesota Press.

Augé, Marc. 1995. *Non-places: Introduction to an Anthropology of Supermodernity*. London: Verso.

Bhabha, Homi. 1992. 'The world and the home'. *Social Text,* 31/32: 141–53.

Botting, Fred. 2007. 'Gothic culture'. In *The Routledge Companion to Gothic,* eds Emma McEvoy and Catherine Spooner. Abingdon: Routledge, 199–213.

Cresswell, Tim. 2010. *Space: A Short Introduction.* Malden, MA: Blackwell.

Falcon, Richard. 1998. 'The discreet harm of the bourgeoisie'. *Sight & Sound,* 8.5: 10–12.

Durham, Scott. 2010. 'Code unknown: Haneke's serial realism'. In *On Michael Haneke,* eds Brian Price and John David Rhodes. Detroit: Wayne State University Press, 245–65.

Freud, Sigmund. 1955. 'The "Uncanny"'. *Standard Edition,* Vol. XVII, trans. James Strachey. London: Hogarth Press, 217–56.

Galt, Rosalind. 2010. 'The functionary of mankind: Haneke and Europe'. In *On Michael Haneke,* eds Brian Price and John David Rhodes. Detroit: Wayne State University Press, 221–42.

Hart, Gail. 2006. 'Michael Haneke's *Funny Games* and Schiller's coercive classicism'. *Modern Austrian Literature,* 39.2: 63–75.

Jameson, Fredric. 1992. *The Geopolitical Aesthetic: Cinema and Space in the World System.* Durham, NC: Duke University Press.

Kermode, Mark. 1998. 'Funny Games'. *Sight & Sound,* 8: 44–5.

Kristeva, Julia. 1982. *Powers of Horror: An Essay on Abjection.* New York: Columbia University Press.

Morrow, Fiona. 2001. 'All pain and no gain'. *Independent,* 2 November, 11.

Polan, Dana. 1996. 'Globalism's localisms'. In *Global-local. Cultural Production and the Transnational Imaginary,* eds Rob Wilson and Wimal Dissanayake. Durham, NC: Duke University Press, 261–83.

Rhodes, John David. 2010. 'The spectacle of skepticism: Haneke's long takes'. In *On Michael Haneke,* eds Brian Price and John David Rhodes. Detroit: Wayne State University Press, 87–102.

Royle, Nicholas. 2003. *The Uncanny: An Introduction.* Manchester: Manchester University Press.

Rutherford, Jonathan. 1990. 'The third space. Interview with Homi Bhabha'. In *Identity. Community, Culture, Difference,* ed. Jonathon Rutherford. London: Lawrence and Wishart, 207–21.

Sassen, Saskia. 2001 (2000). 'Spatialities and temporalities of the global: elements for a theorization'. In *Globalization,* ed. Arjun Appadurai. Durham, NC: Duke University Press, 260–78.

Sfora, David. 1996. 'Uneasy domesticity in the films of Michael Haneke'. *Studies in European Cinema,* 3.2: 93–104.

Shohat, Ella, and Robert Stam. 1996. 'From the imperial family to the transnational imaginary: media spectatorship in the age of globalization'. In *Global-local. Cultural Production and the Transnational Imaginary,* eds Rob Wilson and Wimal Dissanayake. Durham, NC: Duke University Press, 145-70.

Speck, Oliver C. 2010. *Funny Frames. The Filmic Concepts of Michael Haneke.* London: Continuum.

Urs, Jenny, and Susanne Weingarten. 1997. 'Kino ist immer Vergewaltigung'. *Spiegel,* 38: 146–7.

Vertovec, Steven. 2009. *Transnationalism.* Oxford: Routledge.

Virilio, Paul. 1994. *The Vision Machine*. Bloomington: Indiana University Press.
Wheatley, Catherine. 2009. *Michael Haneke's Cinema. The Ethic of the Image*. New York: Berghahn.

Internet sources

Jones, Bronwyn. 2011. 'More than a master of everyday horror: The films of Michael Haneke'. www.thehighhat.com/Nitrate/004/haneke.html. Accessed 2 August 2011.

Filmography

Caché. 2005. Michael Haneke, dir. Sony.
Funny Games. 1997. Michael Haneke, dir. Attitude Films.
Funny Games U.S. 2008. Michael Haneke, dir. Warner Independent.
Ju-On / The Grudge. 2003. Takashi Shimizu, dir. Toei.
Ringu. 1998. Hideo Nakata, dir. Metro Tartan / Universal.
Scream series. 1996-2011. Wes Craven, dir. Dimension Films.
The Shining. 1980. Stanley Kubrick, dir. Warner Bros.

9

Colette Balmain

Pan-Asian gothic

In their introduction to *Rogue Flows: Trans-Asian Cultural Traffic*, Iwabuchi, Muecke and Thomas suggest that 'the globalisation of media and popular/consumer culture is still based upon an assumption of unbeatable Western (American) domination, and the arguments are focussed on how the Rest resist, imitate or appropriate the West' (2004: 9). In these terms manifestations of the gothic within a global marketplace would simply be identifiable through their relationship to Western gothic forms or modes. However a close examination of pan-Asian gothic demonstrates that the relationship between East and West is not one of hierarchal dominance, but one in which the relationship between the local and the global is complex, conflicting and continually changing and one that demands a new way of thinking about the gothic in an age of globalisation and cosmopolitanism: one which is best expressed by the term *globalgothic*.

The films discussed in this chapter are the award-winning portmanteau *Kwaidan* (*Kaidan*, Masaki Kobayashi, Japan: 1964) and *A Tale of Two Sisters* (*Janghwa Hongryeon*, Kim Jee-woon, South Korea: 2003), two films that exemplify the merging of the global with the local in the construction of pan-Asian gothic. *Kwaidan*, a Japanese film, is based upon the translation of traditional Japanese mythology via Lafcadio Hearn (1850–1904), a Western journalist and writer, and *A Tale of Two Sisters* was remade as *The Uninvited* (Charles and Thomas Guard, US/Canada/Germany: 2009), an act of remediation which dilutes the horror of Kim's film for a more teenage-friendly audience while restructuring the Korean folktale (*Janghwa Hongreyon jeon*) on which

A Tale of Two Sisters is based. With its modern setting, *A Tale of Two Sisters* may seem to be a very different expression of gothic from that of *Kwaidan*, which locates its ghostly haunting in the premodern past, before enforced modernisation and democratisation during the Allied Occupation (1942–52). However, both films construct a pan-Asian gothic, in which the local and/or locale gives rise to ghostly returns, returns whose very existence can be interpreted in part as an act of resistance to the domination of Western cultures across Asia. In *The Fantastic in Modern Japanese Literature*, Susan Napier argues that for Japanese writers and directors the fantastic as a mode provides a mechanism through which to subvert the law of the father, which is clearly aligned with the discourse of the West. She points to the significance of the return to 'indigenous folk traditions' and 'rural myths' as a central part of this resistance, arguing that the 'impulse towards the fantastic is a literary discovery of a lost imaginary', a place 'before the law of the father forces the infant into the world of the Symbolic' (Napier, 1996: 11). Here the law of the father or the West seeks to remake the 'Other' in its own image through the twin mechanisms of physical and psychical globalisation. In her discussion of 'Global Hollywood', Anne Cieko points out that the discourse of globalisation 'suggests a complex overlapping and interconnectedness between Hollywood (the dominant "Western" model) and the global. The possible implication for contemporary Asian cinema is that it is effaced, subsumed, or marginalised in such a structure' (2006: 24).

The return to the premodern and oral traditions, a key component of pan-Asian Gothic, can be read as a resistance to the global at the level of the local. However, the global is already imbricated within the local, as Chow points out in her insightful analysis of film as ethnography (2010a: 148–71) utilising Mulvey's now iconic essay on gender and power in Hollywood cinema, 'Visual pleasure and narrative cinema'. While the return to the past in Japanese cinema of the 1950s and 1960s functioned as a form of reimagining of national identity outside of the contaminating influence of Western forms, tied up as they were with the shame of defeat and unconditional surrender demanded by the US, at the same time it offered up a Japaneseness associated with exoticism for the desiring gaze of the West in an act of self-Orientalism. As Chow points out elsewhere, we need to think of 'nativism' and 'Orientalism' as '*languages* which can be used by natives and non-natives alike', the consequence of which is that 'natives' are not 'automatically innocent of Orientalism as a mode of discourse' (2010b: 35). In this sense pan-

Asian gothic is neither global nor local as its resistance to Orientalist discourse that gothicises the Orient as a place of exotic and erotic alterity is comprised by the process of resubjectivation, which relies on that Orientalist discourse as the very foundation of difference. As this suggests and as my subsequent discussion of *Kwaidan* and *A Tale of Two Sisters* argues, the concept of the gothic as a global phenomenon is fraught with difficulties in that local variations become meaningless and divorced from their specific cultural context. Instead the term *globalgothic* enables an understanding of the continuity and differences between and within non-Western gothic forms and Western gothic, without repeating the act of physical colonisation by one of ideological imperialism. Pan-Asian gothic is a manifestation of globalgothic rather than global gothic. One way of understanding this is by thinking about globalgothic as glocal gothic, as the concept of the 'glocal' which has largely displaced simplistic theories of the global 'encapsulates the interaction and fusion of global influences and idioms with idiosyncratic local contextual forms of expression' (Iwabuchi, Muecke and Thomas, 2004: 101).

The visuality of pan-Asian gothic

> Although some are set later, during the Meiji Period (1868–1912), Edo Gothic films are generally set during the Edo Period (1603–1867), during which time the Samurai became obsolete. The period setting is important, as it parallels contemporary concerns at the time over the breakdown of social structures in the face of economic expansion and the perceived Westernization of Japanese society. (Balmain 2008: 54)

The 1950s and 1960s saw the emergence of gothic horror cinema in both Japan and South Korea. In Japan this trend was most fully expressed in the period horror films of Nobuo Nakagawa (1905–85), and in South Korea in the more contemporary domestic gothic films of directors such as Kim Ki-young (1922–98) and Lee Yong-min (1916–). The return to a repressed history in the case of Japan (films set in premodern times having been banned by the Occupation) is mirrored by the haunted modernity of South Korean gothic cinema. In his analysis of the films of Kim Ki-young, Chris Berry underlines the contradictory nature of enforced modernity in South Korea, writing that 'the ambivalence of the Korean experience of modernity as imported [is that] it is at once desired and also a submission to the foreign. That which is intended to strengthen Korea is only achieved by submission to the foreign' (Berry, 2007: 110). The seemingly overt critique of modernity in Japanese gothic cinema, or Edo Gothic, which functions as a lament of loss for an ordered society in which set hierarchies defined one's place in the social and economic order, is enabled through the spectacle of a past which had been denied during the Occupation; conversely, it is the spectacle of the present that is gothicised in Korean horror cinema. As Berry concludes in his discussion of modernity in the films of Kim Ki-young, 'one must consider not only a number of different modernities but also a number of different experiences of *those* modernities, expressed in different cinematic patterns' (2007: 110).

As much as Edo gothic was inward-looking, a nostalgic backwards glance at a period long gone, it was at the same time outward-looking, offering up an exotic, even Orientalist, Japaneseness for the desiring gaze of Western audiences. In these films Japaneseness is an aesthetically pleasing spectacle of lush colours, period settings and highly stylised sets accompanied by the haunting sounds of traditional Japanese music. These films deal with suitably gothic motifs including shape-shifting cats (*baneko*); vengeful ghosts (*onryō*); demons; doomed lovers and supernatural seductresses, and they include typical gothic themes such as ancestral secrets; psychological disturbances and supernatural hauntings. In her discussion of the visuality of non-Western cinema, Chow utilises Mulvey's argument around visual pleasure in Hollywood cinema to theorise the mechanisms by which non-Western cultures (whether physically or psychically colonised) represent themselves to the dominant Other utilising images provided by that Other. Chow argues that 'the state of being looked at not only is built into the way non-western cultures are viewed by Western ones; more significantly it is part of the *active* manner in which such cultures represent – ethnographize – themselves'. As such, the state of being the object of the gaze – 'past *objecthood*' – is an integral component of subjectification and therefore 'being-looked-at-ness, rather than the act of looking, constitutes the primary event in cross-cultural representations' (2010a: 153).

Kwaidan provides a paradigmatic example of Chow's thesis about the centrality of 'past *objecthood*' as part of the active manner in which non-Western cultures represent themselves. It is only by understanding the complexity of the relationship between the local and the global, as an object of the colonial gaze which provides the mechanism through which a postcolonial subjectivity is constructed, that Kobayashi's decision to choose a Western interpretation and translation of the original folktales as source material for his film rather than indigenous accounts becomes clear. The four stories that make up *Kwaidan* are taken from their English reiteration in the books of Lafcadio Hearn. Hearn moved to Japan in 1890 and subsequently married the daughter of a Japanese Samurai, not only becoming a naturalised Japanese citizen but also adopting a new Japanese name – Koizumi Yakumo. Hearn's many writings on Japan include *Shadowings* (1900) and *Kwaidan: Stories and Studies of Strange Things* (1903). His almost jingoistic embrace of the more conservative and exotic elements of Japanese culture, including state Shintoism and Japanese folklore, are reflected in his writings, which, while sympathetic to his adopted homeland and marking the first considered account on the part of a Westerner to see Japan from the 'perspective' of the Japanese, recreate an imaginary Japan of superstition and strange customs. As Donald Richie argues, 'Hearn, while reflecting the reality of the country around him, was also constructing his own version of that land – he was creating what Roland Barthes was later to call a "fictive nation," a national system of one's own devising' (1997: 12).

The first story, 'The Black Hair', adapted from 'Reconciliation' in *Shadowings*, tells of a devoted wife (Michiyo Aratama) who is abandoned by her husband (Rentaro Mikuni), for a more profitable alliance with a rich merchant through marriage to his vain and conceited only daughter. When he comes to his senses and returns home, the vengeful ghost of his abandoned wife torments him. The second story, 'Woman of the Snow', is taken from *Kwaidan*. A variation on the legend of the Yuki-Onna, it tells of a young woodcutter (Tatsuya Nakadai) who falls in love with a demonic seductress (Keiko Kishi) after she murders his father one cold and lonely night. She spares the son and takes human form in order to live with him as man and wife until one day he disobeys her injunction not to tell of how they met and she disappears, leaving him to bring up their children on his own. The third, 'Hoichi: The Earless', also from *Kwaidan*, tells of a blind 'biwa' musician (Katsuo Nakamura), who is deceived into providing musical accompaniment to re-enactments of the last battle between the Heike and Genji clans for the ghosts of the dead. The final ghostly narrative, 'In a Cup of Tea', concerns a man who sees a strange face reflected in his cup of tea and is taken from *Kottō: Being Japanese Curios, with Sundry Cobwebs* (1902). Overall, the themes of loyalty and honour provide a cohesive force to these four strange tales while offering up a sumptuous exotic picture of Meiji Japan, which is as influenced by Orientalist discourse as it is by native accounts. At the same time this depiction of past times and utilisation of traditional folklore provides an implicit critique of the enforced democratisation and Westernisation of Japan by the Allied Forces. During the Occupation, popular media were identified as an essential part of the democratisation of Japan, and the CIE (Civil Information and Education Section) was set up to 'encourage the development of ideals associated with American "democracy" while preventing the media from disseminating anything considered unsuitable or dangerous to the Occupation government' (Standish, 2006: 155). Revenge dramas in particular were considered unsuitable as the driving forces – 'loyalty' and 'honour' – were seen as antithetical to the maintenance of democratic society and thus incompatible with the Occupiers' vision of a new and democratic Japan (Standish, 2006: 157). As such *Kwaidan* demonstrates the complexities of the various levels of translation and adaption that are central to pan-Asian gothic texts. In his insightful review for *Midnight Eye,* Dean Bowman highlights these complexities:

> Masaki Kobayashi's episodic compilation of ghost stories, recorded from Japanese oral folk tales at the turn of the century by multicultural expat Lafcadio Hearn, has interestingly undergone many levels of translation: from oral tradition, to text, and then to cinema; but also from Japanese, to English, and then back to Japanese. It could stand as something of an inverted embodiment of Japanese film practice in that period, in which directors were influenced by western cinema, either consciously or as a result of political machinations such as the occupation, but also often turned that influence back upon its source. (2007)

The period setting and premodern themes of loyalty and honour in *Kwaidan* can be seen as an act of rebellion against the West's attempt to turn Japanese cinema into a mirror of its own, while simultaneously negotiating a post-Occupation identity by refracting an exotic Japan through the prism of the Other's mirror. As Chow argues, '"Us" and "them" are no longer safely distinguishable; "viewed object" is now looking at "viewed subject" looking' (Chow, 2010a: 153). In *Kwaidan* as in other Edo gothic films of the time, the visual tapestry of Japan's 'exotic' past was presented as much for the consumption of global audiences as it was for local audiences, its exotic visuality as much a marketing strategy as an attempt to reassert a 'traditional' Japanese identity as part of nationalistic discourses, or *nihonjinron* (theories on the Japanese) which stressed Japaneseness uniqueness (Kubota, 1998: 300–1). Kubota writes, 'Critics have argued that *nihonjinron* is a reaction against a sense of identity loss. Ryuko Kubota points out that Harumi Befu, for example, 'argues that *nihonjinron* as an ideology saves Japanese identity which has been threatened by post-war Westernization and industrialization' (Kubota, 1998: 300).

Gothic translations and transformations

Whereas Japanese cinema had a fairly high profile in the West at the time of *Kwaidan,* with Kurosawa's *Rashomon* in 1950 winning both the Golden Lion at the Venice Film Festival and an Honorary Award as 'the most outstanding foreign language film' at the 24th Academy Awards in 1951, South Korean cinema of the 1950s and 1960s was more of a domestic affair, looking mainly to local rather than global markets. The success of Lee Byeong-il's *The Wedding Day* (*Sijibganeun nal*: 1956) in 1957 at the Asian Film Festival where it won a special award for comedy, and its subsequent entry into both the Berlin and Sydney Film Festivals, demonstrated that South Korean cinema could compete both locally and globally; nevertheless, this early promise would not be fulfilled until the 1980s and 1990s. It is significant, however, that *The Wedding Day* was taken as a model of how South Korean cinema should be in order to compete in the global marketplace, emphasising the importance of the traditional and the local/exotic signifiers of the 'Orient' to international success – something which would ultimately be proved true during the boom of South Korean popular culture in the late 1990s, the Korean Wave (*Hallyu*) – first of all across Asia and then internationally. In the words of the *Korean Film Archive,* 'it gave support to the opinion that in order to win an award in a foreign film festival, expressing "local colors" that delivers [*sic*] the unique colors of Korea to a foreign audience is just as important as, or even more important than, the quality of completion and production. In short, people argued that in order to be persuasive overseas, films should have exotic Korean scenes' ('The Truth of Korean Movies').

However, as Lee Yong-min's 1965 gothic horror *A Devilish Homicide* attests, this exoticism was not free from the influence of Japanese popular culture despite this having been officially banned since the Allies forced Japan out of Korea in 1945 (the ban itself lasted until 1998). Certain scenes bear an uncanny relation to Japanese film versions of the folktale of Oiwa, and in particular to her death scene in cinematic versions of the folktale (which was also a kabuki play of some distinction at the time), including Nobuo Nakagawa's *The Ghost Story of Yotsuya* (1959) – often seen as the seminal version of the folktale/kabuki play – in which a Samurai murders his dutiful wife so that he can forge an alliance with a rich merchant by marrying his beautiful daughter. In particular the death scenes of Oiwa in *The Ghost Story of Yotsuya* and that of Aeja (Do Geum-bong) in *A Devilish Homicide* are remarkably similar, right down to the use of poison, resulting disfigurement and consequent suicide. However 'local colors' were added by making the older sister rather than the husband the villain, working within the popular theme of what Berry terms 'monstrous maids' or 'Myeong-jas'. Monstrous maids in domestic gothic function both as a signifier of the eruption of the 'pre-modern and even primitive rural culture' within modernity and as sexualised objects of (male) desire tied into the new changing social structure and modernity – representing both the promise and the terror ascribed to the imposition of Western modernity and all that it entailed (Berry, 2007: 107–8). In the case of South Korean gothic, Japanese influences were more significant than Western ones, especially as a rigid quota system severely limited the number of foreign films that could be shown during a year, along with the length of time they could be shown for.

Owing to decades of military rule and a stagnant film industry, South Korean film had little global impact until the late 1990s and the pop cultural phenomenon known as *Hallyu* or the Korean Wave. However, horror films were low-budget affairs, aimed mainly at the large teenage female audiences both at home and in Japan, as exemplified by School Horror films such as the 1998 *Whispering Corridors* (*Yeogogoedam*, Park Ki-hyeong), so successful that there have been four sequels, although connected by 'theme' rather than characters. Unlike the relatively cheap and profitable School Horror films, with their first-time directors and mainly unknown casts, Kim Jee-woon's 2003 *A Tale of Two Sisters* is an example of a 'well-made film' – defined as a 'commercial feature that makes use of defined genres and the star system . . . which also contains both a distinctive directorial style and commentary on social issues' (Paquet, 2009: 95). While *A Tale of Two Sisters* utilises oral folklore in a similar manner to *Kwaidan* almost forty years earlier, it does so only to subvert the values and morals contained within the well-known folktale rather than merely reiterate them in line with nationalistic discourses of South Korean identity. The folktale itself tells of a spiteful stepmother and her maltreatment of her two stepdaughters, whom, in order to ensure her son's inheritance, she hounds until they both commit suicide. The sisters return as vengeful ghosts (*yeonsang*) and are pacified only when the truth of their abuse comes to light and the stepmother and her son are put to death for their crimes. While the evil stepmother can be found in folktales throughout the globe, the figure has a specific cultural meaning in traditional South Korean belief systems. As Kendall explains, 'Stepchildren are a tribulation for the second wife. Koreans consider the mother the kind or loving parent . . . In Cinderella fashion, it is assumed that she will pamper her own children but deal harshly with the first wife's issue' (1984: 220).

The first half of *A Tale of Two Sisters* keeps fairly close to the original folktale, with an evil stepmother, Eun-ju, tormenting her two stepdaughters, Su-mi (Im Soo-jung) and Su-yeon (Moon Geun-young), while the father (Mu-Hyun), seems oblivious to what is going on around him. In the second half of the film the narrative veers sharply off course as, in a series of revelations and flashbacks, we discover that both the stepmother, Eun-ju, and the younger sister, Su-yeon, have been nothing more than external projections of Su-mi's internal guilt over the death of her mother and younger sister when she fails to respond to Su-yeon's cries when she becomes trapped in the wardrobe that their mother has hanged herself in – Su-yeon suffocates trapped in the wardrobe under her mother's body. Su-mi is the most gothic of characters, the unreliable narrator through whom the narrative is focalised, and whose version of events is not necessarily to be believed. Here the personal past is a refraction of the historical past, in that Su-mi chooses to deny her complicity by utilising a narrative from the past, the original folktale, as a mechanism of disavowal of the present, pointing to the tension between local and global identities, and tradition and modernity, that is symptomatic of a South Korean ideology that seeks global approval through an expression of 'local color'. It is only evident through repeated viewings that Su-mi is in fact a composite of the three main characters of the folktale and that the resolution of the folktale in which good triumphs over evil is subverted. As Dupuy argues, the 'Korean ghost story reaches a satisfying end, where retribution is meted out and where the ghosts succeed in expelling the malevolent element from the family unit. The film, on the other hand, offers a modern transposition of the fairy tale that eschews such a well-ordered ending' (2007).

Like earlier Korean domestic gothic, *A Tale of Two Sisters* shows the continued influence of Japanese cultural products on local productions. Su-yeon's body in a bag which is dragged across the floor by Eun-ju is reminiscent of similar scenes in Miike's *Audition* (1999), while the vengeful ghost dressed in white with long dark hair obscuring her features – who may or may not be another projection of Su-mi's guilt – is a common, if not the most common, feature, of contemporary pan-Asian gothic cinema. At the same time, as in early Korean domestic gothic, the domestic space is a 'Westernised' space, representative of 'stand-up living culture' which was introduced into Korea in the late nineteenth century. The antique European furniture dictated by the structure of the house, the floral wallpaper in the sister's rooms and the richness of the costumes could be interpreted as visual signifiers of the West. At the same time the floral decoration of Su-mi's and Su-yeon's room is also influenced by the names of the sisters from the original folktale, Rose Flower and Red Lotus, demonstrating the increasing interpenetration of global and local worlds and therefore the 'necessity to locate ways in which the "local and the global are always interlocked and complicitous"' (Robertson, 2005).

The art of the remake, as Charles and Thomas Guard's *The Uninvited* (2009) demonstrates, can be best understood in terms of the processes of internationalisation and localisation. According to Anthony Pym, localisation represents 'a paradigm shift away from a focus on the source text (to which a translation had to be equivalent) and towards a focus on the target purpose or function (since all translations are different from their sources)' (2004: 31). Localisation is associated with internationalisation; it 'minimally covers the process whereby the culture-specific features are taken out of a text in order to minimize the problems of later distributing that text into a series of locales' (Pym, 2004: 31). The lack of overt cultural specifity is what renders some films more likely to be remade than others that are closely connected to their locale/local. As we have seen, Kim's film bears little relation to the folktale which provided the original inspiration: the theme of the dysfunctional family and childhood trauma, the gothic aesthetics, the 'standing up' structure of the 'haunted' house and loss of (national) identity have a universal resonance. In this sense there was little that needed to be changed about the film. It is the sensibility that is changed, the emphasis on melodrama and the, possibly, incestuous relations between Su-mi and her father – foregrounded through the doubling of the stepmother and Su-mi – is removed in order to make it less problematic for the PG-13 audience that the remake was aimed at. In addition the distinctions between good and evil are clearer in *The Uninvited*. Anna (Su-mi) is directly responsible for the death of her mother and sister and is therefore a less sympathetic character. The subtlety of the original film is lost, as the 'twist' is evident early in the film and a story about psychological disintegration becomes one about female monstrosity and madness. The act of translation and localisation functions to foreground what Robertson calls 'the global-local' problematic in his discussion of glocalisation. The relationship between *A Tale of Two Sisters* and *The Uninvited* articulates the way in which 'The local has been globalized; just as the global has been localized' (2005).

Globalgothic?

> From the important publication of Edward W. Said's *Orientalism* in 1978, we have seen analyses of how Euro-American colonialism, travel and exploration have produced 'the rest of the world' for the West. However, it is now time to ask how this 'rest of the world' produced and still produces itself out of the very same colonial experiences, and time to understand how the (post)colonial 'them' unevenly and problematically own the West – and not only when they are 'immigrants' in the great Western metropolitan centres of London and Paris, but even when they actually live in Asia. (Wee, 2004: 143)

The purpose of this chapter has been to investigate the relationship between the global and the local in non-Western forms of gothic, and specifically in relation to Japanese and South Korean gothic, which are examples of what I term pan-Asian gothic, something not heterogeneous, but differently expressed at different times and in different nations. Both *Kwaidan* and *A Tale of Two* Sisters highlight complex relationships between the local and the global, something which can be best understand not in terms of a globalisation theory which assumes an unequal and binary relationship between the West and the Rest, but rather through recourse of contemporary theories of glocalisation. Glocalisation theory argues that we need to consider spatiality and the local/locale over temporality and the global which are associated with theories and debates around globalisation. As Robertson points out, 'we do not so much live in a global age as a number of social scientists, historians and others have recently argued . . . as a glocal one – an age in which the quotidian, *reflexive* synthesis of the local and the global is an ever-present feature and, also, a dilemma of most of human life' (2005).

In discussing the process of cultural translation Chow points out that the word *translation* is linked to both 'tradition' and 'betrayal' (2010a: 154). She warns against getting caught up in questions of authenticity and the 'ideology' of fidelity (2010a: 155), of repeating the colonial moment through the valorisation of a culture than no longer exists, and nostalgia for a traditional culture which ignores the history of oppression and repression that defines that culture. 'Cultural translation', she writes, 'needs to be rethought as the co-temporal exchange and connection between different social groups deploying different sign systems that may not be synthesizable to one particular model of language or representation' (2010a: 166). It is in these terms that I want to argue that pan-Asian gothic functions as an exemplary example of globalgothic, in that it takes us outside a binary system which sees non-Western gothic forms as pale imitations of Western gothic. As we have seen, both *Kwaidan* and *A Tale of Two Sisters* problematise the idea of an indigenous gothic that is defined in terms of a poor copy of Western forms of gothic. Instead both films foreground the imbrication of the local in the global and the global in the local. The primacy of to-be-looked-at-ness as a manner by which former colonial nations (whether it is physical or psychical) redefine their identities outside of the colonial moment by acknowledging their status of object of the gaze of the Other points to the complexities and contradictions in thinking through manifestations of the gothic as either purely indigenous cultural artefacts or pale imitations of an original Western (global) gothic. The display of self-Orientalism as demonstrated by *Kwaidan* and *A Tale of Two Sisters*, the holding up of visuality both as resistance to the logic of domination and as acquiescence to its 'to-be-looked-at-ness', necessitates a different way of thinking about the gothic on a global scale. This way of thinking is best exemplified by the concept of globalgothic, which is not based upon the relationship between an original and a copy but rather seeks to understand the gothic in a global/glocal sense in order to produce new readings and critical strategies appropriate to the contemporary world.

References

Balmain, Colette. 2008. *Introduction to Japanese Horror Film*. Edinburgh: Edinburgh University Press.

Berry, Chris. 2007. 'Scream and scream again: Korean modernity as a house of horrors in the films of Kim Ki-young'. In *Seoul Searching: Culture and Identity in Contemporary Korean Cinema*, ed. Frances Gateward. Binghamton: SUNY Press, 99–114.

Chow, Rey. 2010a. 'Film as ethnography; or, translation between cultures in a post-colonial world'. In *The Rey Chow Reader*, ed. Paul Bowman. New York: Columbia University Press, 148–71.

——. 2010b. 'From writing diaspora: Introduction to leading questions'. In *The Rey Chow Reader*, ed. Paul Bowman. New York: Columbia University Press, 30–47.

Cieko, Anne. 2006. 'Theorizing Asian cinema(s)'. In *Contemporary Asian Cinema*, ed. Anne Cieko. Oxford: Berg, 13–31.

Hearn, Lafcadio. 1900. *Shadowings*. Boston: Little, Brown.

——. 1902. *Kotto: Being Japanese Curios, with Sundry Cobwebs*. Boston: Little, Brown.

——. 1903. *Kwaidan: Stories and Studies of Strange Things*. Boston: Little, Brown.

Iwabuchi, Koichi. 2002. *Recentering Globalization: Popular Culture and Japanese Transnationalism*. Durham, NC: Duke University Press

Iwabuchi, Kochi, Stephen Muecke and Mandy Thomas. 2004. 'Introduction: Siting Asian cultural flows'. In *Rogue Flows: Trans-Asian Cultural Traffic*, eds Kochi Iwabuchi, Stephen Muecke and Mandy Thomas. Hong Kong: Hong Kong University Press, 1–10.

Kendall, Laurel. 1984. 'Wives, lesser wives, and ghosts: Supernatural conflict in a Korean Village'. *Asian Folklore Studies*, 43.2: 215–25.

Kubota, Ryuko. 1998. 'Ideologies of English in Japan'. *World Englishes*, 17.3: 295–306.

Mitchell, Tony. 2004. 'Self-orientalism, reverse orientalism and Pan-Asian pop cultural flows in Dick Lee's *Transit Lounge*'. In *Rogue Flows: Trans-Asian Cultural Traffic*, eds Kochi Iwabuchi, Stephen Muecke and Mandy Thomas. Hong Kong: Hong Kong University Press, 95–118.

Napier, Susan J. 1996. *The Fantastic in Modern Japanese Literature: The Subversion of Modernity*. London: Routledge.

Richie, Donald. 1997. *Lafcadio Hearn's Japan*. Singapore: Tuttle.

Standish, Isolde. 2006. *A New History of Japanese Cinema*. New York: Continuum.

Wee, C. J. W. L. 2004. 'Imagining "New Asia" in the Theatre' In *Rogue Flows: Trans-Asian Cultural Traffic*, eds Kochi Iwabuchi, Stephen Muecke and Mandy Thomas. Hong Kong: Hong Kong University Press, 119–51.

Internet sources

Bowman, Dean. 2007. *'Kwaidan'. Midnight Eye*. 3 July. www.midnighteye.com/reviews/kwaidan.shtml. Accessed 15 February 2012.

Dupuy, Coralline. 2007. 'Why don't you remember? Are you crazy? Korean Gothic and psychosis in *A Tale of Two Sisters*'. *Irish Journal of Gothic and Horror Studies*, 3. November. http://irishgothichorrorjournal.homestead.com/taleoftwosisters.html. Accessed 10 February 2011.

Latour, Bruno. 2005. 'On the difficulty of being glocal'. *ART-e-FACT: STRATEGIES OF RESISTANCE. An online magazine for contemporary art \& culture* 4. http://artefact.mi2.hr/_a04/lang_en/index_en.htm. Accessed 15 February 2012.

Paquet, Darcy. 2004. 'Korean main essay. April 2004'. *Essays from the Far East Film Festival*. http://koreanfilm.org/feff.html. Accessed 15 February 2012.

Pym, Anthony. 2004. 'Localization from the perspective of translation studies'. http://www.elda.org/en/proj/scalla/SCALLA2004/Pymv2.pdf. Accessed 10 February 2011.

Robertson, Roland. 2005. 'The conceptual promise of glocalization: Commonality and diversity'. *ART-e-FACT: STRATEGIES OF RESISTANCE. An online magazine for contemporary art \& culture* 4. http://artefact.mi2.hr/_a04/lang_en/theory_robertson_en.htm. Accessed 22 January 2012.

'The Truth of Korean Movies'. 2009. *Korean Film Archive*: www.koreafilm.org/feature/ans_21.asp. Accessed 15 February 2012.

Filmography

Audition. 1999. Takashi Miike, dir. AFDF.

A Devilish Homicide (*Salinma*). 1965. Lee Yong-min, dir. Jeil Films.

The Ghost Story of Yotsuya (*Tokaido Yotsuya kaidan*) 1959. Nobuo Nakagawa, dir. Shintoho.

Kwaidan (*Kaidan*). 1964. Masaki Kobayashi, dir. Toho.

Rashomon. 1950. Akira Kurosawa, dir. Daiei Films.

A Tale of Two Sisters (*Janghwa, Hongryeon*). 2003. Kim Jee-woon, dir. Cineclik Asia.

The Uninvited. 2009. Charles and Thomas Guard, dirs. Dreamworks.

The Wedding Day (*Sijibganeun nal*). 1956. Lee Byeong-il, dir. Dong A Films.

Whispering Corridors (*Yeogogoedam*). 1998. Park Ki-hyeong, dir. Cinema Service.

10

Glennis Byron

Cannibal culture: Serving the people in Fruit Chan's *Dumplings*

> the central feature of global culture today is the politics of the mutual effort of sameness and difference to cannibalize one another
>
> Arjun Appadurai, *Modernity at Large*

Identity politics has been the primary focus of Hong Kong films and film studies since the early 1990s, engaging with anxieties about the Handover, about 'going home' to a world both alien and familiar. In the run up to the Handover the situation appeared unique. As Ackbar Abbas observed, 'The colonized state, while politically subordinate, is in many crucial respects not in a dependent subaltern position, but is in fact more advanced – in terms of education, technology, access to international networks and so forth – than the colonizing state' (1993: 4).

With the growing relaxation of immigration laws after Handover in 1997, there was a gradual integration of capitalist Hong Kong and socialist China, with residents of Hong Kong visiting or moving to the mainland to take advantage of its resources and cheap labour, and a daily quota of mainlanders being given a one-way permit into Hong Kong. The official rhetoric of 'one country, two systems' was increasingly challenged. At the same time, in the wake of the success of J-Horror, the Hong Kong horror industry was revived, with many films focusing on the reworking of traditional Chinese stories and beliefs in order to revisit identity politics in the context of a post-Handover Hong Kong.

Fruit Chan's *Dumplings* has been one of the most commercially successful of these films, and, by the time it was produced in 2004, the situation Abbas described was no longer quite so clear: administrative borders, as the opening scene of *Dumplings* makes clear with Mei moving her raw materials from Shenzhen to Hong Kong with such ease, were no longer such a sign of division. What makes this particular film of interest in terms of the globalgothic is the way it sets up only to challenge the familiar categories of East and West, tradition and modernity, around which Hong Kong identity politics centred, terms which the conditions of globalisation render meaningless. Simultaneously, through the trope of cannibalism, *Dumplings* critiques globalisation, showing Hong Kong and China merging together, equally driven by the prevailing imperative of the global economy: consumption. Before looking specifically at the film, however, I want to offer a context for my reading of *Dumplings* by looking at some of the ways in which Handover led to the exploitation of such categories as East and West, tradition and modernity, both in demonising China and in promoting Hong Kong.

The death of Hong Kong

Following the Sino-British Joint Declaration of 1994, agreeing that sovereignty would be returned to China in 1997, the future of Hong Kong as a key global city, to use the term later coined by Saskia Sassen, no longer seemed assured. Indeed, for some Handover looked set to be, as the title of a now notorious *Fortune* magazine cover story boldly announced in June 1995, 'The death of Hong Kong' (Kraar, 1995). Under Chinese rule, the article claimed, Hong Kong would lose its role as an international commercial and financial hub: 'The naked truth about Hong Kong's future can be summed up in two words: It's over' (Kraar, 1995).

Almost twelve years to the day later, *Fortune*'s headline told a different story: 'Oops!': 'Well, we were wrong' (Prasso, 2007). Oops indeed. Not only did Hong Kong continue to grow as an international hub but the annual 'Globalization Index' released by Ernst and Young in January 2011 shows that Hong Kong has now overtaken Singapore to become the most globalised economy in the world, ranking first out of the world's sixty largest economies in openness to trade, capital movements and cultural integration (Ernst & Young, 2011).

While *Fortune* may have proved to be spectacularly and oracularly unreliable in this instance, the article nevertheless neatly encapsulates in its discourse some of the major concerns dominating the debates in the run up to Handover. What Abbas saw as unique and problematic, *Fortune* recontains with some comfortably familiar categories: West and East, civilised and primitive, modernity and tradition, global and local. Here it is not the local that is under threat, condemned to be chewed up in the global maw and regurgitated as commodity; rather, the horror of horrors from the perspective of the global economy is the prospect of the 'best city in the world for business' (and I am unable to stop myself from hearing echoes of Brett Easton Ellis's 1991 *American Psycho* here) being dragged back into some kind of primitive violent and chaotic morass (Kraar, 1995). The 'dominant use of English, the universal language of business', *Fortune* warned, would 'give way to far more extensive reliance on Cantonese and Mandarin'. Corruption would take root and spread as Hong Kong became a 'global backwater', and all the connotations of the uncivilised and primitive here are gothickally emphasised with echoes of marauding *banditti*: 'Troops of the People's Liberation Army, which has already formed links with the powerful local criminal gangs known as "triads", will stroll the streets' (Kraar, 1995). Lock up your daughters, please.

Cannibalism and China

Around the same time as *Fortune* was prematurely lamenting the demise of Western civilisation in Hong Kong, fears of Chinese influence were also evident in the revival of the old urban myths about China's supposed cannibalistic practices which began to proliferate on the internet. One of the most disturbing of all these purportedly originated with the now defunct Hong Kong *Eastern Express* in 1994. An article in this English-language newspaper entitled 'Aborted babies sold as health food for $10' supposedly accused Chinese doctors in Shenzhen of foetal cannibalism, of eating and selling foetuses as being good for the skin and general health.[1]

The story assumed increasingly fantastic proportions on the internet, with reports of foetal soup being on the menu in Chinese restaurants. Various unpleasant images and videos were circulated around the world, mostly by individual blogs and email. Many of the images were actually taken from the work of a Beijing performance artist, Zhu Yu, and his show 'Eating People', but the rumours nevertheless continued, and the gullible expressed their outrage.[2] Echoes of walled-up pregnant nuns, these stories rehearse the tired old dialectic of inclusion and exclusion which represents China as barbaric and the West as the site of civilisation and modernity. As one of the last remaining taboos, cannibalism is exploited to insist on absolute difference, to construct and define 'us', the civilised, in opposition to 'them', the primitive.

Brand Hong Kong

While such strategies insist on absolute difference in constructions of East and West in order to demonise China, with Hong Kong difference is usually celebrated, particularly in official and tourist representations. Hong Kong's uniqueness, its attraction, is seen as having much to do with the bringing together of two different worlds. As Abbas observes, Hong Kong is usually represented as 'an East-West city, mixing tradition and modernity like memory and desire' (1994: 445). This, he notes, is enshrined in 'one of the most durable images about Hong Kong', the 'Chinese junk in Victoria Harbour against a backdrop of tall modernistic buildings' – an image, he adds, which 'manages to make a complex space disappear into a one-dimensional image, structured on a facile binarism' (445).

This insistence on Hong Kong as 'an East-West city' is particularly notable post-Handover in the government's 'Brand Hong Kong' initiative, launched in 2001. Here there is an insistence on Hong Kong as a global city, on its modernity and transnationalism: it is 'Asia's World City' as the tag line to the brand logo declares. But simultaneously there is an insistence on what could loosely be considered the 'local' or tradition and the past. Brand Hong Kong's dragon image is intended both to show the continuing link with a historical and cultural icon, to combine modernity and antiquity, and to symbolise the meeting of East and West: the image originally incorporated both the Chinese characters for Hong Kong and the English letters H and K, although these were removed when the brand was updated in 2010. China is still associated with tradition, with the past, Hong Kong with the combination of East and West, with the West representing the modern world. It is, as the tourist board announces: 'A dynamic international metropolis steeped in unique blends of East and West' (Discover Hong Kong).

Fruit Chan's *Dumplings*

Dumplings frequently challenges such official promotions of Hong Kong. While it contains few of the standard short cuts to visually representing the city, when such shots do occur they introduce moments of disturbance. This is shown, for example, in a scene which gestures towards that familiar image of the skyline of Hong Kong harbour with the Chinese junk foregrounded. We begin placed as though for the full tourist experience, in the tram coming down from the wealthy heights of Victoria Peak, and the camera then veers upwards to land us on the top of a luxury high rise hotel offering the traditional view of the skyscrapers across the harbour. But although we see water, which initially produces the illusion we are seeing the harbour, a swimmer soon appears to make it clear it is just the hotel swimming pool. And instead of a traditional boat the wealthy businessman Mr Li is foregrounded. The scene is defamiliarised to question official representations, to suggest they may be equally deceptive and hold little relevance for the modern world.

While this may initially imply the local being replaced by the global, *Dumplings* actually works to confound any such easy distinctions. The only vestiges of a traditional China in this scene are reminiscent of what Arif Dirlik has described as the local as object of the operations of capital, where the 'features of the local' are recognized only to 'incorporate localities into the imperatives of the global' (1996: 34). To return to Brand Hong Kong for a moment, this can also be seen in the extensive guidelines designed to protect the identity of the brand: the logo cannot be changed although there is, the guidelines hasten to add, some flexibility in the specifications to allow it to be used in different situations. 'The Dragon symbol may be used on its own in special circumstances. Examples include gift boxes, watches, lapel pins, etc. In such cases, the Dragon can be reproduced as an engraving, etching, foil stamping, etc.' (Brand Hong Kong). One does not, after all, want to be too particular when there is money to be made. In the high-rise scene in *Dumplings*, whatever might be seen as the local in this scene on top of the high-rise turns out to be a global product. It is something used decoratively, as in the dragons on the fountains, or to serve the 'imperatives of the global' in other ways (Dirlik, 1996: 34). Most notably, this is demonstrated when Mr Li proceeds to crack open and eat the contents of a duck egg with a well-developed embryo, believing this will restore his youthfulness and potency. The scene also suggests what we are soon to find out, that the magic ingredient in the rejuvenating dumplings Mrs Li buys from Mei is a human foetus.

The screenwriter Lilian Lee, who also wrote the novella upon which the film is based, is very likely drawing ironically upon some of the outrageous stories circulating on the internet at the time. Nevertheless,

Dumplings, as the almost obscene slurping and crunching that so often dominates the soundtrack seems to emphasise, appropriates cannibalism as a rhetorical trope. Everything to do with foetal cannibalism is exaggerated in the film to the extent that it becomes, while still repulsive, blackly comedic and unreal: we cringe as we laugh. The trope is used for political critique, and for this there is indeed a long-established tradition in China, as in, for example, Lu Xun's 'Diary of a Madman' (1918), considered the beginning of modern Chinese literature. 'Diary of a Madman' attacks the oppressive nature of traditional Chinese Confucian culture as a 'man-eating' society where the strong devour the weak in an endless cannibalistic banquet. Behind the façade of virtues and proprieties, Lu Xun suggests, barbarism and civilisation become two sides of one coin. And the last line of his story, 'Save the children', assumes particular resonance in the context of *Dumplings*.

As so often today, in *Dumplings* cannibalism is turned around, and, rather than being used to construct the primitive, is instead used to condemn a world driven by consumption, by the prevailing imperative of the global economy. While cannibalism depends upon and enforces absolute division, Maggie Kilgour has argued, because of the 'uncanny relatedness between the body of the self and the body of the other it also dissolv[es] the structure it appears to produce' (1990: 148). China/Hong Kong, tradition/modernity, East/West: all these categories break down in the common drive to consume.

The dissolution of difference is given form in the film through the characters of Mei and Mrs Li. Mei, a sixty-four-year-old with the face and body of a thirty-something, initially might seem to be a ghost of the past. Formerly an abortionist with the PRC, she is a mainlander who attained residency in Hong Kong. Unable to continue practising legitimately as a doctor, she now practises her own version of traditional sympathetic medicine. This, along with such other details as the fact that the actress speaks Mandarin, the official state language, while the others speak Cantonese, and that she sings a supposedly nostalgic revolutionary song, would appear to identify Mei with the Chinese past, with the world of tradition, and she exploits this as giving veracity to her claims for her dumplings: tradition gives her sales talk a boost.

Mrs Li's first visit to Mei also suggests a movement into this older world. The public housing estate is old, run down, utilitarian militaristic numbers stamped upon each block. The ageing Chinese resident here reflects both the future she fears – ageing – and the past with which, we are led to assume, she will soon connect. A series of visual signs relating to beauty technology suggest that the higher Mrs Li climbs towards Mei's flat the closer she comes to the practices of this past. She asks for directions in a hairdresser's shop, full of old and rather dangerous-looking dryers. Then someone is shown practising 'threading', perhaps the most ancient method of hair removal, with the customer's face covered with pearl powder, used for centuries to produce a brighter and more youthful skin. The final step is into Mei's barred flat, and into the world of cannibalism, according to Mei one of China's most ancient traditions.

But as the repeated camera shots that linger on the figurines displayed in her flat suggest, Mei is far more than a figure of the past. Mao figurines mingle with the Daoist goddess of nativity and mercy, revolutionary peasants consort with the Virgin Mary, and the ancient Japanese lucky 'welcoming cat' sits down with Hello Kitty. Mei, this seems to suggest, will exploit whatever ideology serves her best. She is not just part of China's planned economy past, she is the product of the new China, of the new market economy; she is still, in the words of Mao's directive, serving the people, but now in response to market forces rather than government controls. Mei exploits both the Chinese mainlanders who abort under the one child policy and the rich Hong Kong socialites, processing the waste products of the former to capitalise on the desires of the latter for youth and beauty. Thoroughly adapted to the new market economy, she understands supply and demand, and where there is desire there is snake oil. The history of cannibalism in China that she delivers to Mr Li is nothing but sales talk. She relies on his gullibility and his ignorance of a China that is, for him, a mythical entity. The supposed local once again is nothing more than a commodity to exploit. Even the revolutionary song she sings is integrated into her sales pitch.

It is particularly significant that Mei cooks up the human foetus in the form of dumplings, something unfortunately rather lost in translation. The original title is 饺子 jiǎozǐ (Mandarin/pinyin) or Gaau ji (Cantonese), the word for the crescent-shaped dumplings that Mei serves. Jiǎozǐ has the shape of ancient *yuan bao* (gold or silver ingots) and the pronunciation takes after the word for the earliest paper money that first appeared in China in the tenth century ('Traditions concerning money'). The word consequently links the most traditional of all Chinese foods with the capitalist world, confounding any easy distinctions between tradition and modernity.

The film also breaks down difference in the way it connects Mei, as new China, with Mrs Li, representative of Hong Kong, something effected primarily through the film's use of space, mirrors and reflections. The women are initially distinguished by both the clothes they wear and their body language. Mei is confident, flexible and comfortable in her body: her clothes are casual and chaotic; Mrs Li is uncomfortable with herself, and, despite the expensive perfectly matched rigouts, appears frumpish. Where they do not differ is in their apparent age, and when Mei asks her to guess how old she is, as the camera moves in a shot-reverse-shot from one woman's face to the other, their skin appears much the same. Many reviewers expressed puzzlement over the casting and presentation of the pop singer Miriam Yeung as Mrs Li, since she is actually eight years younger than Bai Ling, the actress who plays Mei. But this seems to be the point. Mrs Li is already youthful; what she lacks is confidence and control. There is absolutely no physical change in her as a result of consuming the dumplings, except that her clothing seems to become slightly less frumpy: at one point she even sports the colourful leggings that come to be associated with Mei. Such signs suggest a slow seduction, a seduction that will conclude with Mrs Li becoming Mei. The film suggests that the only difference is that Mei has power, and Mrs Li's change is only psychological: she thinks she is gaining power through a new youthfulness, and so behaves accordingly, and therefore confirming, if not in the way we originally understood it, Mei's promotional claim that, if a woman wants to rejuvenate, she has to start from the inside.

Mrs Li's first taste of the dumplings shows awareness of what she is consuming; only her desperate need to retain her philandering husband allows her to control her revulsion. She has clandestinely gone to a place she finds abhorrent in order to carry out an act she finds abhorrent, committed herself to a Faustian pact. Increasing complicity and the erosion of scruples are suggested both through the manipulation of space and through the use of reflection. Mrs Li, while curious, is protected from seeing what she is eating in its recognisable form by the wall dividing the kitchen from the living room. But the barriers are flimsy, like the many curtains shown which barely offer concealment. There is one point when Mei crosses the boundary of the kitchen and confronts Mrs Li with the tiny orange foetus, but the film nevertheless initially underplays the relatedness of foetus and human and, with such images as Mei eating orange melon balls, rather connects foetus with food. Seduction is an incremental process, and after each swallow Mrs Li becomes more accepting. As she develops a psychological and physical addiction and demands the 'potent stuff', the five-month-old foetus that will speed up the process, her increasing need propels her past the barrier of reluctance. This is a moment emphasised by a close-up of her stiletto-clad foot stepping into the kitchen. At this point both Mrs Li and the audience for the first time see the foetus not only in its original unminced and uncooked form but also at a stage when the visual connection with the human form is quite evident. What Kilgour describes as 'the uncanny relatedness between the body of the self and the body of the other' is made all too clear.

Mrs Li runs, repulsed and close to vomiting in the gutter outside. Kristeva's abjection might initially come to mind here.[3] But it is significant that she controls this; she purges only her remaining scruples, and returns. At this moment the blind man who appears to turn to look at her as she turns to look up to Mei's flat suggests her own willed moral blindness, and the dissolution of the difference between the two women begins to be enacted visually. In one of many important mirror shots Mei is reflected caressing her body as Mrs Li returns. It is a key transitional moment as the two women turn in a synchronised movement to look at the foetus, now shown in a dish in a manner suggestive of the most familiar representation of the embryo in the womb. With a disturbing shift in camera angle we see the complicity of the two women as though from the view of the foetus. 'It was a boy' says Mei, showing the penis, 'a boy', echoes Mrs Li. Life and the dumpling are commodities and the boy child gold.

This time the dumplings are served in the circular pattern traditionally used to represent family reunion. Apart from the obvious irony of a 'family reunion' involving the actual consumption of the child, there is also the suggestion of the reunion of child with motherland, of Hong Kong with China, of Mrs Li and Mei. Mrs Li's psychological change is confirmed as she soon reproduces the distinctive self-caressing gesture of Mei. But the fact that the change is really only on the inside is also confirmed by the stench that subsequently comes from her body, a stench that, like her rashes and headaches, identifies an inner corruption. When Mei, fearing arrest, is forced to make a quick exit back to mainland China, she leaves behind the cleaver used in her preparations. In the penultimate scene the identification of the two women becomes complete as Mrs Li wipes the cleaver, preparing to cut up the five-month-old foetus of her husband's mistress, and as she swings down the cleaver and the blood splashes up on her face, the soundtrack plays the music of the revolutionary song Mei sings.

The film, then, ultimately suggests that the simple binaries of East and West, tradition and modernity, have no relevance in contemporary Hong Kong. In a decidedly negative portrayal of the new society, the film through the merging of identities shows China as learning to incorporate the pragmatic and cultural elements of Hong Kong while insidiously corrupting, imparting its own value system into the growing collective identity that will quickly become China, not Hong Kong and China. While Mei is ultimately forced to return to mainland China, to the 'motherland' as the shot of her moving through the tunnel might emphasise, it really does not matter any more: she can work both worlds: her lunch box and frying pan will serve her equally well.

Notes

1 I must add that I have seen no evidence for the existence of this article, simply 'reproduced excerpts' on various websites, and the few critics who have mentioned the article have not been able to provide exact details about its publication. As far as I can see, its very existence is questionably tied up in urban myth.
2 For more on Zhu Yu, and his show 'Eating People', see Rojas, 2002.
3 Emile Yueh-yu Yeh and Neda Hei-tung Ng (2009) do read *Dumplings* in terms of Kristeva's abject and the China/mother – Hong Kong/child relationship.

References

Abbas, Ackbar. 1993. 'The last emporium: verse and cultural space'. *positions*, 1.1: 1–23.

——. 1994. 'Building on disappearance: Hong Kong architecture and the city'. *Public Culture*, 6: 441–59.

Appadurai, Arjun. 1996. *Modernity at Large: Cultural Dimensions of Globalization*. Minneapolis: University of Minnesota Press.

Dirlik, Arif. 1996. 'The global in the local'. In *Global/Local: Cultural Production and the Transnational Imaginary*, eds Rob Wilson and Wimial Dissanayake. Durham, NC: Duke University Press, 21–45.

Kilgour, Maggie. 1990. *From Communion to Cannibalism: An Anatomy of Metaphors of Incorporation*. Princeton: Princeton University Press.

Sassen, Saskia. 2001. *The Global City: New York, London, Tokyo*. Princeton: Princeton University Press.

Xun, Lu. 1990 (1918). *'Diary of a Madman' and Other Stories*, trans. William A Lyell. Honolulu: University of Hawaii Press.

Yeh, Emilie Yueh-yu, and Neda Hei-tung Ng. 2009. 'Magic, medicine, cannibalism: The China demon in Hong Kong horror'. In *Horror to the Extreme: Changing Boundaries in Asian Cinema*, eds Jinhee Choi and Mitsuyo Wada-Marciano. Hong Kong: Hong Kong University Press, 145–60.

Internet sources

Brand Hong Kong. www.brandhk.gov.hk/. Accessed 7 September 2010.

Discover Hong Kong: Official Travel Guide. www.discoverhongkong.com/eng/. Accessed 8 September 2011.

Ernst & Young. 2011. 'Hong Kong tops the globalization index'. Press Release, 24 January. www.ey.com/CN/en/Newsroom/News-releases/2011_Hong-Kong-tops-The-Globalization-Index. Accessed 5 September 2011.

Kraar, Louis. 1995. 'The death of Hong Kong'. *Fortune Magazine,* 26 June. http://money.cnn.com/magazines/fortune/fortune_archive/1995/06/26/203948/index.htm. Accessed 5 September 2011.

Prasso, Sheridan. 2007. 'Oops. Hong Kong is hardly dead'. *Fortune Magazine,* 9 July. http://money.cnn.com/magazines/fortune/fortune_archive/2007/07/09/100122332/index.htm. Accessed 5 September 2011.

Rojas, Carlos. 2002. 'Cannibalism and the Chinese body politic: hermeneutics and violence in cross-cultural perception'. *Postmodern Culture,* 21.3. http://pmc.iath.virginia.edu/text-only/issue.502/12.3rojas.txt. Accessed 1 August 2010.

'Traditions concerning money'. Travel China Guide. www.travelchinaguide.com/intro/focus/currency5.htm. Accessed 6 September 2011.

Filmography

Dumplings. 2004. Fruit Chan, dir. Applause Pictures.

11

Katarzyna Ancuta

Ghost skins: Globalising the supernatural in contemporary Thai horror film

One of the most prolific of film genres since the early days of cinema, horror is also one of the major forms in which the gothic was manifested in the twentieth century and can be found in virtually every cinema of the world. As the genre developed, it has shown an increasing 'intensification of global interconnectedness', demonstrated in those 'persistent cultural interactions and exchange' that Jonathan Xavier Inda and Renato Rosaldo note are entailed in current definitions of globalisation (2008: 4). But does this mean that we can stipulate the existence of a separate category of globalgothic horror and, if so, what would be the potential consequences? The case of Thai horror cinema is a good starting point for discussion, since both 'gothic' and 'horror' are labels foreign to the Thai language, suggesting that what we identify as Thai horror cinema evolved on its own, local terms. Still, there is no denying that the increasing globalisation of the Thai economy and, in consequence, the Thai film industry has had a strong impact on contemporary Thai horror films, affecting not only their production and distribution methods but also their themes, their representations of the uncanny and, more generally, their basic narrative structures.

This chapter discusses the effects of globalisation on the changing cinematic representation of the central local figure of fear, the spirit of the violently dead, or *phii tai hong*, and examines the potential of contemporary Thai horror film to redefine its supernatural characters as 'global ghosts'. My primary example is Sophon Sukdapisit's debut feature *Coming Soon* (*Program na vinyan arkhad*), released in Thailand in 2008. Sukdapisit's flirtation with horror started when he co-wrote the highly successful Thai horror film *Shutter* (*Shutter got tit vinyan*, 2004) with its directors, Parkpoom Wongpoom and Banjong Pisanthanakun, and then wrote the script for their second film, *Alone* (*Fad*), in 2007. By the start of June 2011 Sukdapisit's *Ladda Land* (2011) had become the highest grossing Thai horror production ever, with box-office figures reaching almost US$4 million in Thailand alone.[1]

Scare locally sell globally

Thai horror films, known in Thai as *nung phii*, or ghost films, can roughly be divided into three groups. The most local category comprises horror comedies, featuring specifically Thai spiritual entities, such as *phii krasue* (the filth-eating spirit in the shape of a flying female head with entrails) or *phii pob* (the liver-devouring hungry ghost), whose representations do not fare well beyond Thailand, or South-East Asia. Thai horror comedies utilise local modes of narrative and frequently rely on the personal charisma of local comedians, the value of which is usually lost on outsiders. The second group comprises Thai gore films with stories of Khmer black magic used as an excuse for plots featuring graphic bodily destruction. Often hastily made low-budget productions, these films seldom reach the standards that would allow them to sell on international markets. The final group consists of films about vengeful spirits of the violently dead, or *phii tai hong*, the most terrifying of Thai ghosts. These are the most 'serious' of all domestic horror productions, and the closest to what a non-Thai audience would usually expect of a horror film.

The Thai understanding of the horror genre is clearly not completely compatible with definitions typically found in film theory textbooks, even if to a certain extent the two overlap. This contradicts the popular assumption that peripheral cinema evolves mostly through the process of copying and mimicking successful mainstream Western productions which, being crucial vehicles of globalisation, facilitate the one-sided economic and cultural transfer from the centre/West to the periphery. Although it is hard to deny that 'there is indeed a power geometry to the processes of globalization' (Inda and Rosaldo, 2008: 15), the Thai case demonstrates that the periphery talks back: 'foreign cultural forms . . . become customized . . . interpreted, translated, and appropriated according to local conditions of reception' (Inda and Rosaldo, 2008: 18). The local becomes 'the place where global flows are consumed, incorporated, and resisted . . . where the global flows fragment and are transformed into something place bound and particular' (Tsing, 2008: 77).

The two basic effects of globalisation, unification and fragmentation (Kinnvall, 2002: 5), in a sense define contemporary Thai cinema as it struggles to secure its position in the world. Since 1997 Thai cinema has received international recognition, with Thai films winning prestigious awards at international festivals, finding international distributors and selling on international markets. It is also plain to see that, while avant-garde festival films enjoy the attention of the critics, the real marketability of Thai films is measured by distribution contracts which tend to favour genre films, horror and martial arts action in particular. Nonzee Nimibutr's *Nang Nak* (1999), the story of a devoted ghost-wife who refuses to abandon her husband after her death, set a box-office record for a Thai production and received wide international exposure through the festival circuit (Chaiworaporn and Knee, 2006: 62). It was also the first Thai film to find an international distributor. The director of *Ong Bak* (2003), Prachya Pinkaew, recalls:

> the success of *Nang Nak* was a turning point for Thai cinema, as investors started getting interested in investing their money in the film production. The film . . . became the first Thai film to sell abroad. It was the first time I heard that Thai films can sell. *Nang Nak* was bought by a foreign distributor. I don't know how much they paid for it but I know it was very little. But all the Thai directors were really happy – we had hope that Thai films could sell. (Pinkaew, 2007: 87)

Chaiworaporn and Knee attribute the success of *Nang Nak* to its ability to compete with Hollywood productions at home by 'employing higher production values than those associated with Thai horror films in decades past while simultaneously making use of indigenous story materials' (2006: 62). A similar strategy – local content with Western mode of production – was employed by the makers of the most internationally known Thai horror film to date, *Shutter*, the only Thai film credited with its own Hollywood remake. What seems different in this case, however, is that the enthusiastic reception of *Shutter* outside Thailand owed much to the increased appetites of global horror audiences for Asian horror films, spawned by the boom of Japanese horror in the early 2000s. Well aware of the phenomenon, the makers of *Shutter* did not shy away from J-Horror references, a strategy they repeated later in *Alone*, but this time with reference to Korean horror. *Shutter*, *Alone* and other recent Thai horror films responded to the local–global dynamics by negotiating the internal and external interpretations of the generic formula in accordance with what Arjun Appadurai calls the global 'politics of the mutual effort of sameness and difference to cannibalize one another' (2008: 59). As a result of that exchange, Thai horror films presented an attractive package of 'the triumphantly universal and the resiliently particular' (Appadurai, 2008: 59) with appeal for both Thai and non-Thai audiences.

Coming Soon by Sophon Sukdapisit is no different in that respect. The film fits well into the local formula, as it tells a simple ghost story that can be interpreted quite literally: an angry ghost of a dead actress materialises in this world to kill those directly and indirectly responsible for her death. At the same time the film invites several more metaphorical interpretations, which can be seen as a sign of the modernisation of Thai horror and a bow towards potential Western viewers, generally stereotyped by Thai film directors as more rational and sophisticated than local audiences. The shift from a literal to a metaphorical reading of the film is made easier by the fact that its plot explores the multilayered concept of cinema, from setting the action in a haunted cinema building, to discussing the filmmaking profession, legal and illegal film distribution and the medium of film itself. By structuring its plot around the concepts of the gaze and perception, with specific instances of seeing, watching, performing, filming, projecting and reproducing often appearing in the context of power and control, *Coming Soon* is haunted by several metaphorical 'ghosts' quite as potent as the literal one.

Much of the metaphorical reading focuses on the complicated relationship between reality and illusion. Seen from this perspective, the medium of film produces 'ghostly' images of life: actors are like 'ghosts' in that they imitate the living through their performance; pirated and legal copies of the film are 'ghosts' of the original; the camera has the power to stop time and capture the 'ghosts' of the living in a glorious, though deathlike moment of immortality. Added to this can be the usual psychoanalytical readings of ghosts in terms of individual guilt (the ghost of the past that represents one's guilty conscience) and national or group trauma (the collective horror fans' guilt for deriving enjoyment from watching graphic accounts of other people's suffering, or the collective Asian or Thai guilt for being amongst the top-ranking nations with regard to film piracy and copyright infringement).

In a typically Thai fashion, the plot of *Coming Soon* overflows with extravagant twists and turns. Sukdapisit presents a three-layered narrative in which 'real-life' events inspire a film that becomes a plot of another film and additionally gets videotaped for the purpose of illegal distribution. The opening scene introduces a deformed madwoman who blinds and kills village children and dies lynched by an angry mob minutes later. The camera then zooms out to reveal a cinema screen and Sukdapisit's audience is thus invited to a private viewing of an upcoming Thai horror film together with its anonymous filmmakers. With the screening still in progress, the ghost of the old woman from the film begins to haunt the theatre premises, eliminating the filmmakers and cinema staff one by one. And yet while initially we are led to believe the film is haunted by the ghost of the madwoman whose life inspired the film within the film, eventually it is revealed that the ghost is actually the vengeful spirit of an unlucky actress who died in an accident on set and whose death throes were edited as part of the picture. Enraged that people want to profit from, or be entertained by, her death, the ghost vows to exact her revenge on the filmmakers, cinema staff, pirates, cinema audience and, as is hinted in the closing scene, future DVD distributors, DVD owners, the audience of Sukdapisit's *Coming Soon* and, by extension, probably also anybody who foolishly decides to write an article about it.

With its Chinese-box narrative structure, *Coming Soon* relies heavily on the repetition and reproduction of genre elements, such as settings, characters or iconography. But as actions get replayed and patterns repeated, the familiar is simultaneously reinforced and reinvented, making room for new interpretations. By focusing his attention on a Thai ghost film as inspiration for his more 'universal' horror film, Sukdapisit distances himself from the local productions, which, ironically, are presented as potentially dangerous and undistributable. At the same time, however, as a cinematic commentary on the Thai directors' plea to protect Thai cinema against piracy, *Coming Soon* remains resiliently local in its interests.

Ghosts in the age of mechanical reproduction

Globalisation is often said to thrive on interconnections, where many things are said 'to circulate, ranging from people to money; cultures to information; and television programs, to international protocols, to the process called globalization itself' (Tsing, 2008: 75). With its ever-increasing scale and speed, and the awareness that the globe is rapidly shrinking (Kinnvall, 2002: 5), global culture relies on technology, implementing a variety of informatisation and digitalisation processes, such as those that allow for replication and reproduction on a mass scale. The two issues that seem particularly relevant for the discussion of Sukdapisit's *Coming Soon* are the notion of content replication – the repetition of ideas, themes and plots within the genre boundaries in Thailand and globally – and the possibility of product duplication – that is, film reproduction for the sake of legal and illegal distribution, specifically in the context of film piracy in Asia.

Akin to pornography, horror does not hide its enthusiastic approach to repetition. Horror sequels play to equally large audiences as horror originals. *Friday the 13th* is currently twelve episodes and counting; *A Nightmare on Elm Street* has its tenth film in the making; the Hong Kong series *Troublesome Night* (*Ying yang lu*) reached nineteen full-length volumes in 2003; and in 2011 Thai fans celebrated the release of the fifteenth part of *Baan Phii Pob*. Horror audiences are the last to protest about plot similarities or repetitive monster designs; in fact, you are more likely to find fan sites with complaints that the werewolf had the wrong teeth, that the vampires glittered, or that the *onryo*[2] had a fringe. Ghost films are no different in this respect, easily replicating culturally specific spirits and localised stories of haunting and retribution. What sets ghosts apart from vampires, werewolves and most other supernatural monsters, however, is the way they function as complex mechanisms for negotiating the fear of death. They are, therefore, inevitably connected with religious viewpoints and culturally shaped concepts of death and the afterlife. Any chance of making ghost films globally successful thus depends on finding ways to reconcile differences in cultural attitudes to ghosts and their representations.

The prevailing acceptance of animistic beliefs and practices in Thailand translates into the common sentiment that ghosts walk among the living on a daily basis. In the eyes of the living, the fact that the realms of the material and the spiritual manage to coexist in relative harmony is evidence that the world of the spirits, like human society, is regulated by a system of laws and rules respected at least by the majority of its inhabitants. These rules, delineating the spirits' appearance, their environment, their habits, potential behaviours and the ways in which they communicate with the living, are passed on from generation to generation in oral lore and reinforced in the form of rituals. Needless to say, to be seen as authentic, cinematic spirits must exhibit the required attributes and adhere to the required rules. And since both are always culturally specific, the more 'correct' the portrayal of indigenous spirits, the more likely it is to alienate or puzzle outsiders.

The ghost in Sukdapisit's *Coming Soon* has been fashioned to fit the

Thai category of *phii tai hong*. *Phii tai hong* are commonly believed to be the most frightening and dangerous of all Thai spirits, since they bear a grudge against the living resulting from the anger and confusion felt at the moment of their untimely death. In Thai beliefs the Keeper of the Dead, *Yom Phraa Baan*, is said to sign a contract with every person, specifying a predestined time to die. In case of premature departure, as a result of accident, suicide or murder, the spirit is forced to remain earthbound until the date the contract runs out (Guelden, 1995: 55). During this time, the ghost receives little sympathy: in Thai culture 'bad death' is believed to be the result of the bad karma one accumulates in one's current and previous lives. Unable to deal with its sudden and often violent death and the indifference of the living, *phii tai hong* is expected to lash out at anyone who happens to be in the vicinity, regardless of whether or not they contributed to its demise.

The ghost in *Coming Soon* died in an accident while shooting a death scene for a film. Using the film to cross over, she can appear everywhere the film is projected and then attach herself to the people she wants to follow. Since the actress died in full character costume and makeup, the ghost retains the appearance of the character, consequently eradicating any potential differences between the actual madwoman lynched, the actress who portrayed her in the film and the traditional anthropomorphic representation of a Thai cinematic vengeful spirit. The ghost first exacts her revenge on the filmmakers who failed to check the safety of the equipment used on set. Then she moves on to pursue the cinema staff, especially those involved with film piracy and the gangsters they work for. The connection is especially obvious in Thai, since pirated films are also commonly called *nung phii* (ghost films), the 'ghostly' attribute here referring to the bad quality of the image rather than the contents. Last but not least, the ghost turns her attention to the cinema audience, with a lack of discrimination characteristic of a grudge-bearing *phii tai hong*.

The fact that the ghost materialises within the medium of film and incorporates its victims into the fabric of the film has one more interesting association in terms of Thai culture. Thai ghost lore contains frequent references to ceremonies involving human sacrifice, in which people are buried alive so that their spirits can guard the foundations of the building (*phii fao luum*) or hidden treasure (*phii fao sab*) for eternity.[3] The concept of a ghost trapped within the very medium of film can be seen as reminiscent of those kinds of sacrifices, especially if the film's plot is read in the context of the intellectual property rights debate that seems to be gaining momentum in Thailand. According to the *Havocscope* online database of black market activities, in 2011 Thailand ranked ninth in the world in terms of countries suffering losses caused by film piracy, with the figures of Bt10–12 billion, or well over US$300 million, a year ('Movie piracy losses by country'). As Thailand remains on the US's 'Priority Watch List' as a country with intellectual property policies that do not meet US standards, local filmmakers and film distributors continue to exert pressure on the Thai government to enforce the law against film piracy.

According to *The Nation*, 'DVD and film piracy [in Thailand] is estimated to be worth more than Bt12 billion a year. The legal DVD market amounts to just 10 per cent of that' (Thongtep, 2011). And, although in the eyes of the public, film piracy in poor countries, such as Thailand, is to a certain extent justified by the high costs of foreign DVDs, it is also clear that Thai films, released without English subtitles, get pirated specifically for the Thai market, showing lack of support of the local film industry. Correcting this behaviour is seen as an absolute priority, even if it involves rather unusual techniques. In 2005 the Ronin Team signed their horror film *Art of the Devil 2* (*Long khong*) with a warning that a Khmer curse will befall anyone who tries to pirate the film and it will haunt them until the day they die. Sukdapisit's sentinel ghost sends a similarly clear message to the viewers of *Coming Soon*: forever bound to the celluloid, she will continue guarding the film against anyone trying to steal it from its rightful owners.

At the same time, however, it is hard to deny that the final words of the ghost, 'Do you want to see me die?', are addressed to the entire audience and that her resentment does not stop at illegal copies of the film but targets the idea of film reproduction as such. In his seminal work on the effects of technology on art appreciation, Walter Benjamin speculated that modern-day reproduction technologies that make a work of art, and especially film, available to mass audiences produce a change in the mode of participation: concentration is replaced by distraction, and films, seen as not requiring attention, play to the absent-minded audience (Benjamin, 1998: 249). In 'the global culture of the hyperreal' (Appadurai, 2008: 49), film and its digitalised duplicates are more commonly *consumed* than *appreciated* by their audience, ready to move on to another item on the list even before the credits have rolled. The mystical 'aura' of the work of art, of which Benjamin wrote, disappears; there is nothing unique in the experience. The life and death of an actress who died for the sake of the film is completely meaningless to the audience. The ghost within the film is but an illusion of a ghost.

Generating global ghosts

In their function as complex mechanisms for coping with death, ghosts are necessarily culture-bound. The search for 'global ghosts', a brand of 'new cross-cultural monstrosities' produced in the process of 'the literature and film of different countries feeding off each other' (Byron, 2008: 33), must begin by locating the common denominator universalising the ghostly experience. To do so we need to examine the visual representation of ghosts and their functions in the supernatural narrative. A cross-cultural dualistic construction of life after death involves anthropomorphisation of the afterlife and its inhabitants based on the projection of the patterns of the living and their categories and relations in this world on to the next and is prone to further rationalisation to include significant differences allowing people to distinguish between the two dimensions (Berta, 2007). An example of such a rationalisation would be the custom of 'feeding the dead'. While in many cultures food offerings are given to the deceased, they are expected not actually to consume the food in its earthly form like ordinary humans but rather to feed on its smoke or essence. A semiotic analysis of ghost films, however, reveals that, while Asian films visualise their ghosts as iconic representations of the living, Western productions prefer to capitalise on the SFX- and CGFX-enhanced symbolic or indexical representations of difference. The Western ghost was originally conceived of as a revenant, 'a corporeal creature, a substantial person acting like a human being because he or she is to all appearances a human being, though one returned from the Otherworld' (Buchan, 1986: 145), and this image was strengthened by nineteenth-century exercises in spectral photography. However, their subsequent characterisation as 'imaginary' and 'irrational' has made it somewhat obligatory to visualise them as immaterial creatures beyond human physicality. And yet the cross-cultural success of such films as *The Sixth Sense* (1999) and *The Others* (2001) proves that the anthropomorphic image of the ghost is likely to be accepted by any audience.

This brings into discussion the function of ghosts within the narrative structure. Among the classic reasons why ghosts choose to cling on to the scraps of their former existence are the dead person's need to reveal the cause of his or her death, to bring the guilty party to justice or help the living cope with grief (Buchan, 1986: 147, 154). Underlying all these is the fear of the fallibility of memory, the dread that one day we will all be forgotten, together with our achievements and misfortunes. Thai ghosts additionally perform two more culturally specific functions: they protect and grant favours to their family members and they act as agents of retribution. The first function, derived from the Chinese cult of ancestors which assumes the continuity of the family irrespective of whether its members are dead or alive, positions ghosts as family elders and spiritual protectors that have every right to influence the decisions of the living. The second is based on Buddhist teachings and linked to the notion of karma, or the accumulation of good and bad deeds during one's life cycle that influences one's afterlife and future reincarnations. Though Buddhism describes ghosts as unlucky creatures unable to let go of their earthly emotions and, consequently, plunging into a hell of their own making, ghosts are also envisioned as forces of retribution restoring order in the universe. Still, it is widely expected that at some point ghosts should relinquish their avenging mission and understand that, like everything else, their suffering is nothing but illusion, not worth holding on to. Only then will the ghost be at peace and able to reincarnate or follow on to the path of nirvana.

The hybridisation of ghosts in the age of globalisation has led to the establishment of new patterns both in the ways ghosts are portrayed and in the reasons for their actualisation. While it is clear that general audiences are likely to accept both the anthropomorphic and non-anthropomorphic renditions of spirits, 'global' ghosts assert their existence through their immersion in new media technologies, thanks to which they become units of digitalised information and part of the scientific and economic order to which modern civilisations subscribe. The ghost in *Coming Soon* merges with the medium of film. Other Thai global ghosts have been known to explore video, *The House* (*Baan phii sing*); television, *Ghost Game* (*Laa thaa phii*); photography, *Shutter*; and mobile phone technology, *Loneliness* (*Ngao*). Global ghosts tend to favour the Asian model, allowing for the randomisation of their actions and abandoning the 'save the virtuous and punish the wicked' pedagogical principle of much traditional Western horror. This has not been entirely unexpected. In 1968, Romero's zombies ate their way indiscriminately through good and bad alike, and Rosemary's baby made it obvious that even the innocent can become a vessel of evil. But although a majority of Western celluloid ghosts prefer to leave accidental bystanders alone, the concept of a spirit blinded by rage and bearing the grudge against all the living, globalised courtesy of J-Horror, seems to have caught on as potentially more frightening.

The Buddhist model demanding the rehabilitation and enlightenment of the spirits seems to fail with the global horror audiences who expect their ghosts to exact violent revenge but care substantially less about their spiritual well-being. New Thai filmmakers are acutely aware of that: all the Thai ghost films that have been specifically marketed for international distribution deny their ghosts any possibility of redemption. In *Shutter* the spirit of Natre ignores her Buddhist funeral rites and continues to haunt her lover, depicted rather graphically as permanently mounted on his shoulders. In *The House* the ghost succeeds in possessing the main heroine and turning her into a murderer and thus claiming more lives. In *Coming Soon* the fury of the ghost is meant to act as protection from the pirates. In contrast the films that use the concept of a ghost to deliver the Buddhist lesson of life's impermanence, such as *The Coffin* (*Long tor tai*, 2008) or *Ghost Mother* (*Phii lieng luk khon*, 2008), while obviously acceptable as examples of local or peripheral horror productions, are less likely to appeal to the global audience.

Sukdapisit's *Coming Soon* succeeds in creating a simultaneously local and global figure of horror. Its local aspect is instantly recognisable to anybody familiar with Thai supernatural mythology, and the history of Thai horror. On a global level the ghost personifies a more universalised, hybridised cinematic vengeful spirit representative of the latest stage of globalisation in the cinema marked by the export of Western production values, Hollywood-influenced genre traditions and the increasing influence of Japan and Korea as new horror production centres. This makes our call for globalgothic horror legitimate. Given that, as Andrew Hock Soon Ng observes, 'transgressing taboos, complicity with evil, the dread of life, violence, and the return of the repressed . . . are not specific to any culture or people' (2008: 1), this is not an entirely unexpected conclusion. While the expression of these sentiments has been the topic of indigenous literatures, art and cinema for quite a while, the encroaching globalisation of culture has resulted in the crystallisation of new hybridised 'global' forms that deserve to be explored in their complexity. These forms are not simply instances of Western cultural imperialism but rather confirm that the processes of globalisation involve a conscious negotiation of values in which the localities have the last word, shaping and transforming foreign influences to fit their specific contexts. Sophon's Sukdapisit's *Coming Soon* is at the same time an example of a local Thai horror production and a case in point to support the call for globalgothic horror.

Notes

1 See *Ladda Land* at *Box Office Mojo*. http://boxofficemojo.com/movies/intl/?page=&country=TH&wk=2011W35&id=_fLADDALAND01.
2 The Japanese long-haired vengeful spirit popularised outside of Japan by films such as Hideo Nakata's *Ringu* (1998) and Takashi Shimizu's *Ju-On* (2003).
3 Construction sacrifice seems to be the most common cause of violent death in this case. According to a local legend, four commoners were buried alive under Bangkok city pillar (*lak muang*), because their names, Yuu, Yong, Man, Kong, combined into an auspicious saying that, roughly translated, means 'this city shall stay strong for eternity'. Guelden accounts for a similar story that replaces (un)luckily named villagers with soldiers (1995: 90) and mentions other sources claiming that three further victims were sacrificed and buried alive under Bangkok city gates in the early nineteenth century (91).

References

Appadurai, Arjun. 2008 (1990). 'Disjuncture and difference in the global cultural economy'. In *The Anthropology of Globalization: A Reader*, eds Jonathan Xavier Inda and Renato Rosaldo. Oxford: Blackwell, 47–65.

Benjamin, Walter. 1998 (1968).'The work of art in the age of mechanical reproduction', trans. Harry Zohn. In *Continental Philosophy: An Anthology*, eds William McNeill and Karen S. Feldman. Oxford: Blackwell, 244–52.

Buchan, David. 1986. 'Tale roles and revenants: A morphology of ghosts'. *Western Folklore*, 45.2: 143–60.

Byron, Glennis. 2008. '"Where meaning collapses": Tunku Halim's *Dark Demon Rising* as global gothic'. In *Asian Gothic: Essays on Literature, Film and Anime*, ed. Andrew Hock Soon Ng. Jefferson, NC: McFarland, 19–31.

Chaiworaporn, Anchalee, and Adam Knee. 2006. 'Thailand: Revival in an age of globalization'. In *Contemporary Asian Cinema: Popular Culture in a Global Frame*, ed. Anne Tereska Ciecko. New York: Berg, 58–70.

Guelden, Marlane. 1995. *Thailand: Into the Spirit World*. Bangkok: Asia Books.

Inda, Jonathan Xavier, and Renato Rosaldo. 2008. 'Tracking global flows'. In *The Anthropology of Globalization: A Reader*, eds Jonathan Xavier Inda and Renato Rosaldo. Oxford: Blackwell, 3–46.

Kinnvall, Catarina. 2002. 'Analyzing the global–local nexus'. In *Globalization and Democratization in Asia: The Construction of Identity*, eds Catarina Kinnvall and Kristina Jönsson. London: Routledge, 3–18.

Ng, Andrew Hock Soon. 2008. 'Introduction'. In *Asian Gothic: Essays on Literature, Film and Anime*, ed. Andrew Hock Soon Ng. Jefferson, NC: McFarland, 1–15.

Pinkaew, Prachya. 2007. 'In conversation with Sronrasilp Ngoenwichit'. *Asian Journal of Literature, Culture and Society*, 1.1: 86–97.

Tsing, Anna. 2008 (2000). 'The global situation'. In *The Anthropology of Globalization: A Reader*, eds Jonathan Xavier Inda and Renato Rosaldo. Oxford: Blackwell, 66–98.

Internet sources

Berta, Peter. 2007.'Afterlife in cross-cultural perspective'. *Encyclopedia of Death and Dying*. www.deathreference.com/A-Bi/Afterlife-in-Cross-Cultural Perspective.html. Accessed 5 August 2011.

Ladda Land. Box Office Mojo http://boxofficemojo.com/movies/intl/?page=&country=TH&wk=2011W35&id=_fLADDALAND01. Accessed September 2011.

'Movie piracy losses by country'. *Havocscope Black Markets*. Online database of black market activities. www.havocscope.com/movie-piracy-losses-bycountry/. Accessed 6 September 2011.

Thongtep, Watchiranont. 2011. 'Distributors struggle against pirate DVD industry'. *The Nation*, 27 June. www.nationmultimedia.com/home/Distributors-struggle-against-pirate-DVD-industry-30158746.html. Accessed 30 June 2011.

Filmography

Alone (*Fad*). 2007. Parkpoom Wongpoom and Banjong Pisanthanakun, dirs. GTH.

Art of the Devil 2 (*Long khong*). 2005. The Ronin Team, dirs. Five Star Productions.

Baan phii pob. 1989. Sri Sawat, dir. Production company unknown.

The Coffin (*Long tor tai*). 2008. Ekachai Uekrongtham, dir. Arclight Films.

Coming Soon (*Program na vinyan arkhad*). 2008. Sophon Sukdapisit, dir. GMM Tai Hub.

Friday the 13th. 1980. Sean S. Cunningham, dir. Paramount.

Ghost Game (*Laa thaa phii*). 2006. Sarawut Wichiensarn, dir. NGR.

Ghost Mother (*Phii lieng luk khon*). 2007. Theeratorn Siriphunvaraporn, dir. Tai Seng.

The Grudge (*Ju-On*). 2003. Takashi Shimizu, dir. Toei.

The House (*Baan phii sing*). 2007. Monthon Arayangkoon, dir. Avant.

Ladda Land. 2011. Sophon Sakdaphisit, dir. GHT & Jorkwang Films.

Loneliness (*Ngao*). 2008. Youngyut Tongkontund, dir. GTH.

Nang Nak. 2009. Nonzee Nimibutr, dir. Buddy Film and Video Company.

A Nightmare on Elm Street. 1984. Wes Craven, dir. New Line Cinema.

Ong Bak. 2003. Prachya Pinkaew, dir. Baa-Ram-Ewe.

The Others. 2001. Alejandro Amenábar, dir. Dimension Films / Warner Bros.

The Ring (*Ringu*). 1998. Hideo Nakata, dir. Metro Tartan / Universal.

Shutter (*Shutter got tit vinyan*). 2004. Parkpoom Wongpoo and Banjong Pisanthanakun, dirs. GMM Grammy.

The Sixth Sense. 1999. M. Night Shyamalan, dir. Spyglass Entertainment.

Troublesome Night (*Yin yang lu*). 1997. Steve Cheng, Victor Tam and Herman Yau, dirs. CBE.

12

James Campbell

From *Sleepy Hollow* to *Silent Hill*: American gothic to globalgothic

In describing the 'new' race of Americans, several years after the Declaration of Independence, as 'a mixture of English, Scotch, Irish, French, Dutch, Germans and Swedes', Hector St Jean de Crèvecoeur affirmed the then popular theory of the 'melting pot', the idea that former colonial distinctions would gradually be erased through intermarriage among the country's white settlers (Crèvecoeur, 1998: 42). This process of white cultural homogenisation, referred to as 'Americanisation' in the early nineteenth century, would later be negatively connected to the idea of globalisation as American cultural imperialism in the late twentieth. Globalisation itself has since come to be viewed as multidirectional and non-hierarchic, an intensification of older, border-crossing processes that could herald the end of the nation state. Indeed, transatlantic and transpacific cultural exchange; interactions with the indigenous, Native American population; the admission of African culture, via slavery; the mainstream acceptance of marginalised non-white American identities in the late twentieth century; and recognition of the role of hybridisation in creating America's local and regional cultures, define America, over the course of its history, as a site of global cultural convergence. In recognition of America's cultural diversity, studies of American gothic have embraced a plurality of regional and transregional 'gothics', each of which is informed by a broader consensus that 'the gothic disrupts the dream world of national myth with the nightmares of history' (Goddu, 1997: 10). In so far as this echoes Leslie Fiedler's description of the gothic in America as 'a literature of darkness and the grotesque in a land of light and affirmation' (1997: 29), it polarises the 'American dream' and 'American nightmare' to a degree that suggests that the gothic not only disrupts but also defines, through opposition, national and regional cultural myths.

Tracing the development, rise and decline of American gothic and the overlapping transition to a globalgothic in which America is but a part leads me to discuss two canonical, antebellum-era American gothic texts, and one contemporary instance with close ties to these, concluding with a final example of a globalgothic 'America' made in Japan. Each suggests the American nation state to be built atop unstable foundations, as representatives of white patriarchy, about whom there is something ridiculous, even monstrous and/or spectral, become hysterical in response to forces beyond their comprehension. These 'forces' include not only those spectres of the subaltern already familiar to American gothic studies but also the effects of globalisation, as subjects become passive within a semantic fog littered with signs of transnationalism that range, over time, from European classicism to Japanese pop culture. This suggests a continuity between American gothic – which is always at least implicitly hybrid – and globalgothic, which foregrounds hybridisation, between their respective depictions of the intersection of decentred subjectivities with decentralised cultural production. But it is also at this point that the two become radically distinct, as the intensification of multidirectional flows in globalgothic aids the creation of a fictional 'American' locality that simply makes no sense in relation to American gothic.

In othering 'white America', both American gothic and globalgothic texts confirm that this part, however dominant, does not represent the whole. And yet it, and many of the 'dreams' and 'nightmares' associated with it, continue to circulate, globally, as, in Beck's terms, 'zombie categories which are dead [yet] still alive' (Beck and Beck-Gernsheim, 2002: 203). This can be seen in the way that Washington Irving's 'The Legend of Sleepy Hollow' (1820), a text that offers an insight into the development of America's regional and national cultural myths and gothic fictions, continues through its various adaptations and appropriations to promote some of the oldest and most misleading of these myths to an increasingly global audience. First published in *The Sketch Book of Geoffrey Crayon, Gent.* (1819–20), and widely credited with having helped to establish the American short story as both a literary form and a commercial enterprise, the tale's success is clearly registered in the *Sketch Book*'s being better known today as *The Legend of Sleepy Hollow and Other Stories.*

Meanwhile, North Tarrytown, renamed 'Sleepy Hollow' in 1996 in honour of (and, presumably, in a bid to capitalise upon) its fictional counterpart, is where 'The Legend Lives™', through tourist attractions and the annual appearance of Irving's Headless Horseman as leader of the Hallowe'en revels, uniting tourists and locals alike in celebration of a holiday and text synonymous with the conspicuous consumption of 'sugared suppositions' (Irving, 2001: 308). In a comment reiterated by others, 'Linda', a fan of the Disneyworld Florida theme park, claims that knowing that its 'Sleepy Hollow' restaurant is modelled after Irving's Sunnyside home will enrich her reception, will 'make buying a funnel cake even more enjoyable' (Duncan, 2010). Walter Benjamin would claim such individuals to be lost within a phantasmagoria of capitalist spectacle, to have made themselves receptive to propaganda (Benjamin, 2002: 18). In this way the park's 'preservation' of Irving's legacy recalls Irving's attempt to preserve the cultural legacy of the colonial Dutch through the works of his authorial alter-ego, the New York historian Diedrich Knickerbocker.

Irving depicts the Hollow in his original tale as a tribal community frozen in time, its 'population, manners, and customs' untouched by 'the great torrent of migration and improvement' affecting 'parts', though not the whole of the new republic (Irving, 2001: 295). Years later, in an 1839 article simply entitled 'Sleepy Hollow', Irving's Geoffrey Crayon laments the arrival of 'civilization' in the region and its impact on local culture. 'Instead of the primitive garbs of homespun manufacture, and antique Dutch fashion' he finds contemporary French fashions now prevail, while 'the intrusion of taste, and literature, and the English language, in this once unsophisticated Dutch neighborhood' threatens to corrupt the innocence or ignorance of his noble savages (333). Furthermore, he fears that the opening of a bank, connecting town to nation, will see the community 'deluged with wealth' (334), modernised to the point that future visitors will 'pronounce all that I have recorded of that once favored region, a fable' (335).

Crayon's lament is meant to be ironic, since the original 'record' was presented as a fable, a 'legend'. In fact it was a self-reflexive commercial fiction, reproduced and circulated until it became a 'legend' by popular consent. Less a ghost story than a story about the telling of ghost stories, it relates how the townsfolk came to share their 'marvellous tales of ghosts and goblins' with the Yankee schoolmaster Ichabod Crane, who in return tells them 'anecdotes of witchcraft', and of the 'direful omens and portentous sights and sounds in the air, which prevailed in the earlier times of Connecticut' (299). Reconciling colonial rivals by conjoining their respective regional oral literatures is a small but significant step towards building a transregional and national literature. But when Ichabod is chased out of town, the furniture he formerly possessed, which 'belonged to the community', is reclaimed and his 'magic books' and writings burnt (318). The Yankee is rejected, preparatory to the reinscription of the town's borders. But this local resistance to Yankee influence meets its own resistance, as Crane, in turn, becomes the subject of local legend.

'There was a contagion in the very air that blew from that haunted region; it breathed forth an atmosphere of dreams and fancies infecting all the land' (312): converting Crane's books to smoke only draws attention to this, to how everything in the Hollow is transmitted through the 'air', via word-of-mouth. Likewise, in the years following its publication, the name of 'Sleepy Hollow' would spread to townships in Illinois and California, inspiring street names in Roanoke and Falls Church, Virginia; in Bethel, Connecticut; and in Longwood, Florida. It has inspired a nationwide myth of the exceptional small-town community, enchanted and enchanting, that in more recent years has taken up residence in the Pacific North-West, in television series such as the ABC network's *Twin Peaks* (1990–91) and CBS's *Northern Exposure* (1990–95). The exceptionalism of these various fictional communities rests on the distinctiveness of their respective 'local tales, haunted spots, and twilight superstitions' (Irving, 2001: 294). But at the time claiming that America's few ghosts resided in its 'long established Dutch communities', and that other areas were too recently settled (311), Irving made 'Sleepy Hollow' an exception that proved the 'rule', the popular myth that endures to this day: that America lacks the history necessary for cultural production (4). In doing so, he privileges one culture at the expense of others, both indigenous and imported.

This first becomes apparent as Irving wonders whether the source of the region's enchantment was its being 'bewitched' by 'an old Indian chief' or 'a high German doctor during the early days of the settlement' (294). Foregrounding the tulip tree and the headless Hessian, signs of the region's Dutch and revolutionary history (312), Irving clearly favours the colonial legacy, reducing the Native American inheritance to a single commodity: 'Indian corn' (301). Tim Burton's 1999 film adaptation, as a part of its generally diminishing portrayal of Dutch culture, replaces the tulip tree with a 'Tree of the Dead'. But it is the exclusion of Native American culture that seems both more pointed and complete, given that its only reference in the film is in the 'Indian trail' leading to this 'dead' sign. There are plenty of references to Native America in a 1980 NBC TV-movie adaptation: Crane's schoolhouse is said to be built atop 'an old Indian cemetery', its resident barn owl possessed by the spirit of 'Chief Running Buffalo', while according to the Dutch school-caretaker, who dons headdress and war-paint at one stage for a lark, the region most definitely was bewitched by an 'Algonquin medicine man'. Reducing Native American culture to jokes, clichés and stereotypes, the film, like Burton's, and like Irving's original text, reifies white America by burying its predecessors beneath misrepresentative signs.

For Kenneth Reed, Irving, 'unwilling to show concern over the slavery issue', also contributed to 'the propagation of certain myths illustrating the black man as a happy, lazy, superstitious, altogether ridiculous animal' (1970: 43). But there is nothing innocuous about the slaves seen outside Van Tassel's farmhouse. Even as they form a window display of 'shining' faces and 'rows of ivory', confirming their status as commodities, they are also depicted as consumers, devouring the sight of Ichabod on the dance floor – a spectacle ripe for ridicule, according to Charles Crow, who sees the slaves' 'ambiguous grins' as signifying 'admiration, or more likely derision' (2009: 31). Immediately following their appearance, Ichabod goes from being 'Saint Vitus himself' to 'the flogger of urchins', displacing on to the children a reminder of slavery (310). A similar moment occurs in the tale's 1839 sequel, as Geoffrey Crayon recalls visiting 'an old goblin-looking mill, situated among rocks and water falls', a picturesque scene of fairytale enchantment somewhat at odds with the concomitant march of 'progress' he elsewhere laments. 'A horse shoe, nailed to the door to keep off witches and evil spirits', a practice common to many cultures, betrays no evidence of the region's localisation of African folkways. But it is at that moment that 'an old negro thrust his head, all dabbled with flour, out of a hole . . . and grinned, and rolled his eyes, and looked like the very hobgoblin of the place' (331).

In its bizarrely literal whitewashing of the old man's ethnicity, the text insists upon his otherness whilst promoting, once again, an ambiguous mix of humour and horror. 'Fixed upon' by Knickerbocker 'as the very one to give him that invaluable kind of information, never to be acquired from books', Crayon claims it was this 'African sage' and a 'good dame' that told him Crane's story (331). This contradicts Knickerbocker's original postscript, where he claimed to have heard it from 'a pleasant, shabby, gentlemanly old fellow', presenting the story for the approval of New York's 'sagest and most illustrious burghers' (319). His poverty and 'air of infinite deference' (320) mark the writer's alienation from the hegemonic order and his desire to join it, to establish a defining image, through the tale's additional association with Irving, Crayon and Knickerbocker, of the fledgling white male American author struggling for recognition in the new republic. Giving fictive credit to the subaltern may strengthen the tale's appearance of being 'authentic' folklore, but the subaltern does not speak, does not have a truly convincing claim to the story created by Irving.

In discussing his film adaptation, Tim Burton echoes Irving's claim that America lacked 'the accumulated treasures of age' (Irving, 2001: 4), when stating that it did not have 'the wealth of stories, folk tales and fairy tales that there are in other countries' (Burton, 2000). This might explain the 'Europeanness' of the film, its cast and its debt to gothic, as Burton's Ichabod (Johnny Depp) recalls his parents in flashbacks that evoke the earliest gothic novels, in the villainous patriarch's pursuit of his mother, while the New York courts are shown using distinctly European 'medieval devices of torture'. The Horseman (Christopher Walken), depicted as a real ghost, combines the 'Spectre Bridegroom' tradition prevalent in European folklore, balladry, and late eighteenth- to early nineteenth-century romantic and gothic literature with the contemporary American 'slasher' – a juxtaposition that further plays up the myth of American culture as ahistorical. Burton's Hollow becomes a gothic America in microcosm, with New England and the South entering the film via their popular association with witchcraft and voodoo, while the 'western woods' reign in the frontier experience. His Dutchmen may seem passably 'authentic', since their accents are not recognisably 'American', but casting so many English actors re-enacts, however inadvertently, the original Yankee cultural absorption of the Dutch. Elsewhere, the Irish/Gaelic Killians and Doctor Lancaster – an English name for the Scottish actor Ian McDiarmid, here speaking in his native accent – suggest a more diverse, though still exclusively white construction of American identity, echoing Crèvecoeur.

The abundance of jack o' lanterns on display is another of the film's anachronisms, the practice only having entered America via Irish mass immigration in the 1840s. Their carved grins supplant the slaves' grinning 'rows of ivory', and, in so far as this draws attention to the fact that there are no African-American performers to be found in Burton's film, it recalls one of the prevailing themes of American gothic studies, the idea that its texts are 'haunted by race' (Goddu, 1997: 7). Only those familiar with the texts are liable to experience this 'haunting', as it depends on close textual comparison. When used to punctuate the film's strange blend of slapstick horror and comedy, the lanterns recall the original tale's ambiguous mix of humour and horror, as exemplified in the grotesque, racist spectacles described above. They underscore not only the fakeness of those misrepresentations but also the absence of a direct correlation between a text and 'real history', a world beyond textual representation. Following its commodification in the Unites States, the lantern becomes a ubiquitous signifier of Halloween in global popular culture, and like McDonald's 'golden arches' promotes global anxieties regarding Americanisation (O'Donnell and Foley, 2009). Synonymous with gleeful, conspicuous consumption and twentieth-century pop culture manifestations of the Headless Horseman, the jack o' lantern establishes multiple continuities between Irving's text and its various adaptations. But by making Burton's film a more successful 'cover-up' than Irving's original tale, in marking its passage from American gothic to globalgothic, the jack o' lantern wards off the spectre of the subaltern.

Compared to Irving, an author eclipsed by his own success, Edgar Allan Poe stands as a figurehead, as the country's 'premier American gothicist' (Oates, 1996: 4), his name and image continuing to thrive thanks to a Poe industry in America that has spawned all manner of strange and surprising adaptations, loosely inspired by, and directly based upon, his work, his image and his biography. It all adds up to an overwhelming impression that America 'owns' Poe, and suggests that one reason his work continues to be branded as 'American' is, at least in part, because the vast extent of his critical and commercial legacy already happens to be located there. Poe, in fact, abhorred the concept of 'literary nationalism'; believing 'the world at large' the 'only proper stage' for a writer (Poe, 2006: 577), he chose to set the bulk of his works in a quasi-European gothic dreamscape. Faced with the 'problem' of Poe, a 'literary un-American committee' of mid-twentieth-century Americanist scholars tried, but failed, to expel him from the country's literary canon (Sanford, 1968: 54), while other critics got round the 'problem' by tying his works' Europeanness to a myth of the antebellum South, in which Poe briefly resided, as the 'Old World' resisting assimilation into the 'New' (Goddu, 1997: 76–7).

In his introduction to *Tales of the Grotesque and Arabesque* (1840), Poe addressed accusations of '"Germanism" and gloom' by remarking that literary 'Germanism' was simply a popular style, coined by German artists and appropriated by others, like himself, for commercial gain: 'terror', he remarked, was 'not of Germany, but of the soul' (Poe, 1984: 129). Relating 'The Fall of the House of Usher' (1839) to literary Germanism, Dennis Perry and Carl Sederholm cite E. T. A. Hoffmann's 'Das Majorat' (1817) and Heinrich Clauren's *Das Raubschloss* (1812) as likely sources for a number of the tale's names and events (2009: 8). That their claim for the influence of Charles Brockden Brown's *Edgar Huntley* (1799) is far less particularised suggests both a desire and a struggle to locate at least one American source for the tale, in order to justify their branding it 'American Gothic' (10–11). Like most critics they understand 'American Gothic' to refer to any gothic text produced by an 'American'. It is by such reasoning that Henry James's *The Turn of the Screw* (1898) – a novella written and set in England, and which references only English texts – comes to appear in nearly all major studies of 'American Gothic'.

Such an arbitrary approach to nation-branding texts overlooks the possibility of authors' making alternative, possibly multiple, or possibly no national identifications (Crow, 2009: 15–16). It suggests that their work is somehow essentially 'American'. But would anyone ignorant of their authorship be able to guess Poe's or James's nationality from their works? Meredith McGill has written extensively on the antebellum 'culture of reprinting', which saw the transnational circulation and anonymous republication of texts (piracy, in today's terms) give birth to an American mass market. She notes how the anonymous reprinting of 'Usher' in the London periodical *Bentley's Miscellany*, and later in the *Boston Notion*, under the heading 'From Bentley's Miscellany', could have led Stateside readers to suppose the tale's author to be English (McGill, 1995: 282–3). While not 'globalgothic' – preceding, as it does, the advent of today's closely interconnected global marketplace where speed is of the essence – Poe's work was certainly transnational, in terms of its content and appeal, circulating throughout Europe to reach as far as Japan before the close of the nineteenth century.

On entering the House of Usher, the narrator or reader must pass through or over a 'Gothic archway', lined with 'sombre tapestries' and 'phantasmagoric armorial trophies'. These 'familiar' yet 'unfamiliar' surroundings have a vaguely European, medieval aspect to them (Poe, 2003: 93), more concretely expressed in Roderick Usher's library.

Books constitute 'no small portion of the mental existence of the invalid', and when read as a sign system – 'Belphegor', 'Machiavelli', 'Heaven and Hell', 'Subterranean Voyage', 'Chiromancy' and a 'book in quarto Gothic' – they complement the tale's depiction of Usher as gloomy, anxious and introspective, weighed down by a 'gothic' imagination. Mixed in, and contrasting with this, 'the Journey into the Blue Distance of Tieck', 'the City of the Sun of Campanella' and tales of 'the old African Satyrs and Ægipans' suggest a lighter, airier aspect to Usher's imagination, as he tries to dream himself free of the house (101). Poe's global popularity and Oriental–Occidental hybrid gothic texts may pave the way for globalgothic, but he does not construe globalisation as something to be frightened of; rather, he portrays it as a possible antidote, to appropriate one of his terms, to gothic 'gloomth'.

Those who can afford to live in more or less splendid isolation, housebound if they so choose (a much greater number now than in Poe's day), and who seek to escape reality by indulging in escapist fantasies, may find it possible to sympathise with Usher. In a neat reversal, it was, for the child hero of Tim Burton's *Vincent* (1982), precisely that claustrophobic atmosphere of gothic gloomth that offered the desired release from the mundane reality of American suburbia. Similarly, in 'Usher II' (1950), Ray Bradbury relocates the house to the moon, thereby identifying Poe's text as 'out of this world'. Modelled after twentieth-century haunted house or fun house theme-park attractions, spaces where shrieks of terror and laughter coincide, it positions Poe alongside the Brothers Grimm, Lewis Carroll, Washington Irving and other world fantasists. In declaring the house 'open for business', Bradbury offers not only a neat rejoinder to those critics who have traditionally sought to 'close' Poe's text but a declaration of openness, of receptiveness to the idea of global cultural convergence (Bradbury, 2008: 126–7).

Stephen King's *The Mist* (1980), by contrast, maintains a narrow focus on minds closed to a world beyond America. Supposed but never confirmed to be the byproduct of an accident at the nearby 'Arrowhead Project' – an ominous name, recalling the Manhattan Project (1942–46), which saw the development of the first atomic bomb – the eponymous mist appears one morning in the town of Bridgton, Maine, without warning (King, 2007: 27–8). The exact scale of the catastrophe that follows is never ascertained, as the text shifts from Bridgton's initial descent into chaos following a power cut, only to focus more intensely on those trapped inside a local supermarket, surrounded by monsters within and without. Accepting that 'people become aware of the dynamics of some new system, in which they are seized, only later on and gradually' (Jameson, 1991: xix), that 'epochal changes are occurring', but that 'these changes exist more in people's consciousness, and on paper, than in behaviour and social conditions' (Beck and Beck-Gernsheim, 2002: 203), it is possible to read the text as a fictional representation of the felt imaginative impact of globalisation. It is something the text and its characters prove 'powerless either to interrogate or to resist' – a trait not uncommon to works that do explicitly seek to discuss globalisation and its effects (Annesley, 2006: 68).

The Mist opens on the home of the Drayton family and their American flag lying 'limp against its pole' (King, 2007: 10), the first phallus in a series. From noting a 'lonely, phallic kielbasa sausage' (49), to saying that 'Giving your wife a gun' could seem 'ludicrously symbolic' (106), family man David Drayton betrays stereotypical masculine anxieties to comically absurd effect. Inheriting his father's house and flag (11–12); believing that a husband is his wife's 'proprietor' (131); and viewing neighbour Norton as a 'father figure of the Western world' (87), David confirms a portrait, and becomes the text's leading representative, of America as postwar White Anglo-Saxon Protestant patriarchy. This is a country divided, as signalled from the outset by David's 'boundary dispute' with Norton (11), and in the community's enmity towards the nation's military-industrial complex. The most striking instance of the latter follows the discovery of two dead soldiers affiliated with the Project, as it prompts David and store clerk Ollie Weeks to compare them to American soldiers who collected human ears during the Vietnam War, and to Nazi war criminals (139). Nothing is offered to justify the excessive readings of the text's paranoid citizens, as they indulge in telling conspiracy theories. Flag-waving patriotism and nationalist myth have been superseded by paranoiac counter-myths, expressing a loss of faith in government, society and, on a larger scale, humanity.

Norton believes he lost the boundary dispute because he was 'an out-of-towner' (11). Telling David 'it's your town', he expresses envy and resentment at not being welcomed into the community, despite extensive investment (89). But David is not particularly well liked either among the people of Bridgton. 'I know you're a big-shot artist with connections in New York and Hollywood', says the local mechanic Jim Grondin to David, 'but that doesn't make you any different from anyone else, in my book' (71). Clearly it does, since it was Jim who raised the subject; and Jim's later calling Norton 'a cheap New York shyster' further suggests 'New York' to be the trigger for a class-based antagonism Norton exacerbates when calling Jim and his friends 'hicks' (90). Elsewhere Ollie's resistance to interacting with 'out-of-staters', calling them 'strangers', highlights a division between locals and tourists (120). The only positive instance of community spirit comes when Dan Miller, a tourist from Massachusetts, rallies together a group large enough to make the market into a fortress (103).

Filtered through Drayton's perception, his artistic background and sensitivity to Mrs Carmody's 'gothic pronouncements' (23), the monsters in *The Mist* are characterised, often simultaneously, as grotesque harbingers of a biblical apocalypse, and as unconvincing, commercial 'fakes'. One, 'no ordinary earthly spider blown up to horror-movie size', trails 'puddles of sticky black stuff', like oil, adding a touch of Hollywood fakery to its appearance (161). Another resembles a 'ninety-eight-cent rubber-joke novelty' (90); others, 'strange creations of vinyl and plastic you can buy for $1.89' (122). Even the dead soldiers resemble 'a kid's Halloween trick' (136). *The Mist*'s grotesque parody of consumer culture finds its most blatant expression in the disembodied tentacles that instinctually grab whatever they can, from dog food to people (78). Drayton half-consciously attributes these 'novelties' to an unseen, omnipotent manipulator, to an Old Testament God (18) and to his repressed 'inner child' (134), speculations that mark a withdrawal from both reality and society. In this he is no different from the other trapped shoppers and staff, hyperconsumers who are opening cans of beer on almost every other page, and taking large quantities of sleeping pills (130). Withdrawing into 'a dope-dream' (95), they recall the 'drowsy, dreamy' Sleepy Hollow townsfolk (Irving, 2001: 294), and Roderick Usher, whose behaviour likewise resembles that of a 'lost drunkard' and 'eater of opium' (Poe, 2003: 95). They become 'like ghosts' (66), 'uneasy phantoms' (110), looking out of the windows 'in an uneasy, speculative way' (95), 'gutless and lost' (108).

In such scenes the mist, which from its first appearance prevented the Draytons from being able to see beyond their own backyard, exacerbates the ignorance and insularity engendered in national isolationism (28). The impending, incomprehensible threat it signifies is globalisation. This is suggested by David's half-expecting to encounter Japanese B-movie monster 'Ghidra' in the borderless wasteland of the novella's conclusion (184), and by his response to an object he discovers shortly after the power cut, when rifling through a cupboard looking for candles. It lies beyond the 'half-ounce of grass' enjoyed by David and his wife, not to mention the WASP parents in *Poltergeist* (1982); past 'Billy's wind-up set of chattering teeth', the text's first reference to joke novelty products; and 'under a Sears catalogue', a prestigious marker of American consumer culture since the first was published in 1888. It is 'a Kewpie doll from Taiwan', and it startles Drayton into repeating himself: 'I found the candles behind the Kewpie doll with its glazed dead man's eyes' (14–15). This drawn-out encounter with the kewpie doll seems significant; a 'dead' sign, guarding and concealing a source of enlightenment, it recalls the jack o' lantern discussed earlier. The problems and anxieties of interpretation that icon engendered become even more pressing when attached to an object viewed outside its national context. With no additional information available to facilitate a reading, Drayton grabs the candles and leaves.

In its provoking unease the doll foreshadows the monsters' subsequent appearance as killer commodities, and suggests that the globalisation of the marketplace and all it entails is something neither Drayton nor America can afford to ignore. This last point dawns on David when he reflects that 'Federal Foods, Inc., with its stores in Bridgton, North Windham, and Portland, might not even exist anymore' – has, in all likelihood, been put out of business by the monsters doubling as cheap commodities and 'alien' consumers. Even 'the Eastern Seaboard might no longer exist' (98), if borders are becoming permeable 'lines in mist' (94). Threatening family, community and nation with some nebulous conception of globalisation as invasion, in addition to crumbling local and national infrastructures, the novella ends by insisting on the importance of hope in the face of adversity (190). It is a hope that Drayton and his followers can learn to navigate this new landscape of torn-up roads, criss-crossed with tentacles and fallen trees, the landscape of 'the new global cultural economy', 'a complex, overlapping, disjunctive order that cannot any longer be understood in terms of existing center-periphery models' (Appadurai, 1996: 32–3).

Both a product and a reflection of this new 'order', Konami's *Silent Hill* (1999), a console game for the PSOne, set in America but made in Japan for a global market, closely recalls the tone, setting and atmosphere of *The Mist* and 'Usher'. It comes as no surprise then, that King's *Mist* should be cited as a key influence by the game's all-Japanese production crew Team Silent, in *Ushinawareta kioku* (*Lost Memories*): *Silent Hill Chronicle.*[1] A number of the game's monsters, its giant insects, disembodied tentacles and pterodactyls, can be traced back to *The Mist*. They also share an influence: as King compares his monsters to the work of Hieronymos Bosch (122, 170), the *Chronicle* cites Bosch alongside another Dutch artist, Pieter Brueghel the Younger, as well as the Anglo-Irish artist Francis Bacon and Spanish surrealist Salvador Dalí. Next to this wide-ranging European eclecticism they list only one American artist, the 'realist' Andrew Wyeth. 'America', 'Japan' and, most intriguingly, 'Europe' are constructed within the game as a heterogeneous, Oriental–Occidental globalgothic blend that simply cannot be called 'American gothic'.

The creator Keiichiro Toyama claims that the game 'was supposed [to] have a "modern American novel" type of atmosphere' (Toyama, 1999: 24), possibly in the hope of capturing something of the global appeal of Stephen King. It certainly does appear to pay homage to American writers, artists and mass culture through its countless obscure allusions, mostly in the form of signs quoted out of context, like 'REDRUM' from King's *The Shining* (1977), and more especially in local business signs, like Cut Rite Chainsaws, lifted from *The Texas Chainsaw Massacre 2* (1986). But the game in fact bears little resemblance to the texts it quotes. Naming streets after American writers known to have produced not just gothic or horror fiction but work in genres and fields not obviously relevant to the game, and citing, in the *Chronicle*, high-profile American auteurs like David Lynch, Stanley Kubrick and Terry Gilliam, whose recognition abroad has always eclipsed their home reception, the game's producers encourage the audience to view the game as an exceptional, 'avant-garde' text. There is also its defamiliarisation of the commercial landscape to consider: distorting familiar, global 'American' brand logos so that, for example, Coca-Cola becomes 'Coce-Cole', and McDonald's, 'Mec Burger'. 'McDonald's, of course, does not inherently represent "America"' (Iwabuchi, 2002: 28), something the distortion of these signs underlines by transforming them into something unfamiliar, 'un-American'. There are enough signs on display to ensure the player should recognise this as an 'American' setting, though any sense of 'Americanness' the game might stand to engender is always marginal and always compromised.

The *Chronicle* also cites, in addition to American and European works, the influence of numerous Japanese writers and artists, including Kunio Yanagita, Junji Ito and Kobo Abe, attributing to them the game's atmosphere, though they are nowhere referenced within it.

If 'to put emphasis on cultural Japanese characteristics within art and fiction' is to produce 'an Orientalist vision of Japan' (Picard, 2009: 95), then the game's producers have done just that, via the Shinto shrine beneath Green Lion Antiques, and the *dojo* in the house on Levin Street. Elsewhere, a store called 'Ichiron's Drugs' signals the Japanese appropriation of a traditional American 'mom and pop' drugstore, of American cultural signifiers. Another, mistranslated as 'No. 1 Foto in 1 Ora', introduces another trace of otherness into this not 'all-American' town. Through these various references, and the *Chronicle*'s claim that the map was modelled on the towns of Towadako and Tazawako in Aomori and Akita Prefectures, Team Silent make a show of disclosing the game's 'true' Japanese nature, as if it were concealed beneath its veneer of 'fake' Americanness. In fact they create 'Japan' as much as they create 'America', othering both in the process.

Like most critics Team Silent privilege an American–Japanese dichotomy when discussing the game and its sequels (Bettenhausen, 2007: 73), a move that neglects its no less significant, if even more incoherent Europeanness. Inflected with signs of a mixed European 'heritage', the game confirms Takayuki Tatsumi's argument that, in its strategies, Japanese Occidentalism resembles Western Orientalism in the way it conflates and exoticises cultures (Tatsumi, 2006: 4). Consider the game's 'Balkan Church', an incongruous landmark with no obvious connection to the Balkans, haunted by the local cultist Dahlia Gillespie, a character resembling a European gypsy stereotype, named after one of the ex-wives of the Italian horror director Dario Argento, whose work is referenced throughout the game. As a verb, 'balkanise' means 'to divide (a region) into a number of smaller and often mutually hostile units'.[2] To describe *Silent Hill* as a 'balkanised' text, then, is to attribute a metonymic function to the church, a composite structure promoting various cultural 'odours' and 'fragrances'.[3] Any attempt to read these, however, is complicated by the sheer density of references, coupled with the use of 'odourless' signs throughout the game, which evade association with particular nation states or regions.[4] The game's sign systems can only be loosely defined: a mix of pagan, medieval, Gnostic and Catholic iconography suggests Europe and the gothic, and it is the fusion of this system with the equally mystifying systems of Orientalism and (un)American mass culture described above that defines the game's distinctive globalgothic aesthetic.

Following Team Silent's disbandment in 2004, *Silent Hill* has gone on to become a truly global transmedia franchise, with the first film adaptation, an American–French–Canadian–Japanese co-production (dir. Christopher Gans, 2006), followed by a succession of games by American and European external developers. But while Czech-based producers Vatra Games advertise what they call a Czech cultural influence in their contribution to the franchise, *Silent Hill: Downpour* (2012), recognising the necessity of including a trace of Europe in creating an 'authentic' *Silent Hill* experience (Turi, 2011), most discussions of the game still privilege a perceived American–Japanese cultural dichotomy. Prior to the release of the first American instalment, *Silent Hill: Homecoming* (2008), many echoed the games reviewer Leigh Alexander's fear that 'American developers might not be able to retain the distinctly Japanese spirit of the series', and her claim that 'the West and the East have distinctly different approaches to creating fear in entertainment media, uniquely rooted in their respective cultural histories'. Her Orientalist/Occidentalist reading of recent cultural trends also leads her to criticise Japanese horror games for being 'a little [too] surreal and disjointed', and to see Western investment and influence as an opportunity to force these games into being less elliptical (Alexander, 2008). And yet the supposedly 'Eastern' traits she cites as potential weaknesses could also be regarded as strengths to consumers who enjoy surreal, disjointed narratives, with the repetitious, timeless and placeless qualities of nightmare: qualities that have never been exclusive to the East, nor ever lacking in the West.

With the most interesting developments in American gothic and horror cultural production presently occurring in niche markets within the book, film, gaming and comic book industries, it is unfortunate that it should be the recent surfeit of lacklustre, high-budget American remakes – of American horror cinema 'classics', and of the 'modern classics' of world horror cinema – that stand to define America's international reputation in this field. Not only do they exacerbate the stigma already attached to the culture industries, they create the erroneous impression that America is in a state of cultural exhaustion. While the encroachment of globalisation has been a subject of anxiety in both national gothic and globalgothic texts, it is, finally, the latter that, exemplifying its ability to inspire variety and novelty through hybridisation, best stand to intimate fears regarding the decline of globalisation. Viewed from this angle, and from within the context of a global recession, *Silent Hill*'s abandoned streets and shopping malls, reflecting both Western and Westernised societies, combine with its stagnant atmosphere to deliver an eerily prescient, post-apocalyptic vision of a world beyond the collapse of local, national and global economies.

Notes

1 Available only in Japan as an addendum to *Silent Hill 3 Official Complete Guide* (2003), Tokyo: Konami, NTT Publications. All references are to an English fan-translation by 'wallofdeath': http://silenthillchronicle.net/.
2 'Balkan, adj.' *OED Online*. December 2011. Oxford University Press. www.oed.com/view/Entry/14891?redirectedFrom=balkan. Accessed 25 January 2012.
3 Cultural 'odour' refers to 'the way in which cultural features of a country' and 'images or ideas' of national identity are associated 'with a particular product', while cultural 'fragrance' is more concerned with 'widely disseminated symbolic images of the country' (Iwabuchi, 2002: 27).
4 See the local businesses 'Ghoul', 'Wind' and 'The Mirage'; the hollowed-out, post-industrial landscape of the 'Otherworld'; and composer Akira Yamaoka's ambient industrial score.

References

Annesley, James. 2006. *Fictions of Globalization: Consumption, the Market and the Contemporary American Novel.* London: Continuum.

Appadurai, Arjun. 1996. *Modernity at Large: Cultural Dimensions of Globalization.* Minneapolis: University of Minnesota Press.

Beck, Ulrich, and Elisabeth Beck-Gernsheim. 2002. *Individualization: Institutionalized Individualism and Its Social and Political Consequences.* London: Sage.

Benjamin, Walter. 2002. *The Arcades Project,* trans. Howard Eiland and Kevin McLaughlin. Cambridge, MA: The Belknap Press of Harvard University Press.

Bettenhausen, Shane. 2007. 'American gothic'. *Electronic Gaming Monthly,* October: 73–80.

Bradbury, Ray. 2008 (1951). *The Illustrated Man.* London: HarperVoyager.

Crèvecoeur, Hector St Jean de. 1998 (1782). *Letters from an American Farmer.* Oxford: Oxford University Press.

Crow, Charles L. 2009. *History of the Gothic: American Gothic.* Cardiff: University of Wales Press.

Fiedler, Leslie A. 1997 (1960). *Love and Death in the American Novel.* Champaign, IL: Dalkey Archive Press.

Giles, Paul. 2011. *The Global Remapping of American Literature.* Princeton, NJ: Princeton University Press.

Goddu, Teresa A. 1997. *Gothic America: Narrative, History, and Nation.* New York: Columbia University Press.

Irving, Washington. 2001 (1819–20). *The Legend of Sleepy Hollow and Other Stories or, The Sketch Book of Geoffrey Crayon, Gent.* New York: Random House.

Iwabuchi, Koichi. 2002. *Recentering Globalization: Popular Culture and Japanese Transnationalism.* Durham, NC: Duke University Press.

Jameson, Fredric. 1991. *Postmodernism, Or, The Cultural Logic of Late Capitalism*. London: Verso.

King, Stephen. 2007. *The Mist. Skeleton Crew*. London: Hodder.

McGill, Meredith. 1995. 'Poe, literary nationalism, and authorial identity'. In *The American Face of Edgar Allan Poe*, eds. Shawn Rosenheim and Stephen Rachman. Baltimore, MD: The Johns Hopkins University Press, 271–304.

Oates, Joyce Carol, ed. 1996. *American Gothic Tales*. New York: Plume.

O'Donnell, Hugh, and Michael Foley, eds. 2009. *Treat or Trick? Halloween in a Globalising World*. Newcastle upon Tyne: Cambridge Scholars Publishing.

Perry, Dennis R., and Carl H. Sederholm. 2009. *Poe, 'The House of Usher,' and the American Gothic*. New York: Palgrave Macmillan.

Picard, Martin. 2009. 'Haunting backgrounds: Transnationality and intermediality in Japanese survival horror video games'. *Horror Video Games: Essays on the Fusion of Fear and Play*, ed. Bernard Perron. Jefferson, NC: McFarland, 95–120.

Poe, Edgar Allan. 1984. *Edgar Allan Poe: Poetry and Tales*, ed. Patrick F. Quinn. New York: Library of America.

——. 2003. *The Fall of the House of Usher and Other Writings*, ed. David Galloway. London: Penguin Books.

——. 2006. *The Portable Edgar Allan Poe*, ed. J. Gerald Kennedy. New York: Penguin Group.

Reed, Kenneth T. 1970. 'Washington Irving and the Negro'. *Negro American Literature Forum*, 4.2: 43–4.

Sanford, Charles L. 1968. 'Edgar Allan Poe: A blight upon the landscape'. *American Quarterly*, 20.1: 54–66.

Tatsumi, Takayuki. 2006. *Full Metal Apache: Transactions Between Cyberpunk Japan and Avant-pop America*. Durham, NC: Duke University Press.

Toyama, Keiichiro. 1999. 'Q & A'. *Playstation Magazine*, 3.19: 24–5.

Internet sources

Alexander, Leigh. 2008. 'Does survival horror really still exist?' *Kotaku*, 29 September. http://kotaku.com/5056008/does-survival-horror-really-still-exist. Accessed 7 August 2011.

Burton, Tim. 2000. Interview with Mark Kermode. *Guardian*, 6 January. www.guardian.co.uk/film/2000/jan/06/guardianinterviewsatbfisouthbank3. Accessed 18 June 2011.

Duncan, Gene. 2010. 'The "Sunnyside" of Sleepy Hollow'. *Disney Parks Blog*, 8 July. http://disneyparks.disney.go.com/blog/2010/07/the-sunnyside-of-sleepy-hollow/. Accessed 30 May 2011.

Turi, Tim. 2011. 'Crafting atmosphere: *Silent Hill: Downpour* and the Czech Republic influence'. *GameInformer.com*, 25 January. www.gameinformer.com/games/silent_hill_downpour/b/xbox360/archive/2011/01/25/crafting-atmosphere-silent-hill-downpour-and-the-czech-republic-influence.aspx. Accessed 26 September 2011.

Ushinawareta Kioku (*Lost Memories*): *Silent Hill Chronicle*. 2003. Trans. 'wallofdeath'. http://silenthillchronicle.net. Accessed 7 June 2011.

Visit Sleepy Hollow – A tourist's guide to Sleepy Hollow. Sleepy Hollow Cemetery Historic Fund. www.visitsleepyhollow.com/. Accessed 19 June 2011.

Filmography

The Legend of Sleepy Hollow. 1980. Henning Schellerup, dir. NBC.
Poltergeist. 1982. Tobe Hooper, dir. Metro-Goldwyn-Mayer.
Silent Hill. 2006. Christopher Gans, dir. TriStar Pictures.
Sleepy Hollow. 1999. Tim Burton, dir. Paramount Pictures.
Vincent. 1982. Tim Burton, dir. Buena Vista Distribution.

Games

Silent Hill. 1999. Konami.
Silent Hill: Downpour. 2012. Konami.
Silent Hill: Homecoming. 2008. Konami.

13

Avril Horner

The Dark Knight: Fear, the law and liquid modernity

There are two ways of thinking about globalgothic. The first is to recognise that many different cultures across the world have experienced and continue to share a sense of the uncanny and/or the supernatural which is expressed through multiple forms, including music, art, literature, film and dance. Thus certain tropes (for example, ghosts; sacred space; malfunctioning space; the living dead in the form of vampires and zombies) seem to be repeated across time and space, albeit inflected by different histories, cultural legacies and ideologies. Such a perspective emphasises both the international nature of gothic and the return of the past or repressed in a way well documented by gothic scholars. The other, rather more interesting, way of defining globalgothic is to view it through the lens of late capitalism and emphasise the 'global' rather than the 'gothic'. From this perspective what we see are huge flows and shifts in various forms of energy or energising forces (for example, money, information, communication systems, media empire 'soft power') which, because they are in some ways spectral, are beyond the control of individual countries or states and thus capable of destabilising cultures and societies as well as enriching them. From a rational and optimistic point of view, such a brave new world can bring about much good. Globalisation encourages free trade and labour mobility, enhances political awareness and, via the internet, 'has enabled an increase in real per capital GDP of $500 in mature countries over the last 15 years – it took the industrial revolution 50 years to provide the same results' (Manyika and Roxburgh, 2011: 60).

However, the gothic does not deal, as we know, in the rational and optimistic. Its job is to articulate fear and anxiety and to thrill and chill us with terrible possibilities. Not surprisingly, then, globalgothic focuses on certain negative aspects of globalisation, including corporatism, neo-imperialism and the dangers of living in a high-risk culture that frequently sails perilously close to catastrophe (Beck, 1992). For many the globalised world is one in which individuals feel disempowered: in which the here is now and the past is dead or irrelevant. In globalised societies, Ghassan Hage claims, extensive low-level paranoia is increasingly common:

> In this phobic culture where everything is viewed as either threatening and in need of extermination or threatened and in need of protection, there is an invasion of the order of the border. From the borders of the self to the borders of the family, friendship, neighborhood, nation, and all the way to the borders of Western civilization, everything and everywhere is perceived as a border from which a potentially threatening other can leap. (2003: 86)

Globalgothic draws on such fears and expresses anxiety about the impact and effects of globalisation on cultures, societies and individuals, particularly in relation to loss of control. It is less concerned with the boundary between the quick and the dead, human and machine, self and other, than with new fears and terrors which coagulate around liminality: that is, the impossibility of defining the boundary between polarities such as local/global; place/cyberspace; autonomy/dissolution. Fears concerning loss of control are expressed in globalgothic through a focus on impotence in the face of technology run riot, various forms of viral contagion and the horror of socially induced trauma (caused through terrorism, global warfare or environmental disaster precipitated by global projects). Globalgothic thus frequently overlaps with the dystopian and the apocalyptic. Just as the Second World War and the Cold War each resulted in a spate of apocalypse writing, so the post-millennial surge of interest in apocalyptic fictions testifies to the level of fear resulting from globalisation. Such texts often carry a strong gothic dimension through the translation of humankind into quasi-zombie figures by means of viral contagion, technological control mechanisms or religious fundamentalism. However, although fears concerning globalisation are often channelled through individual characters in such works, the preoccupation is no longer with individual identity in relation to nation, gender and 'race', as it was in nineteenth-century European and American gothic texts, but with identity in relation to forces that are global, sometimes 'spectral' and frequently unpredictable. Globalgothic is, then, inflected by specific anxieties arising from the perception that globalisation is potentially an economic, cultural, technological and political tsunami that might sweep away autonomy at the level both of the individual and of the nation.

It is through this globalgothic lens that I wish to examine Christopher Nolan's *The Dark Knight*. Most reviewers agreed on three things about this film when it was released in 2008. Firstly, and most obviously, it very effectively continues the story of Batman and the Joker, developing and extending the characterisation of the pair from earlier graphic books and films in a sophisticated albeit highly convoluted manner: Chris Tookey suggested in a review of the film that 'The plot is often impossible to follow' (2008). Secondly, the film offers a darker gothic vision of people and politics than that presented in previous Batman productions. Thirdly, Heath Ledger steals the show by creating a particularly sinister and complex version of the Joker, with his interpretation of the character inspired by Malcolm McDowell's performance in *A Clockwork Orange* and Johnny Rotten (John Lydon) of the Sex Pistols. Gotham City is also remade for a twenty-first-century audience: a 'retro-futurist nightmare' in Charles Holland's words (2008: 207), it presents a dystopian image of New York (although the film was shot mainly in Chicago). As David Halbfinger notes in the *New York Times*, 'the creepy shadows and gothic Wayne Manor are gone, replaced by sleek towers, shiny surfaces, bright lighting' (2008). Indeed the very speed and sleekness of the affluent West contributes to the film's nightmare vision of city life; New York in this film could be any modern city packed with gleaming skyscrapers and, as Charles Holland points out, in *The Dark Knight* 'there is no Bat Cave. Instead, Batman works out of a space that is a cross between a corporate office and a contemporary art gallery' (2008: 207). Even though the Joker's energy is entirely driven by an anarchic desire for destruction, 'evil' is not confined to him alone; rather, it has been internalised and disseminated within the polis. The city, sleek and modern on the outside, has been wholly percolated by the mob, and harbours corruption at every level; the law and its arm of order, the police, are riddled with those who have betrayed principle either for personal profit or out of fear. As Bruce Wayne says when discussing justice, law and revenge with Rachel Dawes, 'Your system is broken'. Society has become an urban jungle that can no longer guarantee its citizens protection from violence and social breakdown.

In this respect the film is a typical gothic anti-Enlightenment tale that continues the Western post-industrial gothic narrative of the city as a nightmare space, a narrative that originated in the 'mysteries' fictions of Eugène Sue and G. W. M. Reynolds in the first half of the nineteenth century and found its apotheosis in Stevenson's *Dr Jekyll and Mr Hyde* in 1886. However, in post-millennial urban gothic texts it is the very sophistication of the city, rather than its dark labyrinths, that produces the nightmare: this is a world we know all too well, a world of underground car parks and bleak purpose-built high-rise office blocks housing identical corporate rooms. It is perhaps significant that we see almost nothing of the interior of Commissioner Gordon's family home and nothing at all of Rachel Dawes's flat: the domestic has no place in gothic Gotham. This is life lived in corporate city space; it is American life taken to extremes; it is deregulation in gothic mode. The desire of some characters to uphold justice in such a world means that Gotham is a city at war with itself. The film's emphasis on war and war tactics also, however, reflects recent American nightmares: David Halbfinger asks wryly 'Gotham as Baghdad anyone?' and Charles Holland notes that 'Not only 9/11 but Guantánamo Bay and Abu Ghraid are alluded to, both literally by a boat full of orange boiler-suited criminals and implicitly in the blurred lines between good and evil' (Halbfinger, 2008; Holland, 2008: 207). Critics of quite different political persuasions liken Batman's illegal activities to the state of emergency declared by George W. Bush in his attempt to protect American citizens after 9/11 (Klavan, 2008; Lewis, 2009; McGowan, 2009). As such comments suggest, many American reviewers read the film through the 'War on Terror' and the invasion of Iraq. However, the film's canvas is broader than such responses indicate. While offering a few threads of hope and optimism, *The Dark Knight* generally presents a dystopian version of twenty-first-century American life in which honesty and integrity struggle to survive: 'You thought we could be decent men in an indecent time' says Harvey Dent to Batman. It is, then, ironically appropriate that the two ferries at risk of complete destruction near the end of the film carry the names 'Spirit' and 'Liberty'.

An interesting twenty-first-century version of gothic, *The Dark Knight* reworks classic gothic devices in order to structure its plot dynamic, not only adapting the concept of the city space as threatening but also exploiting the figure of the double or doppelganger. Bruce Wayne has his own double in Batman, of course, but Batman and the Joker also represent a Jungian version of the self that, by definition, always carries a shadow, or dark side. Thus at one point the Joker says to Batman: 'I don't want to kill you; what would I do without you? . . . You *complete* me'; at another he says 'I think you and I are destined to do this forever'. Indeed, Alfred, Bruce Wayne's butler, points out that Batman's war on crime has actually driven the mob to liaise with the Joker; his very effectiveness has drawn the Joker to him. As the 'good' outlaw, Batman is a superhero, an ambiguous figure using violent means to achieve good ends. He is the *Dark* Knight who has to be hunted down and excoriated as well as celebrated; he is thus, by definition, a liminal figure who threatens as well as saves.

The deranged behaviour of the Joker, on the other hand, echoes that of many gothic figures, including Brockden Brown's Theodore Wieland, Lautréamont's Maldoror, Frankenstein's creature, many of Poe's characters and several of Stephen King's, including Jack Torrance in *The Shining*. We are offered little information about him, and some of the information he offers about himself is contradictory; the only constant is that he hated his father, whom he describes as a 'fiend'. Alfred 'explains' the Joker's behaviour by noting that: 'Some men just want to watch the world burn', and indeed the nature of the Joker's killing sprees ('I just do things') and his insistence that he merely wants to send 'a message' have been read by many American commentators in the light of 9/11: that is, as the seemingly anarchic and irrational acts of a terrorist. Harvey Dent asks the people of Gotham: 'Should we give in to this terrorist's demands?' and the Joker at one point sports a garment lined with grenades, reminiscent of a terrorist suicide mission. The ferries episode not only recalls Cold War strategies but also evokes the spectre of someone being able to obliterate a thousand citizens simply by pressing a button. The fact that no one on either boat can actually bring themselves to press the button presupposes, of course, that Americans do not do such things. The film's use of the word 'terrorist' and its emphasis on chance – represented by the disaffected Dent tossing coins and by his statement that 'The only morality in this cruel world is chance' – might also well reflect the average citizen's fear that survival in today's global community is down to luck, although Dent makes his own luck by keeping his father's two-headed coin about his person. In this world of chance, the Joker, like Al Qaida, is never vanquished entirely, only temporarily overcome. He thus works both as an outsider or outlaw and as a grotesque gothic expression of the potential violence and unpredictability of the terrorist, the ultimate cultural 'Other' who has become a global threat. It is perhaps no coincidence that the mobsters are also cultural 'others' in some way: 'The Chechen' and Salvatore Maroni, head of the Falcone family whose methods are those of the Mafia, for example. The two police in the mob's pay, Anna Ramirez and Wuertz, carry names with obvious European origins whereas the names 'Bruce Wayne' and 'Harvey Dent' suggest a more straightforward American lineage, not that there is such a thing of course. There is certainly a post-9/11 nervousness in the film about what Zygmunt Bauman has termed the 'strangers who have come to stay' (2007: 25), a nervousness that plays on the idea of the 'other' as threatening and that gives a gothic twist to the idea of the United States as a glorious mosaic of racial and national identities.

Although Batman is the 'good' outlaw and the Joker, particularly in Heath Ledger's sinister interpretation of the role, is the bad 'outlaw', they are both outlaws. The outlaw, as David Punter has noted, is a common figure in gothic fiction, 'from the *banditti* of the late eighteenth century to the cyber-"cowboys" of William Gibson and the mercenaries and space rovers of Iain M. Banks' (1998: 200). Every culture defines itself and its laws through outlaw figures, and the film engages with the law at many levels. Batman's role raises obvious questions about the efficacy of the law and the ethics of vigilante behaviour, as both Todd Walters (2009) and Todd McGowan (2009) have argued. However, the already complex dynamic between the Joker and Batman is further complicated by the figure of Harvey Dent. Bruce Wayne, who hosts a fund-raising event for him, describes Dent, newly appointed District Attorney, as 'the face of Gotham's bright future'. And, indeed, initially Dent fulfils this promise, invoking the United States Federal Law Racketeer Influenced and Corrupt Organizations Act (RICO) in order to round up the mob and the Joker. Initially a good man, the 'White Knight' who wishes to work through and with the law to save Gotham, he represents a challenge to the Joker who subsequently proves, by organising Rachel's death and manipulating Dent's ensuing emotions, that anyone is corruptible.

Dent's 'fall' into revenge is represented through the gothic trope of the double as split self, made visible later in the film's second half by the two sides of his face, one still handsome in an American chiselled way, the other horribly burned. Good and evil, it seems, are no longer simply separate entities or, indeed, separable. In this sense, as Todd Walters suggests, *The Dark Knight* represents a 'shift in superhero cinema: a turn away from simplistic narratives toward representations of more complex realities' (2009: 43). The film ends with various characters colluding with the lie that Batman was responsible for many deaths in order that the narrative of Dent as the White Knight can remain valid.

As Bruce Wayne says, 'Sometimes the truth isn't enough. Sometimes people deserve more. Sometimes people deserve to have their faith rewarded.' He thus fulfils Alfred's prediction: 'Batman can be the outcast. He can make the choice that no one else can make. The right choice.'

According to Zygmunt Bauman, it is vital in a disintegrating social culture that people can continue to believe in absolute justice, benign states and effective governments, even though such institutions and concepts may have become eroded and weakened by the force of global flows in money and information. In order for the illusion of their strength to be maintained, Batman shoulders responsibility for the murders committed by Dent; as Alfred informs Rachel: 'He's not being a hero. He's being something more.' Batman thus transmutes finally from outlaw into outcast and scapegoat, as predicted by the Joker: 'To them you're just a freak. Like me. They need you right now but when they don't, they'll cast you out like a leper. See, their morals, their code, is a bad joke and dropped at the first sign of trouble. They're only as good as the world allows them to be.' In this respect Batman can be seen as a version of Agamben's Homo Sacer, a man 'worthy of veneration and provoking horror', who can be killed but not sacrificed (Agamben, 1998: 73; 81–6), taking on such a role so that Harvey Dent can be resurrected as The White Knight in order to preserve faith in the law and democracy.[1] The doublings and pairings that the film sets up are thus finally resolved into gruesome triumvirates; indeed, Nolan admitted in interview that '*The Long Halloween* has a great triangular relationship between Harvey Dent and Gordon and Batman, and that's something we very much drew from' (Carroll, 2008). The Batman/Joker/Dent dynamic is arguably even more potent and certainly more important than the love interest in the film, represented by Rachel Dawes who, despite Maggie Gyllenhall's best efforts to give Rachel some spirit, has a role of limited significance, notwithstanding her status as Assistant District Attorney. *The Dark Knight* is a work that openly focuses on men, power and the law despite its flirtation with romantic love.

In fact what *The Dark Knight* illustrates so chillingly are the threats, uncertainties and negative spin-offs that result from what Zygmunt Bauman has termed 'liquid modernity' (2000). This is the term Bauman coined to describe the phase following 'solid' modernity, a phase marked by 'fluidity' rather than fixedness. In this period the flow of time counts more than space and place. It is characterised by, among other things, the erosion of social forms and institutions that, in their fixedness, block speed flows in information, money and technology. The consequent weakening of traditional social networks, such as community and neighbourhood, leaves the individual without the structures through which a life may be organised so that she or he is thrown into a different – and more fragmented – life experience. Individuals within liquid modernity live in the 'now' and must be ready to move fast, abandoning traditional commitments and loyalties if necessary, in order to survive economically and socially. For Bauman the negative spin-offs of this brave new world include alienation, isolation and unhealthy levels of fear and insecurity upon which various late capitalist bodies and governments prey in order to 'sell' security, for example gated properties. He sees us moving into a 'dystopia made to the measure of liquid modernity – one fit to replace the fears recorded in Orwellian and Huxleyan-style nightmares' (Bauman, 2000: 15). Bauman's vision seems to be reflected in *The Dark Knight*, a film that generates a potent, if perhaps only half-consciously realised, fear in the audience: fear of political, economic and judicial impotence in a 'speed-flow' world. Not surprisingly, then, the film itself is characterised in many ways by speed, a feature that drew accusations of incoherence from some reviewers. David Denby, for example, complained in *The New Yorker* that the film's sense of 'constant climax' leads to incoherence (2008) and David Edelstein described the film on National Public Radio as 'spectacularly incoherent', adding, 'I defy you to make spatial sense of a truck/Bat-tank/police car chase, or the climax with Batman, the Joker, hostages, SWAT teams, fake Batmen and Morgan Freeman on some kind of sonar monitoring gizmo' (2008).

However, seen in the context of Bauman's work on liquid modernity and the speed of global flows, such 'incoherence' makes perfect (if abstract) sense. While Nolan makes use of traditional gothic tropes and devices such as the city and the double in ways we quickly recognise, the film also evokes a sense of pandemonium arising from new forms of flow in information, money and technology which result in loss of control and loss of boundaries. It is no coincidence that there are several conversations about control, jurisdiction and boundaries in the film. In response to Bruce Wayne's assertion that the mob 'have crossed the line', Alfred replies 'You crossed the line first'; Bruce Wayne advises Harvey Dent that 'As our new DA, you might want to figure out where your jurisdiction ends' and also informs Alfred that Batman 'has no limits'. The Joker similarly comments that 'Batman has no jurisdiction' and, defining himself against the mob and the police who 'try to control', he advocates the destruction of all limits and jurisdictions: 'Introduce a little anarchy. Upset the established order.' Lau announces that he will go to Hong Kong which is 'far from Dent's jurisdiction', adding 'The Chinese won't extradite a national'.

American superheroes have always wrestled with the inadequacy of the law in the face of injustice, of course. However, *The Dark Knight* takes this formula a step further. The film's emphasis on law – major characters' identities are defined by their relationship with the law – and its constant references to the limits and definitions of legal power can be seen as an expression of anxiety in a global world in which community, state and national control have become unstable and often ineffectual. Such instability is, some theorists argue, an inevitable consequence of liquid modernity. Jiři Přibáň, for example, notes that liquid modernity

> reflects the diminishing role of the spatial dimensions of social life and highlights the central importance of the flow of time and social change. In the time-space duality, it is time associated with change, flexibility, mobility and overall 'lightness' that matters in liquid society. Information moves with the speed of the electronic signal and has eroded territorial state power. Power has become extraterritorial and the powerful are now those able to disengage themselves from local obligations. International law and nation state legal systems significantly contribute to this strategy of disengagement and growing social liquidity. Increasingly mobile and evasive forms of power coincide with new forms of legal regulation and domination. (2007: 1)

The law itself then, by implication, has become the handmaiden of liquid modernity, adjusting its precepts to the profit motive and global flows rather than to the needs and security of a community or a nation. Speed and lightness characterise the moment: as Bauman notes in *Liquid Modernity*: 'Travelling light, rather than holding tightly to things deemed attractive for their reliability and solidity – that is, for their heavy weight, substantiality and unyielding power of resistance – is now the asset of power' (2000: 13). No wonder, then, that Bruce Wayne tells Lucius Fox early in the film that 'I'm carrying too much weight. I need to be lighter', and that his later comment – 'I need a new suit' – follows Fox's suspicions about the fact that Lau Security Investments has 'grown 8 per cent annually like clockwork', adding 'His revenue stream must be off the books, maybe even illegal'. Fox does indeed provide Batman with a suit that enables him to become 'lighter, faster and more agile'. *The Dark Knight* shows us a world in which information and money flows are stopped neither by physical boundaries, such as state borders and national boundaries, nor by metaphysical constructs, such as the law, ethics or an ideal of citizenship. Lucius Fox, a man of integrity, realises what this can lead to: describing the sonar cell system as 'Beautiful. Unethical. Dangerous', he adds 'This is wrong', thereby acknowledging that, even when the end seems to justify the means, such surveillance constitutes a 'violation of civil liberties' (McGowan, 2009).

The film's emphasis on boundaries and control, then, is held in constant tension with global flows that are out of jurisdiction's reach and that recognise no such boundaries. Such flows include technology (the use of a sonar cell system as a form of global surveillance in a post-panoptic world); economic conduits (money flows to and is controlled from Hong Kong; can disappear, evaporate, become spectral); and political movements based on seemingly irrational affiliations (as we have seen, terrorism is evoked in various ways throughout the film). The real anxiety with which *The Dark Knight* engages, then, is the dawn of an age of impotence in which American economic, scientific and political power is rendered ineffectual through global movements and phenomena, including the rise of China as an economic superpower. Consoling in some ways – Lucius Fox represents ethical decision-making in such a world and the Gordons represent the survival of the family – the film nevertheless explores the fear that the traditional power structures of 'solid' modernity have been disrupted and outmoded, leaving modern America vulnerable and fragile. It hardly needs spelling out that the film's narrative resonates strongly with America's changing status concerning economic power and global supremacy after 9/11, the War on Terror and a global recession that has impacted on the West far more than the East. Going with the flows of liquid modernity has distinct economic advantages of course. Citing Clausewitz, Bauman points out that current warfare 'looks increasingly like a "promotion of global free trade by other means"' (2000: 12) – an argument recently developed by Naomi Klein (2008) – but the world of Gotham shows the cost of such complicity. This is, after all, a gothic film, intent on exploring liquid modernity as nightmare rather than as economic opportunity.

Bauman draws attention to Richard Sennett's statement that 'cries for law and order are greatest when . . . communities are most isolated from the other people in the city' (Bauman, 2000: 106, citing Sennett, 1997: 194). What we hear, long and loud, throughout *The Dark Knight* are precisely those cries. Such isolation, according to Bauman, is a product of 'The new individualism, the fading of human bonds and the wilting of solidarity [which] are the other side of the globalization coin . . . Society is no longer protected by the state, or at least, it is unlikely to trust the protection on offer; it is now exposed to the rapacity of forces it does not control and no longer hopes or intends to recapture and subdue' (2007: 35). In such a context the Joker's anarchic behaviour is only a hyperbolic expression of 'the rapacity of forces' that characterise liquid modernity. This, indeed, is the nature of his 'message'; as he says himself: 'I'm not a monster. I'm just ahead of the curve.' Nolan's resurrection of a superhero whose relationship to the law is ambiguous in order to reassert American integrity and strength is impressive but, as René Girard suggests in *La Violence et le sacré* (cited in Bauman, 2000: 194), the use of violence becomes more common as a boundary-drawing device when boundaries themselves, including those of the law, become indistinct and porous. The resulting 'state of exception', supposedly temporary and declared only in times of crisis, can in fact pave the way to a permanent state of emergency, allowing the status and integrity of the law to be further eroded. This, in turn, creates a climate in which fascism and totalitarianism can flourish, as Agamben has argued (Agamben, 2005). The fragility of Gotham City reflects a real fear that all that seemed solid has indeed melted into liquid modernity. If this is the real cause of the 'war' in Gotham City, then Batman has a long fight ahead of him indeed.

Note

1 I owe this connection to Fred Botting.

References

Agamben, Giorgio. 1998. *Homo Sacer: Sovereign Power and Bare Life*, trans. Daniel Heller-Roazen. Stanford: Stanford University Press.

——. 2005. *State of Exception*, trans. Kevin Attell. Chicago: University of Chicago Press.

Bauman, Zygmunt. 2000. *Liquid Modernity*. Cambridge: Polity Press.

——.2007. 'Uncertainty and other liquid-modern fears'. In *Liquid Society and Its Law*, ed. Jiři Přibáň. Ashgate: Aldershot, 17–40.

Beck, Ulrich. 1992. *Risk Society: Towards a New Modernity*, trans. M. Ritter. London: Sage.

Brown, Charles Brockden. 1798. *Weiland; or, the Transformation: An American Tale*. New York: H. Caritat.

Hage, Ghassan. 2003. '"Comes a time we are all enthusiasm": Understanding Palestinian suicide bombers in times of exighophobia'. *Public Culture,* 15.1: 65–89. Cited in Diane Negra. 2009. *What a Girl Wants? Fantasizing the Reclamation of Self in Postfeminism*. London: Routledge.

King, Steven. 1977. *The Shining*. New York: Doubleday.

Klein, Naomi. 2008. *The Shock Doctrine: The Rise of Disaster Capitalism*. London: Penguin.

Lautréamont, Comte de (Isidore Lucien Ducasse). 1868–69. *Les Chants de Maldoror*. Paris: Albert Lacroix.

Přibáň, Jiři, ed. 2007. *Liquid Society and Its Law*. Ashgate: Aldershot.

Punter, David. 1998. *Gothic Pathologies: The Text, the Body and the Law*. Basingstoke: Macmillan.

Reynolds, G. W. M. 1844–56. *The Mysteries of London*. Published weekly.

Sennett, Richard. 1997. *The Uses of Disorder: Personal Identity and City Life*. London: Faber & Faber.

Shelley, Mary. 1818. *Frankenstein, or The Modern Prometheus*. 3 vols. London: Lackington, Hughes, Harding, Mavor and Jones.

Stevenson, Robert Louis. 1866. *The Strange Case of Dr Jekyll and Mr Hyde*. London: Longmans, Green and Co.

Sue, Eugène. 1842–3. *Les Mystères de Paris*. Published serially in *Journal des débats*.

Walters, Todd. 2009. '*The Dark Knight*'. *Philosophy Now*, 73: 42–5.

Internet sources

Carroll, Larry. 2008. 'In "Dark Knight", the often-incompetent Jim Gordon actually knows what he's doing'. *MTV Movie News,* 10 July. www.mtv.com/news/articles/1590648/commissioner-gordon-knows-what-hes-doing-dark-knight.jhtml. Accessed 10 September 2009.

Denby, David. 2008. 'Past shock'. *The New Yorker*, 21 July. www.newyorker.com/arts/critics/cinema/2008/07/21/080721crci_cinema_denby. Accessed 10 September 2009.

Edelstein, David. 2008. 'The dark night: A cheerless blood-drenched allegory'. National Public Radio, 12 July. www.npr.org/templates/story/story.php?storyId=92624890. Accessed 10 September 2009.

Halbfinger, David. M. 2008. 'Batman's burden: A director confronts darkness and death'. *New York Times*, 9 March. www.nytimes.com/2008/03/09/movies/09halb.html. Accessed 10 September 2009.

Holland, Charles. 2008. 'Review of *The Dark Knight*'. *Icon,* 64: 207. www.iconeye.com/read-previous-issues/icon-o64-%7C-october-2008/the-dark-knight. Accessed 10 September 2009.

Klavan, Andrew. 2008. 'What Bush and Batman have in common'. *Wall Street Journal,* 25 July. http://online.wsj.com/article/SB121694247343482821.html?mod=opinion_main_commentaries. Accessed 10 September 2009.

Lewis, Randolph. 2009. '*The Dark Knight* of American empire'. *Jump Cut: A Review of Contemporary Media,* 51. www.ejumpcut.org/archive/jc51.2009/DarkKnightBloch/index.html. Accessed 15 January 2010.

Manyika, James, and Charles Roxburgh. 2011. 'The web makes us richer'. *Prospect*, September. www.prospectmagazine.co.uk/tag/gdp-growth/. Accessed September 2011.

McGowan, Todd. 2009. 'The exceptional darkness of *The Dark Knight*'. *Jump Cut: A Review of Contemporary Media*, 51. www.ejumpcut.org/archive/jc51.2009/dark-KnightKant/index.html. Accessed 20 December 2009.

Tookey, Chris. 2008. '*The Dark Knight* – Holy moly! Batman's a big noise – but loses the plot'. *Daily Mail*, 24 July. www.dailymail.co.uk/tvshowbiz/reviews/article-1037123/Holy-Moly-Batmans-big-noise--loses-plot.html. Accessed 10 September 2009.

Filmography

A Clockwork Orange. 1971. Stanley Kubrick, dir. Warner Bros.

The Dark Knight. 2008. Christopher Nolan, dir. Warner Bros.

Fred Botting

Globalzombie: From *White Zombie* to *World War Z*

In his preface to Franz Fanon's *The Wretched of the Earth*, Jean-Paul Sartre invokes zombies as doubled figures in the construction and critique of colonial power and western humanism:

> Europeans you must open this book and enter into it. After a few steps in the darkness you will see strangers gathered around a fire; come close, and listen, for they are talking of the destiny they will mete out to your trading-centres and to the hired soldiers who defend them. They will see you, perhaps, but they will go on talking among themselves, without even lowering their voices. This indifference strikes home: their fathers, shadowy creatures, *your* creatures, were but dead souls; you who allowed them glimpses of light, to you only did they dare speak, and you did not bother to reply to such zombies. Their sons ignore you; a fire warms them and sheds light around them, and you have not lit it. Now, at a respectful distance, it is you who will feel furtive, nightbound and perished with cold. Turn and turn about; in these shadows from whence a new dawn will break, it is you who are the zombies. (Sartre, 2001: 11–12)

Subaltern and disempowered by their Western masters, zombies stand, initially, for the effects of colonial power: dehumanised and ignored, colonial subjects begin to discover their own fire and voice in revolutionary violence reversing the gaze of their supposed masters and disclosing the latter's lack of soul, feeling or humanity. Writing in 1961, Sartre criticises the underlying monstrosity of Western humanism (to make men, he claims, also requires making slaves and monsters). Reversing zombie positions, for colonised countries, forms the basis of a challenge to and overturning of power relations; it also cuts at the very heart of Western humanistic self-representations.

Over forty years later, to follow Sartre, zombies more than ever are 'us', supposing that the collective pronoun, in a contemporary global context, still retains any purchase in a world in which, ideologically or technologically, differences between humanity and monstrosity are more reversible and difficult to define. Borders separating self and other wear thin in the face of rapid and extensive flows of capital, information, commodities and bodies. Binary oppositions (West–East/North–South) lose definition; geopolitical structures break up, diverse ethnic groupings emerge. Forms of domination change under transnational capital and resistance to or subversion of imposition occurs in the name of local tradition, custom and community. 'Globalgothic', questioning how far Western forms can be adapted to or opened up by specific cultural traditions, traces some of the tensions evinced in postcolonial criticism. But globalgothic does not simply repeat postcolonial questions in asserting local specificities against overpowering and tyrannically imposed political, economic and cultural systems, its empires writing back darkly by invoking the shadowy figures of and beyond Western monstrosity. Hence 'global' and 'gothic' entwine: the difference of world and cultural form (a difference sustained in modernity) becomes an enveloping darkness spreading across borders. There is another sense to globalgothic: if gothic arose as a mirror to the modernity of progress, democracy, enlightened humanism – that is as its violent, exclusionary, tyrannical underside – then globalgothic also has neocolonial economic implications as a brand spreading across the world, another Coke, another McDonald's, another Nike (Goldman and Papson, 1998; Wernick, 1991; Botting, 2004): in this mode, with a swoosh of bats encircling the globe, 'GGI' – Global Goth Inc. – insinuates itself, as advertising slogans do, into everyday discourse ('I'd like to teach the world to goth'; 'I'm gothing it'; 'Just goth it'; 'Vorsprung durch gotik' and so on). Replicating transnational flows of capital and commodities, globalgothic may also hold up a mirror to a world rewritten, its differences of culture and history reformatted by the context of globalisation, suggesting a new, dark age shadowing the new world order of homogenised consumption and corporate cultural and economic control. The two senses of 'globalgothic' sustain a doubleness that refuses division, acknowledging the political complexities emerging with globalisation and confronting the often unbearable contradictions of social, ethical and critical questioning that comes with globalisation's challenge to diverse ways of life and values. Globalgothic registers – albeit anxiously and without assurance

– the shifts and ruptures that disturb all contemporary zones, be they psychic, social, geopolitical or virtual.

Glennis Byron's recent mapping of the contours of globalgothic lays out intercultural relations of an emerging hybrid form, careful to avoid resolving the opposition between a homogenised global system and the specifics of local folklore tradition. Her reading of Tunku Halim's *Dark Demon Rising* identifies how Western, gothic figures of monstrosity are linked to the disturbing simulacra of brands, commodities and urban flows, how they constitute threats to Malaysian rural life and customs. While local demons rise up in resistance, and it seems that tradition wins out in Halim's novel, both poles become prey to a wider, more disturbing sense of meaninglessness and derealisation: the anxiety globalism evokes produces an evacuation and filling of subjective-cultural voids with lifestyle commodities that, apparently, can be resolved only by a return to custom, community and tradition that have been reinvented, fabricated anew. In the vacillation between country and city life, between materialism and spirituality, consumerism and tradition, and with femininity torn between propriety, sexual transgression and economic independence, the ending establishes itself only as another fantasy, a nostalgic return to a rural continuity that never existed, a place that, while seeming to offer reality, coherence and meaning against the horrors of globalism, acknowledges itself to be another fantasy construction.

As rapid derealisation interfects local and global, a crowded, unnerving and transitory space of in-betweenness emerges. Homi Bhabha's *The Location of Culture* engages with postcolonial ambivalences and undecidability, recognising modern culture's plurality. Interstitial, culture is *heimlich* and *unheimlich* at once, its mobility a fraught 'internal liminality' of differentiations, ambivalences, translations (Bhabha, 1994: 149). Lines of demarcation, differentiation and exclusion break up, along with ideas of nation and self-identity: 'cultural globality', for Bhabha, 'is figured in the *in-between* spaces of double-frames: its historical originality marked by a cognitive obscurity; its decentred "subject" signified in the nervous temporality of the transitional, or the emergent provisionality of the "present"' (216).

Bhabha's version of culture offers a position that is relational, plural and mobile. In highlighting issues of cultural translation and liminality, moreover, Bhabha is sensitive to the movement that precedes and undermines fixed structures. His argument has significant bearing on ways to conceptualise globalgothic and its relation to reading and writing practices. It relates, for instance, to a novel engaging with questions of empire, cultural transition, nation and migration, a novel that may or may not be postcolonial, magical realist or, even, gothic: Salman Rushdie's *Shame* (1983). *Shame* tells the story of Indian independence and partition, focusing on the political ramifications and hard realities of military and religious power in a newly formed Pakistan. But that is one of its storylines. It also spins a fabulous yarn about a doctor-voyeur-poet born upside down to three sisters who marries the troubled daughter – Sufiya Zinobia – of one of Pakistan's warring political families. Fiction and history, imagination and monstrosity, tradition, empire and modernity, political oppression and sexual repression: all these collide and interpenetrate in this novel by a man born in India, who moved to Pakistan, was educated in England and, at the time of writing, was living and working in advertising in London. In dealing with identity and migration, the novel moves between cultures and discusses their interrelations in terms of translation. A doubleness characterises the account: in translation meanings are lost and gained.

With the sense of being carried across, translation also impinges upon questions of migration in which history, belonging and tradition are displaced. This, in the novel's terms, is not necessarily a bad thing: discussing how people can become attached to a birthplace, the narrator comments how we pretend we are trees and speak of roots, which 'are a conservative myth, designed to keep us in our places' (Rushdie, 1983: 86). Too much pressure, keeping one in one's place, also describes the novel's main topic: shame. 'Shame' is an untranslatable word, a signifier of the taboos that conjoin cultural identity to both tradition and violence. In the novel its specific pressures on familial, religious and political life in Pakistan spread beyond borders to a terse and brutal reference to honour killings and riots in London. For all its untranslatability – marker of blockage and the stubborn and chunky intransigence of cultural specificity – shame is provided with a distinctly global metaphor: the narrator invites us to imagine shame 'as a liquid', 'a sweet fizzy tooth-rotting drink, stored in a vending machine' (122). Contained in a cup, the analogy suggests, the flows of shame-shamelessness are given outlet. With no cup 'the fluid of shame spills, spreading in a frothy lake across the floor' (122). Without appropriate social forms and rituals, shame fails to maintain bonds, values and traditions. Force-fed myths and ideologies, one pukes in violent abreaction. The metaphor of globalisation indicates one cause of shame. But shame is not only imposed from outside, it emerges as a result of excessive internal pressures in family life, sexual roles and political structures. Like the losses and gains of translation, the axis of shame-shamelessness discloses a movement that is ambivalent and disturbing, producing – in the innocent figure of the daughter – a violent and monstrous excess: Sufiya Zinobia, young, innocent, slow, becomes the receptacle of a family's and a nation's shame, her monstrous acts of destruction pathological and political all at once.

The doubleness and ambivalence that arises in *Shame* seems to assume familiar, almost gothic proportions. David Punter (2000) identifies a Frankensteinian element to Sufiya's monstrosity and reads it, as the novel's narrator suggests, in terms of a modern dialectic of civilisation and barbarism in which monstrosities must be pushed to the outer edges of social life. Excluded, Sufiya remains very much at the centre, born and bred within the citadels of decency and propriety. Yet, described as exterminating angel, werewolf and vampire, identified as both beauty and beast, Jekyll and Hyde, she cannot stay in the realms of fantasy, especially in a novel in which fantasy has already and irrevocably fused with reality. Even when the narrator seems to offer a solution to too much myth, fantasy, shame and corruption, he can only propose as a 'new myth' three very familiar terms: 'liberty, equality, and fraternity'. These, he suggests, compose a 'third' myth (251). But the move to the ideals of enlightened, democratic humanity, a move which restores distinctly modern oppositions and hierarchies, may not, in the terms laid out, be tenable even as myth: the return to humanity, enlightenment and democracy, to the clarity of historical and cultural (Western) ideals and differences, seems to have already been clouded if not undermined in the novel's earlier reference to a French Revolution whose enlightened heroes and dark villains cannot be held apart. The popular figure of Danton merges with the tyrant Robespierre; they become chimerical figures of civilised barbarity and barbaric civilisation, 'Danpierre' and 'Robeston' (240). Doubles are not divisible, it seems, something blocks, and perhaps enables, the easy imposition of obvious oppositions, confounding delineations into the comfortable dualities of good and evil, ego and id, surface and depth, appearance and reality, inner and outer. In *Shame* the invocation of gothic figures prevents any easy separation or resolution of matters of monstrosity. Indeed enlightenment modernity – in gothic commentary – invented its monstrosities from the start as its underside and necessary antithesis. The doublings of *Shame* become visibly and inseparably bound up with a duplicity it cannot shake off. In this respect a novel ostensibly about Pakistan yet also using Western gothic figures and political rhetoric turns questions of globalgothic inward to open up the double face of modernity itself, a double face already busy eating itself.

Enter the zombie. Neglected until recently, paradoxical and remorselessly unattractive, zombies disclose a disturbing internal excess in Western constructions of its self and its others, an excess exacerbated by the economic and cultural upheavals associated with globalisation and intensified by the flows of information, commodities and bodies in which a transnational and corporate mode of capitalism tears up older securities anchoring identity in structures of nation, culture, family, class, work, leaving them, in Ulrich Beck's phrase, as 'zombie categories' (Beck and Beck-Gernstein; 2002). Zombies are modern figures: sites of colonial-global crossings, internal excess and misrecognition. Susan Sontag (1974) links them to aliens and bodysnatchers, results of the dehumanising efficiency of technocratic power rather than figures embodying generic gothic distinctions between primitivism and enlightenment. In American films of the 1930s and 1940s – *King of the Zombies, I Walked with a Zombie* – however, gothic themes are played out in a racialised context: a displaced South, the Caribbean, provides the setting for a sexualised encounter with an otherness exuding colonial anxieties and demanding to be suppressed. This is the ostensible pattern of Victor Halperin's film *White Zombie* (1932). A woman travelling to join her fiancé, an American bank employee in Haiti, meets another American, a plantation owner, onboard. He offers to host their wedding at his villa. He has an ulterior motive, wanting her for himself. He solicits the help of a local voodoo master in order to take possession of her. A special powder renders her unconscious and apparently dead. She is buried, exhumed and taken from her tomb to the castle of the voodoo master, who keeps her for himself, zombifying the plantation owner when he protests. Her bereft fiancé, after a period of disconsolate drunkenness, and with the aid of a local doctor and priest, sets out to rescue and revive her.

On the surface *White Zombie* presents a tale of amorous delusion and possession equating race and sexuality as forms of otherness to be mastered through diabolical possession or be reclaimed by love, rationality or religion: primitivism and superstition are set against civilisation and reason. As the plot moves rapidly through wedding, death and burial, it climaxes in a distinctly gothic location: the lair of the voodoo master is a ruined medieval castle perched on a cliff top. External sublimity – low shots looking up from the shore at the imposing edifice – is reinforced with internal scenes dominated by a grand and gloomy hall, its long arched windows letting in a chiaroscuro of light. Given the Caribbean setting, the gothic scene is extremely strange, as is the casting of its lead actor, Bela Lugosi, who plays the voodoo master 'Murder Legendre'. The European émigré and Hollywood's face of Dracula further imposes the Old World on the New, turning voodoo into a Europeanised, archaic fantasy threatening the clean-cut American couple. The move is strange, and not so much because Vodun is linked to gothic images: the religion emerged as an effect of slavery and colonialism, with various African belief systems, Catholicism and French folklore mixed together. It also served as one of the few points of unity in the successful slave rebellion of the 1790s that threw out the slave masters and established a Republic (see Leyburn, 1966; Simpson, 1940; Hurston, 1938). What is strange about *White Zombie*'s yoking of a gothicised Europe and Europeanised voodoo is its American and imperialist occlusions (see Williams, 1983). In 1932 Haiti had already been under US occupation for seventeen years. Marines invaded in 1915 for a range of reasons: to deal with the insolvency and anarchy following the assassination of the President, and, supposedly, to thwart Germany's intention to take over the country. The invasion led to a period of reconstruction and modernisation, and limited guerrilla resistance, in which a collective peasant economy ceded to changes in property laws and sugar production, and slave labour was employed in road building. In this light an American bank employee, and an American plantation owner, though dressed in the manner of a colonial Englishman, assume greater significance: the film, while avoiding direct acknowledgement of US imperialism, registers via its gothic tropes and images distaste at the abuse of power associated with European modes of colonialism.

For all its gothic trappings the film does not quite manage to cast everything into a past associated with Europe. It engages with the then modernity of film form, as, in Walter Benjamin's critique, one of the most striking technical manifestations of crowded urban existence. Murder Legendre is not only a master of voodoo spells and potions who dwells in a Gothic castle: he is also a mill owner who puts his zombies to work carrying sacks of cane and turning the enormous grinding wheel that refines it into sugar. His mill, though lit darkly and shot through railings to suggest the atmosphere of a Piranesi print, is a place of industry. He even recommends zombies to the plantation owner on commercial grounds: tireless, obedient, slavish, neither eating nor sleeping, they are the ideal workers for the long hours and mechanised routines of productive labour. In looking back, gothically, and yet forward, in its context of industrial and cinematic production, *White Zombie* discloses the some of the features of 'Gothic modernism' that Tom Gunning (2000) analyses in Lang's *Metropolis*: the film stages a conflict between gothic and modernity in which its very modern images of industrialised society, social control and scientific innovation are set against the dark underworld of the workplaces and the monstrous machines of mechanical production, stark presentations of modern, Fordist productive relations. The modernity of the zombie, inscribed by conditions of mechanical production and represented by the most modern mode of mechanical reproduction (cinema), thus crystallises as the very image of mass society developing in the early twentieth century (Tulloch, 1977).

Mass society, mass consumption, mass culture: the pattern is set for readings of zombies, Romero's *Night of the Living Dead* and *Dawn of the Dead* being two of the most influential. The former, released in 1968, presents the mass conformism of the 1950s under pressure from the mass protests of the Civil Rights and anti-Vietnam movements. Mass media are foregrounded in the film: radio and television become a focus for the survivors who avidly watch news reports and interviews with government officials, scientists and the military arguing over the cause of the phenomenon and the solution. Terms like 'mass murder epidemic' and 'mass hysteria' underline the question of mass culture and conformism – and associate it with zombies – while at the same time the humans remain captivated by the television screen. *Dawn of the Dead* (1978) traces further changes in the political and economic climate. Its famous central location, the shopping mall, brings questions of consumption to the fore in which the move from industrial production – characterised by mass labour, useful rationality and conservative, prudent morality – gives way to luxurious, wasteful consumption and non-productive expenditures of credit cards, advertising, and service industries (Goux, 1990). The film begins with scenes of mass media failure and social breakdown. On arriving at its celebrated centrepiece, the zombie-filled mall, the small group of survivors survey the scene of shambling, animated corpses in bemusement as much as fear: 'what are they doing; where are they going?' asks one: their origins obscure, their amblings senseless, their otherness briefly intact. Another replies with a phrase that becomes the film's refrain: 'they're us', just doing what they used to do in an important place in their lives, directed by the residues of memory and instinct. 'They're us': like the zombies window shopping their way around the mall, the survivors do the same. 'They're us': the zombie consumer identification is reinforced by shots of survivors exchanging looks with zombies through shop windows, one group the mirror of another. 'They're us': identification discloses a difference, minimal though it may be. When the survivors turn on the automated facilities of the mall and the lights, escalators, fountains, announcements, and, as a comic soundtrack, the muzak, all start working, the zombies who had previously been threatening shadows are rendered figures of fun: their lack of co-ordination, lack of reflexes and ungainliness are exaggerated, their inability to negotiate their environment played up as they fall over, fall into fountains and fall off escalators. Buffoons, clowns, lumbering fools, these consumer zombies are thrown by a world of automation, hapless in the face of the simplest machinery.

They're us, but not quite. They never seem satisfied, nor achieve the fullness of consumption or completion of death, just repeating ad nauseam. Zombies are aimless, useless, destructive (Modleski, 1986: 158); they have 'no positive connotations whatsoever' (Wood, 1986: 118). Their negativity associated, in terms of the skill sets of post-industrial corporate capital, with 'already-exhausted sources of value', they are the 'dead weight' of a labour force of no use to an economy of outsourced manufacturing and high staffing costs: lumbering, redundant, they slow down capital's investments and returns; they are those workers 'consumed and cast aside' by the move towards post-industrial consumer services (Shaviro, 2002: 263–8). They are the 'disenfranchised underclass of the material world . . . a projection of postmodern capitalism's anxiety about *itself*' (Beard, 1993: 30). Compare Romero's zombies to the fast, sophisticated, adaptable and sexy cyborg-vampires celebrated in the flight to posthuman virtuality: fast, agile, forever young, they have the vocational skills of the new networked creative and cultural economy of impermanent self-employment, flexibility, technological innovation and enterprise (Latham, 2002). Zombies are us: figures of unproductive expenditure, too slow, lumbering and inflexible to cope, too corporeal and disconnected to be anything other than the jetsam of a virtual dematerialisation entailed in the flight of globalisation.

The new frontiers marked out in this shift do not solely follow the lines of inclusion and exclusion of geopolitical and imperial borders: within what is called the 'First World', the homeless, unemployed, elderly, sick, travellers and beggars form an interior outside, an unbearable internal excess (Žižek, 1993: 222). For Michel Serres, in his account of new communications technologies, the destitute become angels of a new state of being: 'the wretched of the earth are messengers of an extraordinary state which is unknown to us. They roam the streets, they keep a low profile, they don't say much, they reach out a hand, they disappear . . . and then suddenly re-appear on a street corner: they are phantoms but they are real, in the sense that they pierce through our illusory realities' (Serres, 1995: 20). Figures of a techno-economic reconfiguration of reality, these 'angels' haunt the inside with the approach of something unknown, left behind, yet to come . . .

On a global scale the living dead represent the dejecta of post-industrialism, or the mass of individuated bodies in sweatshops or crossing seas and borders, without identities or papers, hungry for useful, paid employment, eager to feed families or flee cycles of oppression, war and starvation. Max Brooks's *World War Z* (2006), written as supplement to a UN report documenting human testimonies on the suffering, devastation and rebuilding of the zombie war, charts the emergence and overcoming of global swarms of living dead. These swarms in part constitute reactionary images of Western fears of immigrants and asylum seekers; they also manifest the excessive, wasteful, destructive effects of global capital as it transforms lives within Western borders, rendering the differentiated post-industrial mass powerless, useless, stupid, voracious consumers spending without meaning and direction. While insisting on recovering that most problematic of characteristics – the human factor – in the face of zombie swarms, the novel also takes great pleasure in imagining total destruction of the emergent new world order. A zombie apocalypse, a global destruction like a biblical, cold war or planetary meltdown, is not, in Brooks's terms, such a bad idea. He has spent rather a long time, too long perhaps, working on the details: his *Zombie Survival Guide* (2003) itemises the dos and don'ts, the strategy, equipment and training for living in a world overrun with zombies. Within Brooks's curious humour lurk strong traces of survivalism and militia-minded anti-governmental independence (though Brooks lives in New York not Montana). If his novel recoils from the excesses and uncertainties of the emergent new world order, its return to communal, practical values involves, enjoys even, huge sacrifices of lives and cultures in which global monstrosity leads to different geopolitical patterns and ways of living.

There are all sorts of nasty and ambivalent political edges: not only in the spectacle of mass destruction and cultural collapse but also in its cruel mockery of the zombie-like stupidity of fellow citizens.

Enjoyment, of course, is never a wholesome process, though it is integral to the constitution of what, otherwise, would be porous or incomplete subjective, cultural and ideological boundaries. It is, moreover, a feature of gothic fictions from the start (Townshend, 2007).What Lacan calls 'Other enjoyment' or the 'theft of enjoyment' explains how beings deal with excess and otherness, a model that can be applied to racism (Miller, 1988: 125; Žižek, 1993: 203). Immigrants, for example, are contradictorily represented as working either too hard or too little, taking too much from our health service or not paying enough tax: the construction does not say much about immigrant groups, but discloses inner tensions in the host culture and its value systems. The other serves as a screen on which to project those internal anxieties and enables the venting of tensions that become unbearable, that chew one up from within (obesity, smoking, anti-social behaviour).

In *World War Z* enjoyment takes various forms: there are nasty pleasures in comments on the way that US citizens fleeing north from the zombie hordes take all sorts of useless consumer items – laptops, hairdryers, GameCubes – rather than warm clothes and food. The hierarchies of a culture of disposable wealth, goods and services are overthrown: like the waste of consumer society, the executives, reps, analysts who have no useful skills for survival, are recycled, retrained by the immigrant carpenters and machinists they used to employ. They, however, learn to find meaning in productive labour and rediscover a sense of community. Technological excess, too, is tempered: all the weaponry of advanced military acquisitions, the platform of 'netrocentric' or 'hyperwar', 'don't mean shit' (92) in the face of relentless zombie hordes. Military failure is watched on TV. In another incident a group of celebrities holed up in a luxurious villa bunker on a New York island watch people being consumed in the streets on TV while broadcasting to a live audience. They are soon besieged, not by zombies but by human viewers. Global capitalism is shown to be a 'crapshoot' in which entrepreneurs can make millions exploiting fear by marketing drugs that were never effective against the virus causing zombification. Capital, virus, advertising, information, migration cohere as a metaphor for globalisation's destructive flows. Enjoyment, in these instances, has an expulsive direction, an expenditure of unbearably unproductive figures, energies and activities, a release from or exhaustion caused by too much information, too many commodities, too many contradictions. It relishes manifestations of the uselessness and corruption of systems of state and ideological protection, all powerless against the zombie swarms they exploited or failed to manage.

Other episodes disclose a darker political undercurrent to enjoyment. For all the testimony from around the world, many of the accounts, particularly of the process of rebuilding, centre on the US, though it is divested of any gloss of imagined global superiority. In locating the origins of the zombie contagion in China and its spread in the migrations from the East, enjoyment is projected outwards in fears of population expansion and economic power. These fears stem not from threatened superiority but from its loss: only as China and India become the new economic superpowers (as the novel notes) does US imperialism turn on itself and a political morality disgusted at other countries' excesses – pollution, oil consumption, human rights abuses – finds outlet. Other readings presented in the novel argue that zombies constitute an act of vengeance against the 'First World' allowing other economies to develop and prosper. The most successful countries, again announcing a political ambivalence, are those that have pursued isolationist paths, whether enforced or otherwise. Israel erects another fence (though is beset by internal discord); Cuba keeps the swarms at bay; South Africa, revising an apartheid plan to deal with mass black uprising, drafts a global policy for survival: its rationale being that millions of humans will have to be sacrificed. At the end the global map is redrawn: Cuba, in a pleasing irony, has become the commercial and financial powerhouse of the recovering world economy while the US struggles to establish a viable currency; a 'Holy Russian Empire' and a United States of Southern Africa have emerged. The US, however, seems to have recovered some of its older values (self-reliance, sacrifice, hard work, community) and a new sense of freedom. Despite the scale of sacrifice and suffering, it almost seems worth it: close to the end of the book a wheelchair-bound, Pakistani-American sculptor observes: 'I'm not going to say the war was a good thing. I'm not that much of a sick fuck, but you've got to admit that it did bring people together' (336). It is perhaps a sick idea to restore a human community through killing billions, as if the only sense of unity comes at the cost of global disintegration.

World War Z turns away from globalisation by turning on its excesses, tracing its own violent self-consumption and the destructive drives it generates. Zombies perform a multiple function in this unifying, purgative sacrificial expenditure, a condensation of the homogenised multitude (as individuated mass, virus, wastefulness, consumerist stupidities and pusillanimous politics) produced by global capital: an entirely other and undead system of exploitation from which it is already impossible to extricate oneself. Its excess is zombie jouissance, an enjoyment which remains too much our own. They're us. The identification may be desirable in that they are free from death, self-consciousness, enjoyment. It is also unbearable and demands expulsion. Overdetermined in their cultural and political significance, yet resolutely not human, zombies provide another blank screen for otherness and enjoyment, a return to the oscillation between all-too human and utterly inhuman underlying humanism, another degree zero of otherness against which a degree zero of humanity can be reinvoked. Perhaps it is just nostalgia countering the pressure of multiple and fragmentary global swarms and flows. Or perhaps it is a brief venting of excesses and anxieties. The novel's return to human values and community, recentring the human figure in a global world that thought it had passed beyond humanity, returns to a basic humanist fantasy: that there is an idea of person that transcends myth, culture, ideology. Maybe, in the words of Rushdie's narrator, it is a myth that should be highly recommended. Yet myth, as Barthes noted, is a language that refuses to die, one that turns subjects into 'speaking corpses' (1973: 133). Ambivalent, myth again masks monstrous excesses which humans remain unable to claim as their own – or move beyond.

References

Barthes, Roland. 1973. *Mythologies*, trans. Annette Lavers. London: Cape.

Beard, Steve. 1993. 'No particular place to go', *Sight and Sound*, 3.4: 30–1.

Beck, Ulrich, and Beck-Gernstein, Elisabeth. 2002. *Individualization: Institutionalized Individualism and Its Social and Political Cosequences*. London: Sage.

Benjamin, Walter. 1968. *Illuminations*, trans. Harry Zohn, ed. Hannah Arendt. New York: Schoken Books.

Bhabha, Homi. 1994. *The Location of Culture*. London: Routledge.

Botting, Fred. 2004. 'fcuk speed'. *Culture and Organisation*, 10.1: 37–52.

Brooks, Max. 2003. *World War Z*. London: Duckworth.

——. 2006. *The Zombie Survival Guide*. New York: Three Rivers Press.

Byron, Glennis. 2008. '"Where meaning collapses": Tunku Halim's *Dark Demon Rising* as global gothic'. In *Asian Gothic: Essays on Literature, Film and Anime*, ed. Andrew Hock Soon Ng. Jefferson, NC: McFarland, 19–31.

Goldman, Robert, and Papson, Stephen. 1998. *Nike Culture*. London: Sage.

Goux, Jean-Joseph. 1990. 'General economics and postmodern capitalism'. *Yale French Studies*, 78: 206–24.

Gunning, Tom. 2000. *The Films of Fritz Lang*. London: BFI Publishing.

Hurston, Zora Neale. 1938. *Tell My Horse: Voodoo and Life in Haiti and Jamaica.* Philadelphia: Lippincott.
Lacan, Jacques. 1998. *The Seminar of Jacques Lacan Book XX Encore 1972–1973*, trans. Bruce Fink, ed. Jacques-Alain Miller. New York: Norton.
Latham, Rob. 2002. *Consuming Youth: Vampires, Cyborgs and the Culture of Consumption*. Chicago: University of Chicago Press.
Leyburn, James G. 1966. *The Haitian People*. New Haven, CT: Yale University Press.
Miller, Jacques-Alain. 1988. 'Extimité'. *Prose Studies*, 11.3: 121–31.
Modleski, Tania 1986. 'The terror of pleasure: The contemporary horror film and post-modern theory'. In *Studies in Entertainment: Critical Approaches to Mass Culture*, ed. Tania Modleski. Bloomington: Indiana University Press, 155–66.
Punter, David. 2000. *Postcolonial Imaginings*. London: Sage.
Rushdie, Salman. 1983. *Shame*. London: Picador.
Sartre, Jean-Paul 2001 (1961). 'Preface'. In Franz Fanon, *The Wretched of the Earth*, trans. Constance Farrington. London: Penguin Classics, 7–26.
Serres, Michel. 1995. *Angels: A Modern Myth*, trans. Francis Cowper, ed. Phillippa Hurd. New York: Flammarion.
Shaviro, Steve. 2002. 'Capitalist monsters'. *Historical Materialism*, 10:4: 281–90.
Simpson, George Eaton. 1940. 'Haitian magic'. *Social Forces*, 19.1: 95–100.
Sontag, Susan. 1974 (1966). 'The imagination of disaster'. In *Film Theory and Criticism*, eds Gerald Mast and Marshall Cohen. Oxford: Oxford University Press, 422–37.
Townshend, Dale. 2007. *The Orders of Gothic*. New York: AMS Press.
Tulloch, John. 1977. 'Mimesis or marginality? Collective belief and German Expressionism'. In *Conflict and Control in the Cinema*, ed. John Tullock. Melbourne: Macmillan, 37–68.
Wernick, Andrew. 1991. *Promotional Culture*. London: Sage.
Williams, Tony. 1983. '*White Zombie*: Haitian horror'. *Jump Cut*, 28: 18–20.
Wood, Robin. 1986. *Hollywood from Vietnam to Reagan*. New York: Columbia University Press.
Žižek, Slavoj. 1993. *Tarrying with the Negative*. Durham, NC: Duke University Press.

Filmography

Dawn of the Dead. 1978. George Romero, dir. United Artists.
I Walked with a Zombie. 1943. Jacques Tournier, dir. RKO Radio Pictures.
King of the Zombies. 1941. Jean Yarbrough, dir. Monogram Pictures.
Metropolis. 1927. Fritz Lang, dir. UFA.
Night of the Living Dead. 1968. George Romero, dir. Walter Reade Organization.
White Zombie. 1932. Victor Halperin, dir. United Artists.

15

Charles Shirō Inouye

Globalgothic: Unburying Japanese figurality

The Japanese playwright and novelist Izumi Kyōka (1873–1939) was a fearful man. His fear was dual in nature: both horror and reverence. Without the latter, he would have been no more impressive than Edgar Allan Poe, whose 'The Tell-tale Heart' (1843) takes us to a dark place (which is interesting) and leaves us there (which is not). Both writers were at times histrionic, but I find little hope in the gothic recipe that Poe proffers, whereas in Kyōka it is impossible to miss the structure of deliverance that is implied in, for instance, 'The Holy Man of Mt Kōya' ('Kōya hijiri', 1900), where we sense a return to safety from our trespass in the territory of eros and death.[1]

Possibly because of this reverential, redemptive element, Kyōka is questionably 'gothic', just as the entire category of 'Japanese gothic' is also questionable. If we insist that the gothic is a rebellion against a higher monolithic order, as Henry J. Hughes (2000) has argued, we must wonder how such a revolt could possibly manifest itself on the Archipelago, where the gods are multiple, spatially present and interchangeably good and evil.[2] If Japan had a monolithic order, it was during the brief period between 1868 and 1945. This was, not incidentally, also the age of Hirai Tarō (1894–1965), who styled himself Edogawa Rampo. As the Japanese Poe, Hirai consciously sought to titillate his readers in conventionally gothic ways. But when the disastrous conclusion of the Second World War shattered the monolithic imperial system (*tennō sei*), it made cultural rebellion less horrifying and more repentant, ushering in a postmodern age of monstrous expression that fits our usual understanding of the (modern) gothic only occasionally.

Today, as a dominant source of globalised popular culture, Japan's contributions to the globalgothic force us to rethink the definition of the gothic. To be sure, even in the West, Dracula's coat has become tight in places. In Japan the fit, which never was very good in the first place, clearly needs to be let out and taken up in many places. How to account for the popularity of costume play (*kosupure*), the global reach of J-Horror, and the relentless monstrosity of anime, manga and video gaming? Can this contemporary anti-realism also be called gothic, or is it something altogether different?

Here I will try to understand both fear and the gothic in a broader way, one that follows from nothing less than a new way of framing the modern era. I propose the following premodern-modern-postmodern model:

Animism
Rationalism
Re-animism

According to this pattern, premodern animism was supplanted by modern rationalism, which is now being supplanted by what I will call re-animism – or a resurgence of monster-friendly expression in the postwar period.

In Japan the changing status of animism is relatively easy to follow since it was not suppressed as thoroughly as it was in the Middle East or in Europe. Anciently it was a form of localised polytheistic worship that recognised the anima of impressive things: large trees, rocks, champion sumo wrestlers. In Japan the deities were fundamentally neutral, or capable of being both good and bad. When successfully propitiated by festivals (*matsuri*) and other types of localised worship, they were considered benevolent *kami*. When they were forgotten or otherwise offended, they became destructive monsters or *yōkai* (Komatsu, 2007: 42–8). Importantly, these sacred beings were largely visible and present in this world. Sacred space was, and today still is, marked by a *shimenawa*, a rope with dangling straw and paper tassels that is not a symbol in the formal sense. It does not point to a higher invisible Order, but, rather, to the visible tree, rock or shrine around which it is tied.[3] In the case of the sumo wrestler, the rope becomes a horizontal one, or *yokozuna*.

Monotheism came later. In Japan the brief heyday of worshipping a single god came not when the Jesuits arrived in the sixteenth century but significantly later, in the nineteenth century, when the Meiji Emperor was made symbol and father of the modern Japanese nation. In 1871 the ancient practice of worshipping local gods was organised into a new national religious system known as State Shintō.[4] By way of government policy, Japan's emperor (*tennō*) came to be worshipped as a singularly important divine figure. Naturally, this national development was corrosive to earlier notions of many local gods, whether *kami* or *yōkai*.

Monotheism was a hard sell in Japan. In other parts of the world animism yielded to it more easily. In the Middle East idols in 'high places' were destroyed by iconophobic followers of an omnipotent God. There the idea of an invisible and singular deity gained wide credibility. Judaism spread with comparative ease since its fearful Truth was made symbolic and, therefore, moveable – so unlike the well-rooted green tree and the thick oak that Ezekiel scorned. As for Christianity, the idea of one God combined with the notion of Aristotle's Prime Mover, so that by the time of Augustine of Hippo (354–430) the mundane world looked devotedly up to a sacred intelligence that only rarely deigned to look down. As for the spread of Islam, even the native *jinn* bowed to Allah, another singular God whose influence spread from the Iberian peninsula in the west to Indonesia in the east.

Such a transcendental God could be known by way of a text, and so it was possible to be Jewish anywhere the Torah could travel. The same can be said of the portability of Christianity and Islam. Animism, on the other hand, is by definition not portable. Its assertion of significant space, the sacred that is actually visible and present, is utterly localised and polytheistic. Thus there was nothing like a symbolic heaven to which Japanese animists could aspire. As Joseph Kitagawa argued, the sacred world was the one they lived in, the here and now (1989: 43–58). The land was never a *metaphor* of redemption until modernity rendered it into various forms of abstraction: the nation state (*kokka*), the body politic (*kokutai*), the empire (*dai Nihon teikoku*) and so on. Only then did worship become a matter of 'rational' belief. As it did, monsters became supernatural (or foreign) rather than natural.[5]

In the West the gothic emerges as a form of doubt about the rational scepticism that led to the Enlightenment. In the case of Judaism the conversion to Islam of the Messianic figure Sabbatai Zevi (1626–c.76) opened the way to questioning and to loss of faith. For Christianity René Descartes (1596–1650) famously sought to cure his fear of the mutable by finding his own critical mind (cogito) to be more trustworthy than even God. By comparison Baruch Spinoza (1632–77) was even more assertive about the powers of the human mind. During the ensuing Age of Reason, the hierarchical and absolutist structure of monotheism was not simply cast aside. Its utility was exploited in ways that led to an absolutist structure for Reason, lending to rationality the same chauvinistic impulse that had plagued sectarianism. Man became the measure of *all* things, eagerly climbing into God's jealous throne. No wonder, then, that modernity, like monotheism, abhorred relativism, to say nothing of discouraging the many gods of animism or the hard-to-catalogue eccentricities of the gothic. Nature became answerable to the explanations and empirical demonstrations of science. High and low places alike survived God's wrath, but only to become atomised and mute. Once rationalised, an orderly world could speak for itself only in frightful moments of tortured outburst: romantic, gothic, modernist or otherwise.

Japan modernised, too. My analysis of Japan's expressive culture shows that modern consciousness developed there by way of large-scale shifts in the semiotic field. Studying the period from the sixteenth to the twentieth centuries, I identify three major semiotic trends that aided the development of modern thought: firstly, a shift toward phonocentricity, or a sound orientation of signs; secondly, a shift toward realism, or a homogenisation of signs; and thirdly, a shift toward symbolic framing, or a perspectival use of signs to symbolise the mundane world as a reflection of various ideological formations. What phonocentricity, realism and symbolic framing have in common is a suppression of figurality, or what I define to be the expressive potential of the grapheme.[6]

Why did modern consciousness abhor the grapheme? To ask this question is to begin to understand not only why animism weakened in Japan but also why the gothic has been principally viewed as a rebellion in modernised cultures. In a word gothic expression is typically marked by high figurality: wraiths and monsters, blood and gore. It shares this feature with animism, which, being similarly grapheme-friendly, affirms the particular, visual space of what I call locale: local, lyrically perceived significant space. The principal difference between the two is that animism retains a wider range of fear – both horror and reverence – whereas the modern, 'advanced' focus of what we have traditionally called the gothic seems to have concentrated mostly on horror.

Modernity suppresses the grapheme because modern society is massive, and massiveness can be attained only conceptually: as a sharing of certain ideas and ideological formations that is considerably wider than, for instance, the sharing of a particular tree in a local grove. As Benedict Anderson (1983) has pointed out, the nation state is conceptual in nature. It is not naturally occurring but is something that must be imagined into existence. For this to happen, traditional identification with the concrete particulars of locale and local life must be supplanted by general (and generalising) abstractions. Concepts such as nation, race and society provide the glue that holds modern societies together. While Anderson argues that modernisation is accomplished by way of print capitalism, which supports this kind of imagination, my point is that modernisation required the evolution of many other types of expression as well. As important as printed materials were flags, uniforms, realistic paintings and so on.

Such signs were necessary because they concealed the diversity of understanding that actually occurs when different individuals think about a notion such as the nation. In essence, differences in experience and constitution lead people to grasp these ideas in different ways. Even when we accept the common meaning of a symbol, for instance, the thoughts and emotions it stirs in one person are not identical to those of another. The great utility of something like a flag, then, is that its reduced figurality – the graphic simplicity of circles, stripes and other shapes – establishes a standardised expression that masks over the actual diversity of people's understanding. It asserts an idealised, common comprehension in place of actual, localised reaction. As a symbol a flag *represents and standardises* the meaning of the nation, thereby encouraging a uniformity of response and discouraging nonconformity of the sort that is so often deemed gothic. In sum low figurality conceals differences of understanding, while high figurality reveals them.

Now, if the modern mind appreciates uniformity and conformity, herein lies a great paradox. Why is it that the assertive modern self emerges by way of a suppression of individuality? This tension is perfectly reflected in the way that the Emperor Meiji had to don a Prussian general's uniform in order to become the father of the Japanese nation. Was this change of clothing not an expression of what Edmund Burke in *Reflections on the Revolution in France* called the 'proud submission' of the modern individual to the state (1963: 550)? Clearly, hegemony is born of this need to standardise the imagination and to mobilise the masses in a way that makes the citizen accept surrender as a standard, non-gothic, empowering act. For this reason modern distortion tries to appear as a lack of distortion, despite its profoundly imaginative character. By way of hegemonic expressive systems, such as the realistic novel, a seamless unity of citizenship and patriotism is born. By way of this same modernising effort, the gothic, which finds itself outside the borders of both verisimilitude and traditional monotheistic standards, came to express anxiety and fear in a histrionic, horrible way. It eventually rendered the dual nature of fear singular: all the horror with little of the reverence. No doubt the modern suppression of figurality led to this equating of the high figurality with horror.

Modern culture favours fiction because modernity itself is a fiction, a distortion made to seem normal rather than exceptional. Its verisimilitude follows from a thorough homogenisation of expressive style. Like a novel, the imaginary modern nation is sustained by a semiotic field that masks actual differences of understanding by making them as invisible as sound, by covering them over with realistic consistency and by framing them with ideological symbols. Only when figurality is sufficiently suppressed do we come to accept the profound deceptions of realism as true since there is no longer a way to become aware of them. Enter the gothic, which employs higher figurality to reveal difference and break the spell of modern hegemony. It disturbs the artifices of realism so we begin to see paint strokes rather than a seamless, naturally occurring landscape. White skin ruptures and reveals red blood and pulsing organs. A biting, sucking Dracula moves us *back* to 'primitive' higher figurality.

Figurality's trueness to horror is non-standard. This is its value to gothic expression. It allows distortion to appear as distortion, and truth to be exposed as a lie. It refuses to be washed clean in the clear, purified blood of the nation. Thus it was that the visual field became ever more streamlined as Western Europe moved from animism to Catholicism to Protestantism to Science. The same happened as Japan moved from animism to Shintō to National Learning (*kokugaku*) to State Shintō to Science. Needless to say, the similar cultural trajectory of both was toward the sublimated horror of total war.

In the decades between the First and Second World Wars, an age when Japan sought racial purity, national unity and military invincibility, semiotic extravagance was dismissed as *ero guro nansensu*: 'erotic, grotesque, nonsense'. Such expression was considered modern*ist,* and sometimes gothic, in the sense that it was non-standard. *Ero guro nansensu* was suppressed since successful political mobilisation depended on *limiting* the possible sources of meaning just as it demanded the uniform interpretation of that meaning. This suppression, however, was done in a way that felt empowering. As Walter Benjamin (1968) observed, the age of mechanical reproduction enthralled the masses by giving them a new power of expression. Fascism did not meddle with the reallocation of property, but focused instead on giving everyone a powerful voice. It was an irresistibly seductive voice: authoritatively positioned behind lecterns in vast lecture halls, compellingly amplified and broadcast over wide stretches of space. In this golden age of oration realism also emerged as the ability to account for all space by tying the visual field to the similar fixed point of a single seer.[7] Not only this, but such limited and limiting phonic and graphic perspectives became framed symbolically by various comprehensive ideological systems that gave modern expression a hegemonic vastness, while at the same time establishing clear margins and categories of the unacceptable.

All three of these developments had the common effect of suppressing diversity and encouraging unity by limiting the sources of truth. They made the single speaker into the single seer, who then became a symbol or head signifier of modern reality. Thus we understand how and why Japan's Emperor Meiji, who played no visibly governmental role before the Restoration of 1868, became the ubiquitous father of the nation by 1900. First trotted out on several excursions to meet his people, he then came to rule an entire nation by way of his massively reproduced, ceremonially worshipped photograph. His rule was typically one of thorough representation. He became God, and the politicians, bureaucrats and generals became the priesthood that spoke for him.

Although they eventually did so with great enthusiasm, the Japanese were slow to accept this or any other sort of monotheism. Millennia of animistic practice had taught them to have a more immediate and lyrical relationship with the space of the islands. The spirit-filled grove, the mountain, the waterfall – these localities were all approachable, visual sources of meaning and identity. Lyrically defined as poetically encoded locales, ancient Japan was only gradually discovered by modern travellers. One of the most famous was the poet Matsuo Bashō (1644–94). Writing at a time when the old was slipping away, he resisted the growing subject–object split with his call for *butsuga ichinyō*, the melding of subject and object. As if to arrest the flow of modern life, he called for a poetics that located the seer amid the seen. 'If you wish to write about bamboo, go to the bamboo' (qtd in Shirane, 1998: 261).[8] As modernisation progressed, the Japanese, too, eventually turned from the 'non-symbolic understanding of symbols' to embrace a symbolic order (Kitagawa, 1989: 45).

As this happened, poetic lyricism gave way to prosaic description, and the rhetorical devices of past tense and third person were employed to help the author join the historian in burying the past in a very deep grave, allowing only a corrected *memory* of the dead to confirm rational truths about those living in the present. Surely the design of the modern cenotaph – a slightly rounded base, and slightly narrowing sides – shows how the tremendous depth of this modern burial tries to be a reflection of the equally tremendous height of modern principle. The point here being, of course, that the rotting dead who died for glorious ideals must never be allowed to intrude into the space of the living lest the reasons for their deaths come into question.

In ancient Japan the dead often returned to visit the living, and such events, far from being considered horrible, were well planned and welcome. With the onset of modern consciousness, however, their appearance came increasingly to be non-standard and elaborately expressed. An example of this new expression can be found in Ueda Akinari's 'White Peak' ('Shiramine', 1776), where the ancient trope of the *onryō* (vengeful spirit) is explicated with a delirious eloquence.[9] Having been wronged, the ghost of Emperor Sutoku vows 'to bring the whole world (*ama ga shita*) into chaos' (Akinari, 1973: 334). Far from quietly accepting his misfortune, he becomes no less than 'the king of evil, the leader (*kami*) of more than 300 varieties of demons' who are dedicated to pouring vengeance upon his enemies and changing the course of history (341). For the purpose of describing a dangerously strong-willed Sutoku, Akinari's language is appropriately rich and menacing. It becomes gothic in the classical modern sense, that is, as a horrible exaggeration:

> In the light I could clearly see his highness's features. His august face flushed crimson. His hair hung down to his knees, tangled like a thorn bush. His eyes were turned up, leaving only the whites exposed, and his fevered breath came in painful gasps. His persimmon-coloured robes were covered with soot. His nails had grown as long and sharp as a beast's claws. In every detail he was the impressive, horrifying form of a demon king. (my translation, 342)

Of course premodern dealings with the dead had previously been considered momentous, if not always frightening. The purpose of the *matsuri* (festival) was to placate the dead souls of powerful people whose unchecked vengeance as *onryō* posed a threat to the living. But in Akinari's story we sense something new: a surpassing, modern kind of fear, a horrified grappling with the inexplicable that follows from a loss of reverence.

Is it too much to say that modern consciousness avoided fear altogether, whether horror or reverence? The early psychologist Inoue Enryō (1858–1919) denied the existence of *yōkai*, giving them only a phantom status as expressions of abnormal mental states.[10] If he found the lingering fear of ghosts and monsters primitive and embarrassing, others like Kyōka rejected the modern paradox of 'true fiction' and encouraged fear in its every aspect, both horror and reverence. Importantly, he too was modern to the extent that he attempted to make ghosts appear not in the countryside but in downtown Tokyo, expressing the rebellious spirit of the gothic.[11] But, as I said in the beginning, he retained an abiding reverence for the uncanny, and for this reason he was pushed to the margins of modern Japanese literature. His embracing of ghosts and monsters was a negative reaction to modernity, a point that should not be surprising when we consider that the great blossoming of monstrosity in Japan occurred not in ancient or medieval times but during the Tokugawa period (1600–1868) when positivism started to make itself felt. The wealth of monstrosity represented by the encyclopaedic studies of Toriyama Sekien (1712–88) or the vivid illustrations of Katsushika Hokusai (1760–1849) and numerous other ukiyoe artists is breathtaking. Are their highly monstrous creations not reactive responses to the tightening grip of realism as well as weakening expressions of reverence? Because of the persistent force of animist perception in Japan, their rebellion had an extraordinary vividness and imaginative breadth that Kyōka, for one, desired to keep alive.

As I have said, with the attempted organisation of animistic practices into what came to be known as State Shintō, the gods (and especially the emperor) were given a symbolic status that abstracted them from the space of day-to-day life and drew them into the ideological realm. With the unconditional surrender of the Japanese military in 1945, the hegemonic spell was broken, and the narrative of Japan's invincibility was proved wrong. In the ideological vacuum that followed, many versions of a possible new Japan were proposed. The one relevant to this discussion of the gothic was the resurgence of animism.

For the manga artist and animator Mizuki Shigeru (1922–), restoring Japan's lost monstrosity became a personal, lifelong goal. Upon his return from war he openly and unsparingly critiqued Japan's military establishment in a way that only he, as Japan's most beloved manga artist, could do. He was relentless in his desire to expose the lies that had led to so much suffering: 'I saw too many comrades die', he writes in *War Manga that My Dead Comrades Made Me Draw* (*Naki senyu ga egakaseta senki manga*). 'Even now, I sometimes catch a glimpse of the shades of dead friends standing at my bedside . . . When I think of those who, now without voice, died pitifully in war, I am overcome with anger' (qtd in Penney, 2008; Penney's translation).

In *War and Japan* (*Sensō to Nihon*, 1991) we see where his sympathies lie. Here, scenes of battle and atrocity are done realistically, while it is the monstrous Rat (Nezumiotoko) who delivers the thoughtful moral comment. Like the early modern Akinari, the postmodern Shigeru performs the function of placating *onryō*. When compared to Akinari, however, Shigeru's understanding of *kami* and *yōkai* actually appears *more* traditional and, therefore, less horrific than Akinari's modern gothic. In other words, being postmodern, the supernatural beings that appear in Mizuki's work better reflect the ancient understanding that spirits are neither clearly bad nor good, but flexibly both. As a form of graphic *matsuri*, his words and images resuscitate a balanced realm where, as Plutschow notes, the human is the divine, the divine is human and the interaction of both is intimate (Plutschow, 1996). Man and Rat Man are similarly monstrous players in what Anne Ellison (2006) has called this new age of 'millennial monsters'. Certainly Mizuki's attempt to reanimate postwar Japan lends credence to Oshii Mamoru's sense of the contemporary present as an age of the 'posthuman', demonstrated, for example, by his 1995 film *Ghost in the Shell*. For this reason today's *yōkai* are no longer as threatening as Sutoku or even as the irradiated Godzilla once was. Having inherited much from Toriyama Sekien's encyclopaedic and ludic *Illustrated Night Parade of One Hundred Demons* (*Gazu hyakki yakō*, 1776),[12] Mizuki's creations are well on their way to becoming domesticated monsters of the playful sort that easily fit in a child's pocket.[13]

I would like to suggest that the richness and influence of Japanese soft power today owes much to the way animism survived the modern period and continues to have a growing influence on Japanese popular culture in the postmodern era.[14] Today this resurgence re-animates the world by way of a globally shared, highly visual semiotic field. Grapheme-oriented tools of expression open modern graves and unearth a once buried figurality. Freed from the semiotic constraints of phonocentrism, realism and symbolic framing, post-industrial societies in general seem to be newly monster-rich, each in its own way. What we are calling the globalgothic is a contemporary blossoming of non-realistic expression that is sustained by high figurality and nourished by numerous cross-cultural flows. It has learned to go beyond fear-as-horror to include fear-as-reverence once again. If this is the age of J-Horror and Pokémon, it is also a green age, a time of new reverence for locality.

Japan's dominant expressive form is no longer the realistic novel but the animated film, complete with its affirmation of radical change, metamorphosis and monstrosity. Openly affirming of change, the internal logic of anime is at once ancient and cutting edge. In tone anime is both horrifying and hopeful. On the one hand, we have Otomo Katsuhiro's darkly apocalyptic *Akira* (1988) and the nightmarish *Paprika* (2006) of Kon Satoshi. On the other, we have Miyazaki Hayao's brighter *Nausicaa of the Windy Valley* (*Kaze no tani no Naushika,* 1984), his begrudgingly hopeful *Princess Mononoke* (*Momonoke hime,* 1997) and his even redemptive *Spirited Away* (*Sen to Chihiro no kamikakushi,* 2001), which is the most pointedly monstrous film of all his works to date.

In conclusion, to insist that gothic fear be only horrifying is to remain trapped within a modern expressive regime that is no longer well supported either by contemporary expressive technologies or by a concomitant postwar resurgence of animism. In Japan numerous expressions of high figurality are having the effect of reanimating the present, lending to the globalgothic a complicated, nuanced fear that appears as both horror and reverence.

Notes

1 For an analysis of Kyōka's fear and the archetype of trespass and return see Inouye, 1998.
2 My response to Hughes's argument can be found in Inouye, 2005: 1–6.
3 For more on the *shimenawa* see Inouye, 2008.
4 For more on the evolution of Shintō as a national religion see Hardacre, 1989.
5 Note, for instance, the monstrous caricatures of Roosevelt, Churchill and other enemies by emerging manga artists during the Second World War.
6 At the time of this writing, the manuscript for my *Figurality and the Development of Modern Consciousness* is in process.
7 For the tie between perspective and symbolism see Panofsky, 1991.
8 For more on Matsuo Bashō's aesthetic principles see Shirane, 1998.
9 *Onryō* are the spirits of those who died a wrongful death. They are highly individualistic in the sense that only the strong willed, usually those who held prominent positions in society, become vengeful spirits; and only if they cannot be propitiated by those aware of their possible discontent. See Plutschow, 1996.

10 For more on Enryō's critique of monstrosity see Figal, 1999.
11 For Kyōka's antimodernity see Kawakami, 1999.
12 For Shigeru's indebtedness to Toriyama Sekien see Foster, 2008.
13 To give just one example of a *yōkai* genealogy, Toriyama visualised the legendary *kamaitachi*, or whirlwind, as three clawing weasels (*itachi*) swirling in the air. Mizuki adapted the figure in *Gegege no Kitarō*, where it appears as a human-looking creature with green skin who goes airborne and slices through anything in his way. The trope then gets reinstated in Pokémon, where Sneasel and Weavil make their appearance as weasel-like figures with sharp claws. One type of Pokémon attack is called *kamaitachi*, or razor wind.
14 While inoculating her analysis with a denial of 'animism as an essential, timeless component of Japanese culture', Anne Allison goes on to claim that 'an animist sensibility percolates the postmodern landscape in ways that do not occur in the United States' (2006: 12). Truly, animism manifests itself differently in different places, but it was, and is becoming again, widespread.

References

Akinari, Ueda. 1973 (1776). 'Shiramine'. In *Ugetsu monogatari, Nihon koten bungaku zenshū*. Vol. 48. Tokyo: Shōgakkan, 331–44.

Allison, Anne. 2006. *Millennial Monsters: Japanese Toys and the Global Imagination.* Berkeley: University of California Press.

Anderson, Benedict. 1983. *Imagined Communities: Reflections on the Origin and Spread of Nationalism*. London: Verso.

Benjamin, Walter. 1968. 'The work of art in the age of mechanical reproduction'. In Walter Benjamin, *Illuminations: Essays and Reflections*, trans. Harry Zohn, ed. Hannah Arendt. New York: Harcourt, Brace, Jovanovich, 217–52.

Burke, Edmund. 1963 (1790). *Reflections on the Revolution in France*. In *Edmund Burke: Selected Writings and Speeches*, ed. Peter J. Stanlis. Washington, DC: Regnery Publishing, 511–608.

Figal, Gerald. 1999. *Civilization and Monsters: Spirits of Modernity in Meiji Japan.* Durham, NC: Duke University Press.

Foster, Michael Dylan. 2008. 'The otherworlds of Mizuki Shigeru'. *Mechademia*, 3: 8–28.

Hardacre, Helen. 1989. *Shintō and the State 1868–1988*. Princeton: Princeton University Press.

Hughes, Henry J. 2000. 'Familiarity of the strange: Japan's Gothic tradition'. *Criticism*, 42.1: 59–89.

Inouye, Charles Shirō. 1998. *The Similitude of Blossoms: A Critical Biography of Izumi Kyōka (1873–1939), Japanese Novelist and Playwright*. Cambridge, MA: Harvard University Press.

——. 2005. *In Light of Shadows: More Gothic Tales by Izumi Kyōka*. Honolulu: University of Hawaii Press.

——. 2008. *Evanescence and Form: An Introduction to Japanese Culture*. New York: Palgrave.

Kawakami, Chiyoko. 1999. 'The metropolitan uncanny in the works of Izumi Kyōka:

A counter-discourse on Japan's modernization'. *Harvard Journal of Asiatic Studies*, 59.2: 559–83.

Kitagawa, Joseph. 1989. *On Understanding Japanese Religion*. Princeton: Princeton University Press.

Komatsu Kazuhiko. 2007. *New Thoughts on the Study of Monsters* (*Yōkaigaku shinkō*). Tokyo: Yōsensha.

Panofsky, Erwin. 1991. *Perspective as Symbolic Form*, trans. Christopher Wood. New York: Zone Books.

Mizuki Shigeru. 2007. 'Naki senyu ga egakaseta senki manga' ('War manga that my dead comrades made me draw'). *Aa gyokusai*. Tokyo: Azora Shuppan, 185–6.

Plutschow, Herbert. 1996. *Matsuri: The Festivals of Japan*. Richmond: Japan Library.

——. 2006. *A Reader in Edo Period Travel*. Folkestone: Global Oriental.

Poe, Edgar Allan. 1843. 'The Tell-tale Heart'. *Pioneer*, 1: 29–31.

Shirane, Haruo. 1998. *Traces of Dreams: Landscape, Cultural Memory, and the Poetry of Bashō*. Stanford: Stanford University Press.

Toriyama Sekien. 1776. *Illustrated Night Parade of One Hundred Demons* (*Gazu hyakki yakō*). Tokyo: Kasokawa Shotes.

Internet sources

Mizuki Shigeru. 2008. '*War and Japan*' ('Sensō to Nihon'), 1991. trans. Matthew Penney. *The Asia-Pacific Journal: Japan Focus*. www.japanfocus.org/-Matthew-Penney/2905. Accessed October 2011.

Penney, Matthew. 2008. '*War and Japan*, the non-fiction manga of Mizuki Shigeru'. *The Asia-Pacific Journal: Japan Focus*. www.japanfocus.org/-Matthew-Penney/2905. Accessed October 2011.

Filmography

Akira. 1988. Otomo Katsuhiro, dir. Toho.

Ghost in the Shell. 1995. Oshii Mamoru, dir. Shochiku.

Nausicaa of the Windy Valley (*Kaze no tani no Naushika*). 1984. Miyazaki Hayao, dir. Toei.

Paprika. 2006. Kon Satoshi, dir. Sony.

Princess Mononoke (*Momonoke hime*). 1997. Miyazaki Hayao, dir. Toho.

Spirited Away (*Sen to Chihiro no kamikakushi*). 2001. Miyazaki Hayao, dir. Toho.

Index